M000237486

LAST
FLIGHT TO
STUTTGART

LAST

SEARCHING FOR THE

FLIGHT TO

BOMBER BOYS OF LANCASTER EQ-P

STUTTGART

LISA JEAN RUSS

VICTORIA · VANCOUVER · CALGARY

Copyright © 2018 Lisa Jean Russ

All rights reserved. No part of this publication may be reproduced, stored in
a retrieval system, or transmitted in any form or by any means—electronic,
mechanical, audio recording, or otherwise—without the written permission
of the publisher or a licence from Access Copyright, Toronto, Canada.

Heritage House Publishing Company Ltd.
heritagehouse.ca

Cataloguing information available from Library and Archives Canada

978-1-77203-262-8 (pbk)
978-1-77203-263-5 (epub)

Edited by Jesmine Cham
Proofread by Lesley Cameron
Cover and interior design by Jacqui Thomas
Cover (*top*), title page, and part opener photograph: CGTA5-Mods.com/
    Avro Lancaster Mk-X
Cover photograph (*bottom*): Looking for pieces of EQ-P in a farmer's field,
    2010, by Michael Russ

The interior of this book was produced on 100% post-consumer recycled paper,
processed chlorine free, and printed with vegetable-based inks.

We acknowledge the financial support of the Government of Canada through the
Canada Book Fund (CBF) and the Canada Council for the Arts, and the Province
of British Columbia through the British Columbia Arts Council and the Book
Publishing Tax Credit.

22 21 20 19 18 1 2 3 4 5

Printed in Canada

To the memory of Robert (Bud) George Alfred Burt and to all those who have given their lives in war "for freedom"

Grey goose, grey goose,
Whither flyest thou?
"Eastward, eastward is my flight,
With the cry 'For Freedom's right,'
O'er a stormy wind-tossed sea,
O'er a war-torn Germany,
I've taught my countrymen to fly,
To live, and if they must, to die."

From "Song of the Grey Goose," 1943 (author unknown)
408 Squadron display board, Canadian Memorial T2 Hangar,
Building 17, Yorkshire Air Museum Allied Forces Memorial

Author's Note

Last Flight to Stuttgart tells the story of seven men who fought in the Second World War under Bomber Command and how I came to know them. This crew represents the tens of thousands of men who died in the war protecting our freedom. We remember the illustrious leaders and those who participated in well-known battles, but without the average man serving on the battlefront, wars would never be won. For every leader who has his story told, there are many thousands of servicemen whose stories will never come to light. I have chosen to thank the marginalized and honour their names by telling their story. They are my heroes.

PART 1

MEMORY FAILS ME

Operation 5: Stuttgart

O
n Wednesday, March 15, 1944, the boys flying Lancaster II LL637, coded EQ-P, from 408 "Goose" Squadron of the Royal Canadian Air Force (RCAF), once again found their names listed for bombing operations. Yorkshire's Linton-on-Ouse base readied its bombers, preparing sixteen Lancasters each from Goose Squadron and 426 "Thunderbird" Squadron. The day would follow a familiar routine, with the morning breakfast and the daily Lancaster check by the aircrew readying EQ-P for the night ahead, while the ground crew worked on any outstanding mechanical issues and began preparations for bombing-up. After the numerous stand-downs and scrubs, surely tonight they would fly, signalling the "first heavy raid of the month."[1]

Bud Burt would be going on his first operation if all went as planned. He had been sick when his crew mates went on their first four operational trips and had yet to experience the full effect of flying over enemy territory. Bud probably felt like an "odd bod." Even if his crew mates had given him vivid descriptions of those first ops, it would have done little to quell his nerves. He would be anxious to do his part and get this first op under his belt.

In Sussex, Bud's cousin Kenneth Arthur Burt, a ground crew mechanic on leave from 418 Squadron, boarded a train for York. A few weeks earlier, Bud had dropped in on Kenneth at a station hangar. They had gone out for drinks, and during their chat Bud had promised his cousin a flight in a warbird.[2] Eager to fly, Kenneth hoped to meet up with Bud later in the day.

Meanwhile, the operational crews at Linton-on-Ouse filed into the briefing room for their pre-operation instructions. Their target tonight was Stuttgart, Germany. Bomber Command had planned a heavy attack. Like many of Germany's big cities, Stuttgart harboured an effective rail transportation network and various industrial war factories. Searchlights and anti-aircraft gun batteries, as well as a Luftwaffe fighter base at Echterdingen, defended Stuttgart's citizens and its industrial precinct. Departures at Linton-on-Ouse would commence at 7:00 PM or, in military parlance, 1900 hours.[3] The round trip was expected to take the bombers about seven and a half hours.

Later that afternoon, two crews were scrubbed from the operation because of technical failures.[4] For some, it seemed, the night would be a quiet one. The rest ate their pre-op meal of bacon and eggs, then dressed in their flight gear, taking time to follow their own idiosyncrasies. Some pulled on their gear in a particular order; others donned a special sweater or scarf, a lucky object or a gift from a loved one. Whatever their peculiarity, it had to be done just so, or it was considered an ill omen. They picked up their parachutes, ignoring the standing WAF joke, "Bring it back if it doesn't open,"[5] climbed into the trucks, and headed out to the planes.

EQ-P sat fully loaded with eight 30-pound and nearly three hundred 4-pound incendiary bombs, one 4,000-pound high-capacity "cookie" blast bomb,[6] and 5,400 rounds of .303 small arms ammunition for the airplane's guns.[7] The crews stood around their respective Lancasters in the cold late-winter dusk, having a last smoke, saying silent prayers, rubbing or kissing a talisman for luck, or vomiting over one tire while others urinated for good luck on another. All waited for the signal that the operation was scrubbed or on.

Tonight the operation was a go. The boys of EQ-P climbed aboard in their cumbersome gear, lifted up the ladder, shut the side door of the Lancaster, and headed for their individual stations. Norm Lumgair and Jock Cruickshank, pilot and flight engineer, settled into their seats side by side in the cockpit. It would take two men to get this fully loaded mechanical beast off the ground. As bomb aimer, Bill Taylor was positioned in the nose of the plane. He had two options on takeoff. He could, as was often done, go down into the nose turret. If takeoff failed, however, this was a dangerous location. The safer alternative was to stand behind the pilot and flight engineer, waiting until they got into the air before taking up his position. George Parker, the navigator, sat at his navigation table, just behind Norm. A short distance farther down the cramped fuselage, Larry Doran, the wireless operator, sorted radio operations. Bob Hudson, the mid-upper gunner, strapped himself into the mid-upper turret, while Bud, the tail gunner, slid down the aft end of the fuselage and squeezed himself into the tail turret, shutting the doors between him and the rest of the crew. Settled in the plane, the boys did their pre-flight tests and prepared for takeoff.

Before they could get off the ground, another 408 Squadron Lancaster and crew were scrubbed from the operation on account of technical failure, cutting the squadron's contribution for the night down to thirteen Lancasters.[8] The crews, preoccupied with their own pre-flight tests, paid no attention to those left behind.

With everything in order, Norm signed EQ-P off as "fit to fly." The four-engined bomber waddled along the grass, headed for the runway.

The weather forecast was not a good one, warning of clear skies and high winds.[9] With little cloud cover to hide in, the bombers were vulnerable to attack, which meant the gunners faced a tense night scouring the heavens for night fighters. And while tailwinds had caused an early arrival over their target during an op to Leipzig in February, tonight the winds would hinder their progress. Even so, Bomber Command expected the crews to remain vigilant and stick to the schedule.

The crews were anxious to be off. The first 408 Squadron aircraft departed at 1901,[10] with 426 Squadron starting departures at 1906.[11] Finally EQ-P perched at the end of the runway, ready to take to the skies. At 1918, the bomber ascended into the bleak, cloudless twilight and headed toward the coast, the eleventh Lancaster to take off from Linton-on-Ouse Station, flying as part of the third wave.[12] Thunderbird Squadron's bombers were all in the air by 1930,[13] with the last of Goose Squadron's birds taking up the final position at 1940.[14] The bombers huddled together in the closing dark, a small cluster of geese in an immense flock. In total, 863 aircraft took off from various airfields across England that night, with Canada's 6 Group[15] providing

131 planes for the effort.[16] Of the total aircraft, 617 were Lancaster bombers, joined by 230 Halifaxes and 16 Mosquitos.[17]

The bombers swept "west of London to Selsey Bill near Portsmouth, across the Channel to a position near Deauville, then to points south of Paris and Strasbourg,"[18] almost to the Swiss border, before approaching Stuttgart from the southwest. This atypical route would help the bombers avoid coming in contact with the German night fighters until just before the target. Once the night-fighter force located the bomber stream, however, combat would be fierce.[19] The boys faced a long night ahead.

By now Kenneth had been travelling for more hours than expected after finding himself in the middle of a train delay. When he finally arrived in York, he made his way to 408 Squadron's non-commissioned officers' barracks at Beningbrough Hall, but Bud had already gone. With nothing to do, and with Bud not in need of his bed, Kenneth bunked at the hall, expecting to be awakened by his cousin upon his return.[20] He could use the sleep. Cot or not, the hall was luxurious compared to the typical cold Nissen hut accommodations inhabited by most of the British-based air force. He settled down and went to sleep.

Although the bomber advance, stretching kilometres in breadth and width, was slowed by the wind,[21] there were few issues for the bomber stream to deal with until it was crossing the Vosges Mountains in France. The fertile valley of the Reid or Bas-Rhin region of Alsace, wedged between the Vosges Mountains on one side and the Rhine River and Germany's Black Forest on the other, had been occupied by the Germans since the spring of 1940. As the stream of heavily loaded bombers thundered overhead, about to begin the final leg to the target, German night fighters launched their assault.

The bomber crews remained silent, leaving communication lines open for necessary commands. The gunners moved their guns through quadrants of sky, their eyes trained for that small change in the dark that heralded an approaching aircraft. Their command of "corkscrew starboard (or port), now!" would initiate the pilot's inevitable action to save their lives by plunging the heavily loaded bomber into a controlled twist and dive, hurtling toward the earth below before lifting once again, causing some to lose their supper.

But there was no guarantee that the gunners would see a night fighter before enemy bullets riddled their aircraft and sent them to their deaths. Sometimes undeterred by bullets, and in other instances unnoticed, the Messerschmitt 110 and the Junkers Ju88 night fighters infiltrated the bomber stream, sliding in behind unaware bombers or lining themselves up underneath. Their guns readied for attack, they gained speed and approached their prey. The highly volatile underbelly of the bombers, swollen with explosives and incendiaries, remained weak and unprotected, a blind spot of serious repercussions when searing bullets penetrated the metal. The bomber stream, persistent in its objective to reach the target, continued on, dodging and weaving to evade the night fighters. Some crews who could see the attacked bombers watched helplessly as the sky flashed bright, forced to observe the demise of their mates as flaming fuselages plummeted to the unyielding earth below.

Over Stuttgart, the bombing got off to a bad start. Strong winds delayed the beginning of the attack and also blew the flares, dropped by Pathfinders to mark the target, away from their objective.[22] The markers were "well short of the target,"[23] and Wing Commander (Wg. Cdr.) D.S. Jacobs, flying in 408 Squadron's EQ-H, remarked later that "the markers were not concentrated, there was a considerable discrepancy between the ground markers and the sky-markers."[24]

The bombers passed straight and steady overhead. Stuttgart, unlike Berlin, had few searchlights to illuminate them for the moderate anti-aircraft defences waiting below[25] and the night fighters lurking above, so their hopes and prayers to remain hidden might be answered tonight. Flying at an altitude of between 5,400 and 7,300 metres, they released 402,000 pounds of incendiary bombs and 64,000 pounds of explosives,[26] then lurched upwards, freed of their heavy load. Bodies remained tense as pilots were forced to continue to fly straight through the flak, maintaining their course until the camera recorded their bombing. In those moments they were particularly vulnerable to the night fighters, unable to dodge or weave, and giving the fighters full advantage.

The attack did not replicate the accuracy of Bomber Command's previous operation to Augsburg. During the early stages, the bombers struck the centre of Stuttgart, damaging the educational institution or *Akademie*. Bombs damaged houses in the southwestern suburbs, but the open countryside in the same vicinity, completely off target, received the majority of the hit.[27] And although some crews reported seeing strongly burning fires and a fire glow visible "up to 140 miles on the homeward journey," a good assessment was unattainable because the cloud cover varied from 50 to 100 percent over the target.[28]

The bombers, unburdened from the weight of their bomb load, quickly exited to the north. Each crew's navigator plotted a course for home while the rest of the crew continued their strained surveillance of the sky. Among the stream, some bombers carried incendiaries that had hung up in their bomb bay, a liability in the event of a fighter attack. If the incendiaries were set alight, the aircraft would burn in the air. Some crews found their mechanical air positioning indicator unserviceable, forcing navigators in those aircraft to rely on more ancient navigation techniques, such as a sextant and the stars, to get home. One aircraft lost the use of its rear gun turret, leaving the crew unable to defend itself from approaching night fighters. Their only hope was to avoid being seen.[29]

Night fighters snapped at their tails as the stream turned west, following the bombers out of the illuminated target area and into the darkness, harrying them back along their "homeward leg, which took the bombers north of Paris and Dieppe, across the Channel to Selsey Bill, then to Reading and finally to their various bases."[30]

The number of sorties for the night, 1,116, was a new record for Bomber Command,[31] and in the early morning hours of March 16, 1944, bombers landed across England. Cold and cramped bodies struggled to uncurl themselves from nearly eight tense hours in one position; some had to be helped out of their turrets, so cold and stiff their legs would not work. Exhausted, hungry, and with the ringing of thundering engines still whirring in their ears, the crewmen headed for a hot drink, a cigarette, and a debriefing before they could go to bed.

But not all crews survived to see the light of day. Thirty-seven aircraft were lost on the Stuttgart operation, with another four downed in other areas, their broken and burnt-out fuselages scattered across the bomber route over Germany and France. Most of their nearly 290 crewmen lay dead among their smoking wrecks. A small number, having managed to parachute from their falling aircraft, hearts pounding, attempted to hide, but most were found and taken as prisoners of war. Another small number evaded capture and began the long ordeal of finding a way home with help from resistance groups. All of 408 Squadron's returned aircraft were "successful in reaching the primary,"[32] but only eleven made it to home soil. EQ-E and EQ-P had failed to return and were "presumed lost over the target."[33]

On the morning of March 16, 1944, Kenneth woke up of his own accord in Bud's cot. He asked the air crewman in the cot next to Bud's the whereabouts of his cousin, but the answer was not something he shared with his family until nearly sixty years later. Kenneth was told that Bud's plane had gone down in flames. He left the job of telling the Burt family to the RCAF.[34]

2

Telegrams and Letters,
Shattered Hopes and Dreams

A mong the many telegrams prepared by the RCAF in the days following the Stuttgart operation, seven carried the names of the boys from EQ-P. Ken, Bud's younger brother, can still remember that day. "I saw the telegram guy ride up on his bicycle and lean it against one of the tall trees in our front yard and come to the front door," he said. "I recall later walking to Nelson Street and telling Aunt Ethel the news."[1] Pat, Bob Hudson's sister, has a similar recollection. She and her stepsister answered the door but had to wait what seemed a long time for their mother to return from shopping to reveal the disquieting contents. All the families would read a dreaded form telegram in stark capitals, similar to that received by the Burt family:

> MR ROBERT BURT 140 QUEEN STREET EAST BRAMPTON
> ONTARIO (REPORT DELIVERY)
> FROM RCAF CASUALTIES OFFICE
> DATE 19 MAR
>
> REGRET TO ADVISE THAT YOUR SON R TWO NOUGHT SIX
> FOUR ONE EIGHT SERGEANT ROBERT GEORGE ALFRED BURT
> IS REPORTED MISSING AFTER AIR OPERATIONS OVERSEAS
> MARCH SIXTEENTH STOP LETTER FOLLOWS

A letter to each family soon followed from 408 Squadron overseas, and a second was received from the Air Ministry's Casualties Office in Ottawa, although it took at least a week for the letters to arrive. Today, when technology allows the world to receive news in an instant, it's hard to imagine the week-long roller coaster of emotions they experienced, waiting for the mail day after day, hoping for news that their loved one had been found. Fearing someone would regret to inform them their brother, son, or husband was dead.

With the letters finally in hand, the families found themselves no better off. The correspondence confirmed their fears; their loved one was indeed "missing." They read on to find out that the crew had left the base around 7 PM,[2] but the crew and aircraft "failed to return to its base after a bombing raid over Stuttgart, Germany on the night of March 15 and the early morning of March 16, 1944. There were four other members of the Royal Canadian Air Force in the crew and they also have been reported missing. Since you may wish to know their names and next-of-kin, we are listing them. . . ."[3] The letter offered hope that their loved one was possibly a prisoner of war (POW), which despite being an unhappy thought was better than the contemplation of death. The Casualties Branch and 408 Squadron asked the families to bear with them while they acquired information. The squadron added that it had already gathered the men's effects and shipped them by train to the Central Depository, to be held for six months. If there was no word by then, the items would be shipped home to the families.[4]

Word of the missing airmen spread quickly among family and friends. Ken recalls that Bud's girlfriend, Audrey Harris, "would visit my mother quite often and I would escort her home to Main Street when it was dark."[5] Others sent letters. The same day the Casualties Office had typed the letter to the Burt family, Bud's previous employer, E.L. Vokes, the assistant general manager of Hewetson Shoes Ltd., also wrote to them.

> It came as a great shock to all of us at the factory when we
> heard that Bob[6] was reported missing. However, we all hope
> and pray that better news will arrive as soon as possible for
> your sake, as we realize the anxiety and strain which you
> are at present enduring. You can be assured that our thoughts

*and prayers are with you in this vigil. Bob was very popular
and well thought of around the factory and the community
can ill afford to lose boys of his type. We are certainly looking
forward to receiving better news.*[7]

The families also corresponded among themselves. Pat Parker and
Marjorie Doran, the wives of George Parker and Larry Doran, both
lived in Edmonton, Alberta. For a while their shared locality and sor-
rows helped them cope. They extended their concern to the other crew
families by sending them letters of support. Bud Burt's family received
letters from both women, who expressed their feelings and hopes. The
first to arrive came from Pat:

*Since "Bud" and my husband George Parker, were in the same
crew, I felt, I wanted to drop you a few lines, which I hope may
lessen your terrible shock. News like this, is a hard blow to
bear, especially when it concerns our loved ones. I have every
hope that somewhere they are safe & I only hope that you are
as sure as I am that everything is alright.*

    *I'm sorry that such an occasion should have to prompt my
first letter to you, but I feel, and I know I'll be writing a much
more cheerful one in the near future.*

    *Mrs. Doran whose husband was a member of the crew,
lives here in the city too & is a very dear friend of mine. I think
it has been easier for us, having each other for moral support.*

    *My sincere hopes and prayers are with each of these boys
and their families.*[8]

The second letter, from Marjorie, arrived shortly thereafter:

*I am really at a loss for words to express my feelings, but I
want you to know I am hoping and praying for your son's
safety as well as my husband Larry Doran.*

    *The suspense & anxiety is great but we have so much to
hope for that I'm sure the boys are safe somewhere.*

    *I have handed the information from Ottawa's letter to
our local Red Cross & through them I hope to receive speedier*

news. Any other news I may hear I will forward on to you
immediately.

There is so little we can do it makes one feel helpless,
but I'm sure before long we'll be hearing good news.

In the meantime my thoughts are with you & the
members of your family.[9]

Over the next few months, the families received notification of
their loved one's promotion or commission, which had been granted
before March 16. The arrival of each letter likely caused heart rates
to surge. Mothers, fathers, or wives grasped the unopened envelopes
tightly in their hands, but when they read the air force message,
expressing regret that "no further information has been received,"
they would only have felt more uncertainty.[10] These letters also did not
say how long the wait for information would take, how long the ordeal
of letters would continue, and what emotional toll it would eventually
take on the families. The waiting game had begun.

At the end of August 1944, both Bill Taylor's and Bud Burt's families
received correspondence confirming their worst fears—but not defin-
itively. The International Red Cross in Geneva had obtained German
information that their sons had died on March 15, 1944. The circumstances remained unknown, and because the information came from
"enemy sources," the air force said it was "necessary for the present to
consider your son 'missing believed killed' until confirmed by further
evidence."[11] The report left the families in limbo—they could neither
fully grieve nor believe in miracles.

In November, Bob Hudson's and Jock Cruickshank's families were
informed of the German documents. Bob's mother wrote to her eldest
son, Clarence (Cag), then serving in the Royal Signals, upon receiving
the news:

I don't know how I'm going to write. You must have noticed
when I wrote my last letter to you that I was down in the
depths, and now I feel worse than ever. I had news last
Wednesday that Bob is reported killed, and have been waiting
for a letter giving details. Today I have a letter from the Red
Cross to say that they have an Official Statement from a

German source which says that Bob and three other Sergeants whose names and numbers are all given correctly, lost their lives on the night of March 15th.

There seems to be no reason to doubt this, although there are no details as to how they died or where they are buried, and the Red Cross Committee promise to let us know as soon as they receive any more information.

It's hard Cag, all this after waiting, hoping and praying for eight long weary months. I've tried to be brave, and the old chin has been kept up well outside, but there have been so many times in the last few months that I have just sobbed my heart out when I have been alone in the house. I can't bear it, that's why I have opened my house to the R.A.F. Boys from Wymeswold. They and the yanks helped me through the dark patch in a wonderful way, and it is a great consolation for me to receive lovely letters from Mothers in different parts of this Country and Canada and America, thanking me for what I have done for their boys, and praying for the safe return of my own boys.[12]

For the other families, the waiting game continued. Oddly, the only person to receive a letter with a full list of those named in the German documents was Robert Lumgair (Norm's brother), who was still serving overseas. The German documents revealed that "Sgt. Cruickshank, Sgt. Taylor, Sgt. Hudson, Sgt. Burt, Sgt. Ennis and one other listed as 'unknown' all lost their lives on the 15th March, 1944. Sgt. Ennis is not a member of this crew."

Larry, Norm, and George, who were not named in the letter, continued to be listed as missing.[13] Between December 1944 and February 1945, the Air Ministry sent a letter to the crewmen's relatives, asking if they'd had any further information from their loved one. It went on to say that, "in view of the lapse of time and the absence of any further information . . . the Air Ministry Overseas now proposes to take action to presume [their deaths] for official purposes."[14] Norm's father, who received the letter in December, responded to the Casualties Office in a tone that showed the strain the families were feeling: "We have had no further word from Norman but I might say it would have showed more sympathy after withholding notice so long if you had held it just a little longer or until after Xmas."[15]

In February 1945, Bill's and Bud's families signed for the personal effects their sons had left behind. Bill's belongings came in a carton; Bud's in a brown fibre suitcase. Official death certificates for all seven men were written by February 1945. With these in hand, the families could apply for life insurance payments and begin to settle the dead men's estates, a process that was not completed until almost a year and a half after the men went missing.

In England, Bob's mother opened the box containing her son's effects and discovered some items she was sure belonged to someone else. At the time, she placed them back in the box and put it away. However, when she returned to them later, she removed a notebook, one of the items she didn't recognize, and found a common link. She immediately wrote to Bud's family in Canada:

> I looked through the book and found your address and remembered that Sgt. Burt was one of the names in the Red Cross letter.
>
> Was he your son? If so I know you will be glad to have the book. The only other article amongst my son's belongings that I am not sure about is a Rolls Razor. If that belonged to your boy I will gladly send it on to you. I know it wasn't my Bob's.[16]
>
> What a methodical boy he must have been to have kept such a record of letters received and sent.
>
> In my boy's wallet was a photograph (postcard size) of a Canadian Sgt. A.G. I wonder if that was your boy, in any case there would only be two A.G.s in one crew . . . now that we know the worst I can only say how grieved I am for you all and pray that God has given you strength to bear your sorrow.
>
> My son told me what a "grand bunch of lads" his crew were and I know how proud he was to be serving with Canadians, he had only one other English boy in his crew.[17]

The letters, the effects, and the payments, when they came, were constant reminders, fleetingly reopening the shutters of hope before slamming them shut again, leaving gaping wounds that never quite healed for any of the families. This experience was probably common for most families, especially those who found themselves in receipt of a letter stating their loved one was missing—and there were more than a few such families over the course of the war. As David L. Bashow wrote in his history of Bomber Command:

> The violent, dynamic, and wide-ranging nature of the air war was such that many airmen have no known graves, and the skies over northwest Europe remain their only cemetery. In poignant testimony, the Runnymede Memorial in Britain, dedicated in 1953, is inscribed with the names of 20,000 Commonwealth airmen of the Second World War who have no known place of eternal rest.[18]

The world celebrated Victory in Europe (VE) Day on May 8, 1945, and families of the missing hoped they would finally receive definitive news in one form or another. If their loved one were dead, they might now get official confirmation from the air force. And if he were alive, the lost would be found and brought home to families who waited anxiously for such news.

Since Larry's disappearance, the Doran family had been troubled by the term "missing." They struggled to overcome the sense of being in limbo in which communications with the air force had left them. There was no sense of finality. They couldn't shake their uncertainty, despite the happy news of victory. Shortly after VE Day, their doubts were replaced by hope. A serviceman knocked on the door of the Doran home in Vancouver, asking to speak with Larry. They welcomed him in but explained that Larry had been listed as missing and then officially listed as dead despite no physical proof. Confused, they listened as the serviceman, with the best of intentions, told them that he had met Larry while overseas in England. One night, on a bombing raid, he himself had been shot down over Germany and captured, spending the rest of the war as a prisoner. During his imprisonment he was sure he had seen Larry in another section of the camp but was unable to communicate with him because the guards were beating anyone who talked. With his own liberation, he assumed Larry had also been freed and returned home.[19]

The Dorans heard this story at a most precarious time, when men were returning from overseas, some of whom had been missing and presumed dead. They wondered if Larry, like this man, might actually have survived the war. Might he be coming home any day now, to step over their threshold and back into their lives? Surely he had to be alive if someone had seen him. Despite their expectations, Larry did not appear.

On August 17, 1945, yet another tragedy befell the Doran family when Larry's father, William John Doran, suffered a fatal heart attack at the Tilley Hotel in Tilley, Alberta.[20] William had been on his way home from the RCAF base in Gimli, Manitoba, where he had been on duty with the Royal Engineers, working for the Canadian War Department. He died never knowing what had happened to his son. Within the last nine years, Larry's mother had lost her youngest son and grandson in two separate and unrelated tragedies; her eldest son, Larry, was missing, presumed killed in the war, without even a grave she could visit; and now she would have to bury her husband, who had also died away from home in the service of his country.

That summer the RCAF shipped home the personal effects of George, Larry, and Norm. When George's wife, Pat, received his personal effects, she noticed the date of an unfinished letter: March 15, 1944.[21] She also realized that a number of items were missing, and she wrote to the Estates Branch requesting information regarding his "ring, identification bracelet, pen and pencil, cigarette case and lighter."[22] The writer who responded presumed that "he would have been carrying them with him on his last flight and, therefore, they could not have been recovered. This is, indeed, regretful as these items would be more precious to you than the other personal effects."[23] Denied these "more precious" items, lost in the ravages of war, Pat had few physical items left to cherish or pass to their children.

In November 1945, definite news came for the families of Bill, Bud, Jock, and Bob: "According to information obtained from German documents, your son was buried on March 17th, 1944, in the village cemetery at Hilsenheim, approximately thirty miles south west of Strassbourg [sic], Germany." The letter writer ended by assuring the families the graves would be taken care of.[24] Each of the four families now had the date and place of their son's burial but this served as little consolation for what they had been through.

In January 1946, a new year began without war. Although the letters dwindled in number, they still came. Bud's family received a letter near the end of the month noting "a ring, believing to have belong[ed] to your son," had been received at the Estates Branch in Ottawa from overseas and would be sent to them within a matter of days. Bud's mother was instructed to sign and return a copy of the enclosed inventory when she received the ring.[25] She signed the paper on March 15, the second anniversary of her son's death.

For Pat Parker, now considered a widow, the year was an unsettled one. She sold the home George had bought in Edmonton, Alberta, and travelled with her two young children to BC. In a letter written from Kelowna to Bill Taylor's family, she confided:

> *I feel a little blue at selling my house and leaving all the old familiar things behind, but do hope that with this change, I'll be able to settle and find happiness and peace of mind in myself.*
>
> *Am going on to Vancouver in a week or so and then to Victoria. If I can find a place to live, may stay at the coast for the winter. Gail will be starting to [sic] school in September, so will have to settle somewhere by then. I didn't sell my furniture, as I'm sure that eventually I'll return to Edmonton, so will keep it in storage for a while...*
>
> *The children are growing so fast I can scarcely keep them in clothes.*
>
> *Hello to Florence and Dorothy and hope they'll forgive my laxness in my correspondence, but I do think of you all often. Please write when you can...*
>
> *Am looking forward to the rest of my journey as it will be something for us to remember in years to come.*[26]

Near the end of the year, Bill's, Bud's, and Norm's families received the Operational Wings bestowed on their sons. Over the next year and a half, the RCAF forwarded Larry's, Bud's, George's, Norm's, and Bill's log books to their families. Their individual handwriting in the log books was cut short on that last night, and the bold red word *MISSING* stared back at the family from the last entry on the page.

It took almost four years for some bare details of that fateful night to finally come to light. In March 1948 the families received a letter reporting that investigating officers from the Missing Research and Enquiry Service had visited Hilsenheim, thirty-two kilometres south-west of Strasbourg. Upon interrogating the mayor it was revealed:

> *Your son's aircraft crashed two kilometres from Hilsenheim on the road to Wittisheim which is two miles South East of Hilsenheim. No ceremony of any kind was permitted by the Germans who carried out the burial themselves. The villagers, however, went secretly the following night and placed flowers on the graves, much to the anger of the local German Commandant who threatened to shoot the villagers. Fortunately he did not carry out his threat.*
>
> *The graves were located in the village Cemetery; the first three being inscribed with the names of Pilot Officer Taylor, Sergeant Burt, and Sergeant Hudson. The graves of the four remaining crew members were marked "unknown." Exhumation was carried out, but unfortunately individual identification was not found possible. These graves will therefore be registered collectively.*

The letters ended by noting that headstones would be erected at the graves.[27]

Over a year passed before all the families received one final letter. It noted that the graves of the crew were at last registered and expressed "deepest sympathy" for the loss of their "gallant" loved ones.[28] The upheaval for the families finally ended, nearly five and a half years after the deaths.

3

The Beginning of a Love Affair

On a sunny Saturday afternoon in England, I scanned the shelves and tables heaped high with books in Waterstone's bookstore, looking for something to occupy my time while I waited for my mobile to ring. *I should be home working,* I thought. My desk was still scattered with paperwork, unfinished lesson plans for the school classes I taught. But today I was to meet my pen pal, an Australian soldier I had been emailing for the past several months, who was in England on holiday from his overseas deployment. We had bonded over our shared interests in travel and history, and his sense of humour had helped reduce the stress of my hectic life as a teacher. I looked forward to reading his frequent emails and responding in turn, the reading and writing an enjoyable, creative outlet, an indulgence and escape from work.

My eyes wandered to my wristwatch. I thumbed a book, read a back cover, pulled my phone out of my jacket, and looked down at my wrist yet again. How long should I give the Aussie soldier before I headed home to go back to work? I had no way of knowing if he had even arrived in England, no phone number to call. I huffed. Do I take the next bus home? Or miss it and find myself stuck waiting two more hours for the one after that? I moved back to the table of books I had been through twenty minutes earlier, looking for something, anything, of interest. Then the phone finally rang.

I walked the short distance to the library, where we had agreed to meet. We were just going to have a face-to-face chat, maybe eat a meal together. Nothing more than an impromptu get-together of two friends in between one of their holiday flights. He'd be off to wherever, and I'd be back to my paperwork. As I approached, I smiled hesitantly at the man standing by the library entrance. Clean-cut, no one else standing around. He smiled back, standing face-on in the bright sunlight, hands on hips and a jacket resting on one forearm.

He stuck out his hand. "Hi, I'm Michael. You must be Lisa."

I shifted my own jacket to the other arm as I offered him my hand. There had been only a few men in my life who had bothered to shake my hand.

I suggested we head to the park up the street as it was such a nice day. Finding an empty bench in the busy grounds, we sat down and chatted, getting a feel for one another. Within minutes I leaned back, one leg crooked up onto the bench, arm over the backrest. We conversed for well over an hour, asking and answering questions in turn. Watching the easygoing, relaxed figure, I was struck by a startling revelation. I had found a man I could see myself being friends with for the rest of my life.

Instead of going off to other meetings and activities as he had planned to do, Michael spent the next week with me, meeting me after work, holding my hand as we walked, visiting local museums, cooking me a meal, and falling asleep on my shoulder while I worked evenings on my laptop. As the week ended, I realized he had somehow worked his way into my heart.

Three years later, after numerous long-haul flights, meeting respective parents, a very short engagement, many marathon phone calls to plan an overseas wedding, and the insanity of applying for a spouse visa, I found myself stepping onto a Qantas plane with nothing more than a one-way ticket, a suitcase, and a carry-on bag. A few eyebrows must have been raised when security officers scanned my luggage. It was filled with choice bits of personal treasures from my past, including a collection of special teddy bears, memory sticks, photographs, some necessary clothing, and a copy of my paternal family tree tucked neatly into the front pouch. Having just paid off the last of my student loans, I couldn't afford a shipping container or smaller crates to follow behind, so I gave the meagre contents of my cottage to friends and charity and said goodbye to a cold winter in Britain. When I stepped off the plane a day later, a blistering hot Australian summer greeted me.

Moving to Australia was the best and worst of experiences. I was finally living with my new husband after several months apart due to our respective job commitments, but finding employment in my new homeland proved incredibly difficult. Nearly eight and a half years earlier, when British education scouts spoke at my Canadian university about teaching opportunities overseas, I had eagerly looked into the possibility of teaching abroad and eventually moved to Britain, looking for a new start and maybe some adventure. England was part of my heritage, after all, and I was curious and excited to take a step back into the country my ancestors had come from. I'd had no trouble finding work—too much work. In the back of my mind I envisioned weekends of travelling around the countryside, frequenting old manor houses, delving into my family history. Pressing work commitments taking over every weekend and practically all my free time wasn't exactly what I'd in mind, but it paid the bills.

In Australia, however, the job hunt wasn't going quite the way I had planned. I hadn't realized how restricted employment would be in the government area where we lived. Non-Australians are not permitted to take government employment, and a number of job postings that I might have had a chance at were put off limits by the phrase I'd come to dread: "Australian citizens only should apply."

Michael and I had discussed the stresses of my previous job, and we had made a deal. I could apply for any job I wished but I was not allowed to bring work home. Being a bit of a workaholic, and knowing I would only be able to teach part-time under those conditions, I initially did not see a problem. Part-time or shared teaching positions were common in the British education system. However, in Australia, the idea of two teachers sharing a class was alien—and suspect. When this door closed, I set my sights on working in galleries or museums as an education officer. I would still have the enjoyment of working with students, but in a less stressful way. As well, I would be able to draw on my training in teaching, English, and art history, and develop my interest in various aspects of history. It seemed liked the perfect combination. Even if I couldn't get an education position, I anticipated getting some kind of work, even menial labour, at a museum. I hadn't expected museums to fall under the government restriction.

After several fruitless months—and knowing my lengthy education should have carried me to more than the single job interview I had achieved—I found myself, for the first time in my life, walking into an employment agency to see if they could offer me any advice on my resumé or cover letter. The small communal space began to swallow me whole as I explained my situation, only to find the advisor had no suggestions other than "just keep applying."

The man sitting at the next table, working on a basic resumé, turned, looked me up and down, laughed, and quipped, "If you can't get a job, then what the hell are my chances!" *Better than mine*, I thought. At least he was Australian. I wouldn't be able to call myself an Aussie until four years had passed. I left the office barely able to keep the tears from running down my face. Four years! What was I going to do until then? What was I doing in this place?

I slunk home, defeated, rejected, with pain throbbing through the knot in my shoulders and up my neck. I had no way to prove my worth as a newly arrived wife and resident.

The following morning I got up as usual, made Michael's breakfast and lunch, and kissed him before he left for work. I tried to tell myself it was a new morning, a new day; I should just be positive. I scanned the online job posts, looking for anything, however humble, that would let me gain some Australian work experience. Clicking through the pages there was nothing, nothing, nothing. Only restricted government jobs or work I could not do without prior experience I definitely did not have, like driving a transport truck, plumbing, or cutting hair.

By eleven I was ready to scream. I closed my eyes, leaned back in my chair, and squeezed the bridge of my nose, then pushed myself away from the computer and paced the room. I couldn't go through another day looking at job posts, writing cover letters, and tweaking resumés. I stopped in the centre of the room, aimlessly staring at the closet door.

Taking a few steps, I reached out, slid the door aside, and looked at the pile of books, CDs, and photos. I cringed at the sight of my black portfolio, neatly tucked in the corner, silently snickering "loser" at me, before I averted my eyes and turned to the line of thin folders and other paperwork that actually belonged to me and not my husband . . . who was happily oblivious at work, in a job, a real job, unlike me.

I resisted the urge to grab everything and throw it onto the floor. I'd be the one picking it up, and I doubted that would improve my state of mind. I fingered the paperwork, looking for something, anything, that would take me as far away from Australia and my job search as I could get. Something red caught my eye.

That will do, I thought, pulling out the red folder containing a copy of my paternal family tree. *I need a diversion.*

My father's cousin Marg had started collecting particulars on the Burt family years ago. I had never seemed to have more than one brief weekend a year to delve into her paperwork, and now I decided this would pass the hours nicely. I knew very little about my father's side of the family except the confusion I had felt as an eight-year-old child grappling with the reality of death and remarriage and stepparents when my class at school was given a simple assignment to create a family tree.

"But why isn't Grandpa's last name the same as yours, Dad? The teacher said this side would have your last name and the other side would be under Mom's maiden name." So began what my parents probably felt was the equivalent of the Spanish Inquisition. The initial stark realization that some familiar last names didn't link up, while names I had never heard before, and people I had never met, did go on the tree, bothered me deeply. Who were these people? What did they have to do with me? It had all seemed so confusing and unfair. Why wasn't Grandpa my dad's father? If he wasn't Dad's dad, then why did I call him Grandpa? Why couldn't Grandma So-and-So go on my tree? The never-ending questions of a child continued as I tried to wrap my mind around this strange mix of family.

I can still remember sitting on Grandpa's knee the following weekend and staring at that adoring, smiling face, trying to find the answers. Even though I was young, I was fully aware that asking him directly about his connection to the family tree might be inappropriate. I feared hurting him more than I feared never knowing the answers. But in that struggling silence in my heart, I still wondered how he was on my family tree. I called him Grandpa, and he was technically my grandpa, but he wasn't my dad's dad. He wasn't blood. Worse yet, he wasn't my blood. Who was he then? Who was I? For a very short while I resented the feeling that I had somehow lost something I could not put my finger on. Grandpa was dead, but he was here in front of me, wasn't he?

Over the ensuing years, the confusion and resentment slipped into my unconscious. Then Grandpa died when I was fourteen, and my real grandfather stepped out of the shadows slightly when my grandmother gave me two rings, one belonging to the only grandfather I had ever known and another given to her by her first husband, my dad's father, who had been too ill to go to war and died of meningitis in February 1942. A few pictures followed, but nothing more was said.

Over time I began to understand what constituted real family, which was something much broader than blood ties. My immediate family had countless friends and distant relatives who were not blood but were every bit as blood-bound as any true relatives. That eight-year-old mind still lurked within me, wanting to find the answers to the unspoken past, to faces without history, to find family in blood and non-blood alike. It was one catalyst that would shape the next three years of my life.

Now, as I took the family tree in hand, a number of photocopied photos dropped out of the folder. My great-great-grandfather and my second cousin Bud were among them, and I realized they were prime candidates for interesting research as they had military backgrounds, which I could possibly check online. I thumbed through the pages of relatives and found the few details of Bud's life. He would be easiest to research, having served in the Second World War. And he had always held a special place in my mind, being my dad's cousin and having died so young. Besides, it should be a quick task to gather information on a short-lived life, shouldn't it?

Sitting back down at the computer and settling on my new focus, I entered the Commonwealth War Graves Commission (CWGC) website. I had looked at this site years before and thought it might be the best place to start again. I typed in Bud's real name, Robert George Alfred Burt, and scanned the data for him. Nothing new here. He had been a sergeant and an air gunner in the Royal Canadian Air Force and had died on March 15, 1944, at only twenty years old.[1] As I tapped my fingers on the desk, staring at the screen, it occurred to me that I might be able to link his grave details with those of other men who had died that night.

I clicked on the cemetery information link. Including Bud, there were seven casualties, a full crew for a Lancaster, all of whom died March 15, 1944. I realized, in that moment, that Bud must have been with these men when he died. The cemetery report listed the names and data of Douglas Cruickshank, William Lawrence Doran, Robert Henry Hudson, Norman Andrew Lumgair, George Parker, and William Taylor. These men had known Bud, but all of them were dead.

How could I find out more about them? All I knew about Bud was what my dad had told me when I was a child, but Dad was only a child himself when his cousin died. His knowledge amounted to the proud words "Bud was a tail gunner in a Lancaster bomber," spoken whenever we watched a movie or a documentary on the Second World War. I possessed photocopies of two Second World War-era pictures and a poem Bud had written to his girlfriend not long before he died. Other than that I knew nothing about his life apart from the recorded data in front of me on the CWGC website.

I scrutinized the first of two photocopied photographs in my possession. An optimistic young man stared back at me, dressed in his uniform, cap at a distinct angle. No distinguishing markings on the sleeve or chest—a new recruit. He looked so young.

From my family ancestry information I knew Bud had come from a large family, the third-eldest of nine living children. I wondered how it must have been for his family to see him volunteer for active service. What would they remember? The surviving siblings would be in their early seventies, if not in their eighties. I had never met any of them. If I tracked them down, would they be able—or willing— to tell me anything about this beaming chap? What visions of their brother did they hold?

I clicked on the cemetery photo link and enlarged the photo of the graves. Using the grave number from each crew member's information, I identified Bud's tombstone and determined which crew members belonged to the other graves. Flowers spanned all seven graves as though they had just been laid to rest yesterday, not over sixty-five years ago. Who took care of these men in their final resting place? Had the families visited the graves? Did their relatives know what had happened to these men? Did they know their brother or son or husband lay entombed in Hilsenheim Communal Cemetery . . . which sounded more like a German village cemetery than a graveyard in Bas-Rhin, France? Why was that?

In the second photocopy, Bud stood on the edge of a path, smiling but perhaps a little less naive, his gunner boots and mitts on, a couple of Nissen huts in the background. Who took the picture? Was the photographer still alive? I wondered if Bud had sent this picture with the verse he had penned to his girlfriend while overseas. A Brampton newspaper printed the poem after he was listed as missing.

With the facts from the CWGC to aid my research, I started typing the crew names, squadron, hometowns, and so on into Google. What appeared was beyond my expectations. I had stepped into a world that was oddly familiar, with place names I recognized from both Canada and Britain. I had been to Brampton and Vancouver in Canada, and was not all that far away from York on a trip to the Lake District while living in Britain. These fly boys had ended up far from home, not unlike me, although in different circumstances.

The next thing I knew, I heard the gate creak open; Michael was home. Where had the afternoon gone? I quickly saved the information and set it aside.

The next day I checked the job pages but, finding nothing new, turned my attention back to researching Bud and his crew mates. The work was like a special treat, like warm cookies baked by Mom and eaten straight off the pan, fresh from the oven. For the first time in weeks I felt good. I found countless websites on the war, including forums if I wanted to ask questions, and slowly I began to link information to the boys and how they fit into the war as a whole. One piece of information, a story about the crash on March 15, 1944, which I found on the Wittisheim council website, even mentioned Bud by name.[2] I stared in disbelief, trying to absorb the French tale of events surrounding the crash. I quickly translated the story, which described how Bud had been found in his turret with an axe. According to the article, Bud had been trying to escape his turret by hacking at the turret mountings. Tears rolled down my face as I realized Bud hadn't died sweetly oblivious to his end. He knew his fate rested on whether he could escape his turret. Something had gone terribly wrong.

"You should write a book," Michael commented a few days later when I could no longer keep my revelations to myself and worked up the nerve to show him what I had found while I was supposed to be job hunting. He had to be joking. Was it possible to find enough information to make the crew's story an entire book, a memorial to their short but amazing lives? Right now I was collecting more questions than answers, but my curiosity got the better of me. With my secret out and my husband's little push, I found myself falling deeper and deeper into the past. I had unknowingly taken a job without a wage.

4

Seeking Answers

After Michael left for work each morning, I rummaged through the job ads with new vigour, then gave over the afternoons to research. The boys became my life, a security blanket. They gave me confidence and a sense of belonging, protecting me from my new and strange world that often seemed unfair and unrelenting. Somehow they had my back, and with their support I was able to ride out the storm of a job search that had threatened my sanity.

The research was exciting, but I quickly realized I was going to have to focus my search. What was it I really wanted? When it came down to it, I wanted photographs, to know the boys' individual and collective stories, and to discover what happened that fateful night. Essentially, I wanted to trace their lives from beginning to end, to know the boys inside out.

I wondered what information was available and how easy it would be for me to access considering I was living in Australia. The Internet was a fantastic source, an immediate link between my solitary existence at my computer and the greater world. I couldn't afford to go to every museum, archive, or library that held the information I was searching for—many were located thousands of kilometres away in Canada and Britain. I could, however, search their databases online, email queries, obtain copies of documents (at a cost), and search and leave comments in their public comment area in case someone else was searching as I was. Air force associations, war forums, magazines, and newspapers also led me to people who had similar interests.

These interested people were the most instrumental in bringing me answers. They suggested books and websites I could explore. They handed my contact details to others who had the ability to answer my questions. They kindly offered to check documents when they visited archives, museums, and libraries. They even took notes from reference materials and sent them by email.

Along the way I gathered a number of contacts, many of whom became friends. One person in particular, George McKillop, a Second World War 408 Squadron mechanic who was living in BC, became my mentor despite the distance between us. George read my writing, made suggestions, and, most important, believed in me and gave me the courage to keep going when frustrations were high.

I met George through Kelvin Youngs, who was, at the time, part of the Aircrew Remembrance Society, a non-political society that helps relatives and also collects and preserves information (photographs, documents, and memories) of fallen and missing airmen from all nations who fell during the Second World War. From the moment I sent George my research notes in an email and asked if he could help, he knew I was serious about detailing the lives of the boys. He had no doubts I could achieve my objective, and his unwavering trust was exactly the support I needed over the years of searching out the details of their lives.

When I was trying to find more information on the aircraft, I contacted Floyd Williston, author of *Footless Halls of Air*. In the book was a chapter on Earl Reid, the pilot who flew LL637 in 432 Squadron. Through Floyd, I made contact with Earl Reid's nephew Bob, living in Western Canada. Bob was keen on discovering information about his relative, and he sent me helpful information that was difficult to come by. He also happily ordered microfiche from the archive in Ottawa to be sent out west to a library with a microfiche reader, then drove to the library several times at his own expense so he could help me gather information from 432 and 408 Squadron diaries.

In some cases, people sent me books and newspaper clippings. One individual, Robert Schimanowsky, contacted me after coming across my request for information in *Legion Magazine*. He sent me the book *Boys, Bombs and Brussels Sprouts*. Sadly, not long after, he passed away. George McKillop also loaned me a book, *Call of the Goose*. Both books were directly linked to 408 Squadron and not easily obtainable, making their contribution of great importance. From these, I not only gained a sense of what it was like for the boys to be in the air force, but also acquired further directions for research, such as place names, details of specific raids, and the names of others who had flown in the squadron, whom I could then identify in the squadron diary. The story began to come together.

Acquiring even small pieces of information spurred me to keep digging, but it told me little of the boys' specific characters. I hungered to discover more about Bud and the men he had flown with. I realized their relatives would have the personal stories I could not find on the Internet or in history books. Finding the crew families, however, took a long time.

Early in the search I stumbled upon the Library and Archives Canada (LAC) website. Seeing that LAC held service records from the Second World War, I quickly typed in Bud's name, and up came a reference and volume number. The same was true for the other Canadian boys. I knew I wanted the files, but I held off ordering them at first, hoping maybe to get to Ottawa and access the information at a cheaper rate. I wasn't working and was unwilling to hand over an unspecified amount of cash for an unknown amount of information. I was also unable, from the sparse description, to ascertain what the files might hold, so I had no idea if they would help me locate the families or supply much personal information. Instead, I sat on the knowledge and continued my Internet search.

When I began my search for the families, I quickly discovered, mainly through the CWGC website, that they were scattered to the winds, spread across Canada, down to the southern United States, across the Atlantic Ocean in Britain, and, if I counted myself among the mix, across the Pacific in Australia. I spent countless hours scanning and posting messages on Internet forums, sending letters to their hometown newspapers and magazines, writing emails, and, in a number of cases, making phone calls as a last resort, often with the help of others. There were long waits with no replies and no leads. Patience is truly a virtue when it comes to researching.

In the course of one search, I came across Douglas Cruickshank's name on a memorial in St. Mark's Church in Harrogate, England. It seemed as good a place as any to start, so I emailed the church to ask if the family might still be in the area. Two members of the congregation tried to find a relative, but in the end they sadly said they could only tell me what street he had lived on and the names of two of his siblings. They also generously took time to send a few photographs of the memorial showing his name. It was a brilliant start, and I was pleased with the help total strangers were willing to give me. I continued to search but to no avail, and after several unsuccessful attempts in forums and the like, I set Douglas aside and moved on to see if I could find information on the others.

One day, as I read through the forum section of the Canadian Bomber Command Memorial website, I found a comment posted by Charlie Lumgair, pilot Norm Lumgair's nephew. Even though a number of years had passed since his post, I sent an email and was thrilled to receive a prompt reply. Charlie filled in the details of Norm's early years for me; handed me letters telling the story of Wally Richmond, who was originally the tail gunner of the crew; helped me much later on, via phone calls, to find two more families; and spent hours traipsing about parts of Western Canada to find information for me. Charlie became my long arm, reaching places I could not go.

One might wonder why I did not begin by making straightforward contact with my own relatives for information on Bud. Surely finding a contact for Bud would be, for me, a simple matter of making a phone call. However, with Grandpa Burt passing away at an early age, and my grandmother's subsequent moves and remarriages, our ties to the Burt family had dwindled. I had no recollection of ever meeting a Burt relative. All I had was the family tree sent years earlier by an elderly and very ill cousin of my father. I finally did make contact, however, as a result of a strange turn of events.

Early in my research I read two books from Saskatchewan, *Their Names Live On* and *Age Shall Not Weary Them: Saskatchewan Remembers Its War Dead*, both of which mentioned Bill Taylor, the air bomber on EQ-P. When I emailed the contacts listed in one of the books, two of the messages bounced back, but one went through, and my details were passed on to the Taylor family. Soon after, Laura, Bill's niece, emailed me on the family's behalf. Contact with Bill's remaining siblings, and the wartime photos and letters they shared with me, gave me a fuller context and further depth of understanding. And Laura gave me a list of contacts to other crew families that opened several doors. I was soon in touch with Bob Hudson's family in Britain and Bud's brother Ken Burt, who lived in the southeastern United States.

Ken had spent much time researching Bud and the crash. He had wanted to create a small written memorial to his brother for future generations, but this had never come to fruition. Now he quickly became a much-loved relative, sharing a common goal with me. He supplied notes from his own research at the Canadian archives, which showed me the depth of information the archives held and encouraged me to request some of the records for myself. He also sent me a number of wartime postcards and letters, travelled all the way to Canada to collect information from his sister Evelyne, and took it upon himself to interview Bud's best friend, Jim Mullholland, all for my benefit. Together, we would finish what he had started.

After I received their mailing addresses from Bill Taylor's niece, I wrote to both Pat Johnson (née Hudson, Bob's sister) and Joan Hudson (Bob's sister-in-law, the wife of his younger brother, John) in Britain. Soon after, I received a phone call from Pat. John Hudson, who had died in 2004, had spent time tracking down the story of the crash of EQ-P in Alsace. He even made contact with the Steydli family, who owned the property where the plane went down. John had hoped to unite the crew families for the fiftieth anniversary of the crash in 1994, but although he found the Taylors, he searched in vain for the others. The Hudsons, along with the Taylors and the Steydlis, paid tribute to the boys that year in Hilsenheim, but John had not achieved his dream of meeting all the families and gathering them together. Pat was pleased to give me any information she could, sending me a letter, along with photographs and copies of wartime correspondence, and telling me what she could recall about her brother. Before long, her daughter Barbara chipped in, speeding up the passage of information via the Internet.

Rene and Marie-Thérèse Steydli, who were both witness to the night of March 15, 1944, were also delighted to help, with their children Jean-Paul and Monique translating their French responses into English. The whole family's kindness and support of my research quickly endeared them to me. Remembering and honouring the boys was clearly as important to them as it was to me and the other crew families.

After exhausting Laura's contacts, I continued my search via the Internet, but it was her knowledge that helped me find the other families.

I figured that George, who was married, may have had children. It was common in that era for family to name their children after grandparents and parents. Laura's sister was able to verify this. The family still had a letter from 1946 that had been written to their mother by George Parker's wife. From these I learned George Parker had two children named Gail and George. I was also aware that people tended to remain closer to their roots in that era than they do today. Based on these angles, I turned to the online phone directory to see if any names stood out. There were more than a few. I narrowed down the list, and Charlie Lumgair graciously offered to call around, trying to find a connection. Within days his effort paid off. We had accounted for both George's children.

Gail Parker, George's daughter, was able to give us some information on Larry Doran's wife, Marjorie, and Charlie made some more calls. Although we learned Marjorie had passed away, we received information from Marjorie and Larry's marriage certificate, which noted a Walter Doran had witnessed the wedding. One last time, Charlie looked for Larry's relatives, and once again we were lucky. Larry's brother had died years earlier, but his wife had not changed the phone listing. By this chance alone we found Larry's surviving sister-in-law.

This initial connection with the Doran family required communicating by mail rather than email, so the pace of progress was slow. Charlie, my long arm, helped to speed things up through phone calls and by passing information to me via the Internet. He also made a trek to Bralorne Pioneer Museum to read a 1938 article from the community club's newsletter that identified Larry as a "local personality"; this supplied several leads. Later, after Larry's sister-in-law—my Doran contact—died, and while I was searching independently for more leads, I stumbled upon Larry's nephew Patrick, living in Ireland and commenting in an ancestry forum. With his knowledge of family history, which had become an avid pastime in his retirement, we were able to verify what we knew of Larry and deepen our understanding of his life.

It took just over eight months, but I had finally made contact with all but one of the families. Ironically, the missing family was the one I had begun my search with. Now, with those others accounted for, I had to look for new leads to find Douglas Cruickshank's relatives. The last family couldn't be left out.

5

Making Connections

T wo months earlier, my job search had come to an end when I was offered a part-time position as a pathology clerk. Although there was a steep learning curve, the job turned out to be ideal—close to home, with an early start time, which meant I could be home for lunch and spend my afternoons on research.

Matters soon became more complicated, though, as my own private war experience began to play out. My husband was preparing to be sent overseas yet again, this time to Afghanistan. Although I did not feel he was in the same kind of danger that Bud's crew had faced, this did little to calm my nerves. I now had an inkling how George's and Larry's wives must have felt when their husbands left for Europe. I took comfort in the knowledge that my spouse would be back in about four months if all went well.

I took the day off work to accompany Michael to the airport. As others gathered to send their loved ones away on holiday or home from a visit, I hugged my husband goodbye and sent him to war. I watched him go through the gate and then waited for the plane to roll out onto the tarmac. By this time, all but myself and one other person had left the boarding area. We both looked for the same thing: our loved one's face in the tiny windows of the plane. I counted the ovals, trying to get an idea of his location, but I could not see him, even though I knew he was on the side of the aircraft closest to me. Slowly the plane rolled out of sight in preparation for its ascent. I waited, and soon it reappeared at speed, lifting up into the air and banking to the right before disappearing into the sky.

There was no reason left to stay. He was not going to come back today, tomorrow, or next month, and, like the wives in my research, I might face the reality that he would not come home at all. With that realization I took a taxi home. I was essentially a modern-day war bride, living in a foreign country where I still knew hardly anyone, working at a job outside my comfort zone, with my husband gone to an unknown place in a sandy, rocky war zone.

Work and research would be my consolation. It was time to put in a serious effort to locate the last family. I found the online news page for the area around York where the Cruickshanks had lived, and along with writing to a few local forums, I composed a letter to the editors of the online newspaper, asking if they might be able to help. They happily posted my letter in their virtual paper, and I waited yet again.

Since my husband's departure, my senses had become heightened. Every smell, movement, and sound seemed to be amplified. I was reluctant to partake in the delights of even my favourite meals. The smell made me nauseated and upset my stomach, which ached instead of growled, felt unsettled rather than hungry, became weak and shrunken in sympathy with my sleep-deprived brain. When I tried to sleep, any sound was a disruption, waking me with a start. Once roused, I would stay awake with my mind racing. As a result, sleep was sporadic and would come at the oddest hours. I took it where I could.

I was up early one Saturday, ready to push on with research and writing. By the afternoon, however, my eyes kept closing and my head drooped toward the keyboard more than once. Reluctantly, I decided to take a much-needed nap.

Nearly two and a half hours later I awoke but was lying on the bed, still groggy, when I heard the gate creak open. The doorbell rang and I hopped up, realizing I must look a mess, with my hair flying off in all directions. I pulled it out of its hair band and tried to straighten it before opening the door. I expected a sales pitch awaited me and dreaded having to dismiss it, politely but firmly.

To my surprise and utmost delight, there stood an Australian postie holding a large box in his hands. I knew immediately what was in the box: the service records that I had ordered months earlier. The return address label on the box, marked *Archives, Ottawa*, brought back memories of a childhood in that city and in Quebec for the postie, and about eight years of my early adulthood for me, and we took a few moments to chat about Ottawa. The funny part was that we were standing in the sunny heat of Canberra, Australia, talking about a place that seemed a world away and was still covered in snow.

Back inside the house, I cut the box open with Michael's Leatherman, an all-purpose utility tool that held special meaning for the job, with him serving in Afghanistan. I sat down on the carpet, pulling out the contents with eager anticipation. Here was a glimpse into the lives of four of the seven men—Larry, Bill, George, and Bud (I would get the rest of the files later)—though it was no more than stacks of photocopied paper held together by rubber bands.

That afternoon I perused every sheet of the approximately one thousand pages of documents. I read Larry's file first. Partway through I unexpectedly came across an impression of his fingerprints. Instinctively, my fingers shot forward, placed themselves over his distinct marks, and pressed through an invisible barrier. The upturned ephemeral form radiated into my own. As we touched, a jolt of electric emotion coursed through me before dissipating into the page. I felt the paper in sublime fervour, pressing my hand into his, feeling for the flesh and bone within the page's unseen depths. For a brief moment I had passed through time and space, the past and present, and connected with a man I would never meet but would forever love.

I grabbed the other files and flicked through the pages in search of the others' fingerprints. Drugged by the exhilarating but fleeting emotional manifestation, I needed a second hit. Only Bill Taylor's file produced another set. I smoothed my hand over the page with a mixture of elation and deep sadness. I thought of George Parker's children. They had lost their father at such a young age, in their formative years, with so few photographs, so few physical connections, no memories— but the emotional bond was still so strong. My research had stirred in Gail a flood of sadness, happiness, and pride. My contact with the families had made me distinctly aware that even after all this time, hearts had never fully healed; something inside remained forever broken. How could they ever mend under such circumstances? I wanted to be able to give them something to hold on to, something that was distinctly him. I wanted George Parker's children to experience the same epiphany with their father's fingerprints as I had with Larry Doran's, but George's fingerprints were not there. I looked through his file three times, each time hoping I had somehow missed the single page, but it was not to be. Going though Bud's file, I was again denied.

I thought of my family contacts for Larry and Bill and wondered if they would be blessed with the same feeling. They had probably never seen their relative's service records.

How privileged I felt to be the first to touch their hands in spirit. It was worth every penny it cost to get the records and every day it had taken for them to arrive. The long-awaited beginning had come. I was now face to face with the boys.

The service files proved to be a wealth of information, and my connections with the families were fleshing out the background stories of six of the boys, but I still had not had any response to my queries about family connections to Douglas Cruickshank. I began to wonder if I would be able to learn anything about him. After I talked to other researchers online, it became clear that finding all seven families was highly unlikely. Many people told me I should be happy with details of six of the men, but I wasn't. I needed to complete the crew. I could not leave Douglas and his family out of the research.

The days dragged as I spent time at work, learning my new job, and at home, searching in vain for the Cruickshank family, but the nights flew as I tossed and turned in bed, my mind shifting from thought to thought: What was going on with my husband overseas? How could I remember all the important details of my new duties? Where else could I dig for information on the boys, especially Douglas? As more and more stories of the crew came to light, with the families sharing their own large or scant collection of memories and memorabilia, I'd run through the details I was gathering for each boy. They had done so much living in the short years of their lives.

Douglas lingered in my thoughts like a ghostly apparition with no face and no true form. Although I could gather some information surrounding his trade, I could not develop any sense of his character. Why was his family so hard to find? The church's help had given me hope of finding them but had led to a dead end. Could no one remember what had happened to them? Or, for that matter, could no one recall Douglas growing up in the area? The elusive spectre floated never far from my conscious mind but just out of reach. The thought of leaving him behind while the others had their story told upset me. It just wouldn't be a full story without him.

One night in early March my heart leapt and my eyes flicked wide open as a sudden scratching sound came from the kitchen down the hall. I lay in bed, barely able to hear anything above the *whoosh* of blood pumping through my ears. It took several minutes of strained listening before I realized the noise came from the fridge. I couldn't remember hearing that sound when Michael had been home. I closed my eyes. A car squealed its tires on the street outside, and I tensed. I looked at the clock—1:00—let out a breath, covered my head with the blankets, and closed my eyes once again.

The alarm went off at 5:45, and I groaned, despite having been awake since 3:00. I dragged myself out of bed to prepare for work and, as usual, turned the computer on. With a bowl of cereal in hand, I curled up on the computer chair and opened my email account. Blurry-eyed, I checked my husband's email first. Things overseas had not been great. Not that he could tell me anything, but the television and Internet news happily reported every detail about the war. His comment—"Crazy"—summed it up. I understood.

Scanning through the remaining list of emails, I found one from a sender I did not recognize. It carried the subject line *Sergeant Douglas Cruickshank*, so I opened it, expecting to see general information easily found online. My face broke into a smile and my legs shook uncontrollably as I read a two-sentence email stating a family link with Douglas and ending "Please get back to me."[1]

It turned out a person in an ancestry forum linked to the Cruickshank family tree had noticed my search for the family and informed them. I tucked the final gosling safely under my wing.

With the elusive Cruickshank family finally found, I thought the hard part was done. How wrong I was. Sadly, the sister who held all the knowledge had died just months earlier, and not long after I made contact with the family, the last surviving sibling, living in Scotland, also passed. I had been searching in England when most of the family was in Scotland. No wonder I had struggled to find them, wasting valuable time. The remaining family members, unable to supply much insight into the life of Douglas—who I discovered they referred to as Jock—were learning as much as I. They still had a few photos and his medals, but they did not have his log book, making it impossible to determine his first noted flight or the date he finally became linked with the crew of EQ-P.

To make matters worse, when I applied for both Bob's and Jock's service files, I was met by a shocking roadblock. Not all countries kept detailed records of their Second World War servicemen, but after the completeness of the Canadian service files I had expected something more than three or four pages. British records included only general service information, devoid of comments or anything personal that might convey a sense of personality. Although I could understand that this protected the serviceman, I felt it prevented researchers from ever developing a rounded view of the person, especially as time passed and it became less likely they would find family members who actually remembered the man. I wondered what I could possibly glean from such minimal information.

PART 2

OF WHOM DO YOU SPEAK?

6

The Background of War

In Germany during the 1930s, the desire for power, temporarily quelled by defeat in the First World War, was slowly rebuilding. Soon Europe and the Commonwealth were no longer able to ignore Adolf Hitler's dream of European dominance as Germany spread beyond its borders. When Hitler invaded Poland on September 1, 1939, Britain declared war on Germany. On September 10, 1939, Canada followed suit.

In the late 1930s, Canada was, as it still is, a country of wide open spaces. With no enemy on the back doorstep, it offered the Royal Air Force (RAF) a safe place to build the required structures and runways,[1] with the manpower to train countless pilots and crew before sending them overseas. This, along with the country's ties to Britain and its reputation as a strong recruiter and trainer during the First World War, destined Canada to play a significant role in what would become air warfare in the Second World War.[2]

On October 10, 1939, one month after Canada declared war, the country announced it would supply the training fields for aircrews from Canada, Australia, New Zealand, and Britain. Canada signed the British Commonwealth Air Training Plan (BCATP) on December 17, 1939, and the first of many schools opened on April 29, 1940. Eighteen months later, almost all the training schools were in place and operational.[3]

The training of aircrew was systematic. Although there were changes over the war years to eliminate unnecessary training for some aircrew and to streamline the process of getting men into the aircraft and overseas for operational duty, all aircrew started by enlisting and going first to Manning Depot for basic training in military life. After this, many recruits went on to Initial Training School to learn the fundamentals of flight.[4] Subjects typically included mathematics, armaments (weaponry), signals (radio communications), navigation, airmanship (flying in an efficient and safe manner with the required proficiency, skill, and discipline), drill (marching and taking orders, in this instance), law and discipline, meteorology, aircraft recognition (learning to identify parts of an aircraft in order to determine whether a particular plane was friend or foe),[5] anti-gas training (learning how to protect oneself from poison gas attacks),[6] and Link training (training in a ground cockpit simulator).

From here, depending on the abilities of each individual, recruits went to a streamed school for specific crew trades. Pilots were sent for eight weeks to Elementary Flying Training School (EFTS) to learn the basics of flight, followed by Service Flying Training School, where they learned formation flying and improved the skills learned at the EFTS. If they managed all of this, they were sent to more advanced training establishments, generally located in Britain, where they would develop their skills in larger aircraft and focus on the rigours of flying over heavily defended territory.

The other recruits were posted to various training schools, depending on their specialty. There were schools for navigators and wireless operators, as well as schools devoted to bombing and gunnery.[7]

Much of the recruits' learning was assessed via written, practical, and oral exams, which allowed instructors to gauge the recruits' ability to perform the duties of their given course or trade to a required standard. If they did not pass the exams, they would have to retrain within the trade or remuster (be assigned to new duties) within another trade. It was a demanding workload, and for those wanting to be selected to, or remain within, a specific trade, such as pilot, there was a degree of pressure added to the already high expectations.

Upon completion of the courses and testing at each school, the airmen were given a well-deserved but short break of between four and fourteen days before moving on to the next school or course. Once they had completed all the courses in the BCATP, they would receive, on average, a two-week embarkation leave before heading overseas for more training and duty within a squadron.

At the peak of operation, the BCATP had 231 sites in Canada, 10,894 planes flying for training, and 94 schools in operation. The training program produced approximately 3,000 aircrew personnel per month. All told, 131,533 graduates, including those from Commonwealth and occupied countries, passed through the program. Besides helping to pull the Canadian economy out of the depression of the 1930s, the BCATP trained more than half of the men, almost all volunteers, who became aircrew for combat overseas.[8]

During 1940, Canada also took a step toward becoming an independent nation—still a member of the Commonwealth, but without some of the longstanding colonial bonds—when Britain allowed the country to supply squadrons to Bomber Command for operations. In the years to come, fifteen Canadian squadrons, mainly populated by Canadian servicemen, flew out of the north of England for Bomber Command, with many members having graduated from the BCATP.

Each of the boys who trained within the BCATP and eventually made up the ranks of Bomber Command came with his own individual personality, special talents, and unique history. Among them were the boys who would become the crew of EQ-P.

— 7 —

The Boys of EQ-P

Most of the men who volunteered to fly for the RAF's Bomber Command during the Second World War were in their early twenties. Many were fresh out of school. Several were the children of soldiers lucky enough to have survived the Great War. They lived in an era where word of mouth, handwritten letters, telegrams, newspapers, and radios were the common modes of communication. This was the era of the Great Depression, where work and money were scarce, and crops withered to dust in the heat of the sun, with no rain for respite.

Aircraft were majestic—and even more elusive than the farmers' crops. Before the Second World War, most people, including many of the boys who went on to fly in Allied fighters and bombers, had never been in an aircraft. Only one of the boys from EQ-P, Larry Doran, had flown in a plane prior to signing up for duty. With the influx of BCATP facilities, the air force made the average boy's dream of flying a plane an accessible reality. Dangerous or not, this opportunity proved irresistible to many a young lad.

The boys of EQ-P were representative of the recruits who went through BCATP. They ranged in age from nineteen to thirty and came from a variety of backgrounds—rural and urban; comfortably middle class, working class, poor; large families and small. Some were married with children while others were barely out of school.

Two were British and the others were Canadian, some by way of the United States.

As I attempted to join together several pasts that had been lost to time, I noted many similarities and differences among the boys. On their own, each was a unique individual; as a group, however, they fit into four broad categories that were common to many recruits at the time: young gunner boys, farm lads wanting to be pilots, husbands and fathers, and in the case of one crewman, true servicemen.

» Young Gunner Boys

Four of the seven boys who flew in EQ-P learned the art of gunnery as part of their training, but two specifically took on that trade as their full-time job. Bud and Bob, who grew up on opposite sides of the Atlantic Ocean, both stepped up to the challenge of working in the most confined areas of an aircraft, the rear and mid-upper turrets. The youngest of the men in EQ-P, they had the quick reflexes and sharp eyes necessary for the task of gunnery. In addition to their knowledge of gunnery, they also shared a mischievous side, but their lives growing up were very different.

Tail Gunner—Robert (Bud) George Alfred Burt

Bud was my cousin, my blood, and I had developed a curious bond with him from an early age because of my father's proud words about his role in the war, so it was no surprise that I would be interested in knowing more about him. But I also was fascinated by him because he represented half my family history, a history I did not yet know much about. I had enjoyed writing poetry as a teen, and so Bud's poem also piqued my interest. My research, to my surprise, uncovered quite the character. Bud was an energetic, curious scamp; a teasing, light-hearted mischief-maker with a sense of humour; a friendly, reliable sort just looking for excitement. He didn't seem to take anything too seriously and probably, to his way of thinking, had the world by the tail.

He was born April 8, 1924, in Yale, Michigan, the third of nine children born to Robert Oliver Burt, originally from Brampton, Ontario, and Myrtle Bessie Burt (née Weller) from Croswell, Michigan. Bud's elder sister Evelyne, ninety years old by the time I was doing my research, could still recall a number of playful childhood stories involving her green-eyed, fair-skinned imp of a brother with light brown hair. One day, when Evelyne and Bud were children, they got in their father's car. Bud "released the brake and the car rolled down the driveway incline. . . Someone yelled to Dad, 'Your car is going down the hill,' and Dad came running." Mill Creek flowed at the bottom of the incline. Evelyne recalls, "I was. . . pushed out or I got out before the car went into the creek. Bud was not hurt," but the car ended up in the water. Luckily the creek was shallow at this point and had been dammed by the local woolen mill, which used the water for its manufacturing.[1]

A few years later they moved to a new home, on a property with both a house and a large barn. Bud's father instructed the three eldest Burt children not to go into the barn, but that did not stop Bud and his sister. Curiosity got the better of them. Evelyne admitted, "Bud and I did go into the barn just to investigate. We told no one and kept that as our very own secret."[2]

Around the age of five or six, Bud owned a scooter. He would zoom from one room to another, going lickety-split, completing a large circle within the house. He loved this scooter and propelled it throughout the house for what seemed like hours at a time. One day, he did this when his mother was in the kitchen. "All of a sudden there was a big noise. The door to the basement was open and Bud, in his curiosity, fell down the steps into the basement."[3] According to service records, he had a one-inch scar in the centre of his forehead. No one in his family remembers seeing this scar, and his brother Ken can only attribute it to chicken pox. However, considering his scooter runs, perhaps a speed-driven fall was the culprit.

Later, the family relocated to Brampton, Ontario, where Bud's father had grown up and where many of the Burt family still resided. The family lived at 140 Queen Street East, just a few streets away from a number of cousins. Evelyne remembers that in those days Bud "would always be bringing something home to Mother, for example, an apple, blossom of a weed, etc."[4]

Bud attended Brampton Central Public School and Brampton High School between 1930 and 1941. At the age of nine he earned a mark of 72 percent in the vocal solo class for boys under ten at the

Peel Music Festival in Port Credit, Ontario. Throughout his youth he had an interest in music, but he traded singing for playing an instrument in later years.

Raised during the Depression, with so many siblings and with no television, Bud was lucky to get to the occasional Saturday matinee, a great weekend pastime for children in those days. Over the years, Bud shared his birthday with three of his younger brothers, all born in early April. Their amalgamated birthdays were a time to enjoy the simple pleasures in life, with the family eating general party fare at a long table in order to accommodate the large number of children.[5]

Times were tough, so, like many young people in the area at that time, the Burt siblings made their own fun. Bud enjoyed playing rugby, baseball, and hockey.[6] He also got up to the typical older brother antics of teasing and playing tricks on his younger siblings. At other times he allowed his younger brother Ken to tag along when he went to visit his friend Jim Mulholland. The boys did chin-ups and other moves on a high horizontal bar in a large building on the Mulholland property. Sometimes, to Ken's embarrassment, Bud drove him to school in their father's old maroon Durand, which had a missing back window.[7]

Bud's father joined the Lorne Scots Militia Regiment in 1939 as an Officer Mess Steward.[8] Bud followed in his father's footsteps, enlisting in the 2nd Regimental Battalion on June 11, 1941. Seventeen at the time, he told the regiment he was born August 6, 1923, making the regiment believe he was a year older than he was.[9] He remained with the Lorne Scots as a private for nearly a year and a half and played the drums for one year. Ken believes he made some trips around the area as a member of the pipe and drum band.

Bud was mechanically inclined and liked to focus his attention on an old Ford Model T roadster that sat in the family's backyard. He engaged Ken to help push the car out of the backyard and into the driveway adjacent to the house so he could work on the motor. Ken couldn't remember if Bud ever got the car to start but, typical of Bud's humour, he kept his little brother busy pushing the car.[10]

Bud's mischievous enjoyment often came at his innocent young brother's expense. Hormones and the burgeoning understanding of sex became fodder for humour, as they still do for teen boys today. On the way to school one day, Bud and another lad had a good laugh at

Ken but did not enlighten him when, after overhearing their conversation about a "French safe," he asked, "What is that?"[11] On another day, Bud and a friend decided to play a trick on Ken. They sent him to the friend's mother to ask her what "a piece of tail" was. The woman, being of Polish descent and knowing little English, was as unaware as Ken, who could hear Bud and his friend "roaring with laughter."[12]

In their later teens, Bud and Jim Mulholland spent many a Friday and Saturday night driving around in Jim's car, visiting the nearest dance hall. Sometimes they picked up girls en route; other times they went alone and met girls at the dances. A bottle of wine was never far away. The boys were inseparable and shared their dreams, which, for both of them, involved spreading their wings beyond Brampton.[13]

When Bud finished high school in 1941, he went to work for Hewetson Shoe Factory on Mill Street as a machine operator.[14] His girlfriend, Audrey Harris, also worked at the factory. Bud learned the skills of shoemaking on the job, working with, and gaining knowledge from, experienced employees. He operated machines that cut and joined pieces together, decorated and reinforced parts of the shoe, and finished off the shoe.

As Bud neared his eighteenth birthday, like many young men, he felt some pressure to sign up to do his part in the war. Bud and Jim decided to enlist in a service other than the army. When they turned eighteen, they would be subject to the draft and could end up in the army infantry. Bud, an American by birth, was also at risk of being drafted into the US Army. Bud's father, a teenager during the First World War, had served in the Canadian Navy, and Bud preferred the idea of following in his father's footsteps. Jim, however, wanted to join the air force. The two best friends considered their options over a few drinks. They wanted to stick together, so, having discussed their wishes with Bud's parents, the boys left their future to a coin flip. If Jim won the toss they would join the RCAF; if Bud won they would join the navy. The coin turned in favour of Jim.[15]

True to his word, Bud was struck off strength with the Lorne Scots Militia Regiment (meaning he officially left the unit) on November 22, 1942.[16] The following day, he signed his enlistment agreement and was taken on for flying duties with the RCAF at the No. 1 Manning Depot in Toronto. He had done the required paperwork and had references from a local storekeeper and his public school principal. They recommended Bud as a person of "good character, reliable, and very conscientious,"[17] who was co-operative, pleasing, and "never involved in any trouble at school."[18]

He had never flown before, but this was not uncommon for most men joining at the time. He was deemed to have an athletic physique, standard mentality, good motivation, steady eyes, and a pleasant personality—in fact, the air force interviewer found him humorous. The RCAF considered the alert and co-operative recruit to be someone who would mix well with others and make for passable aircrew. Bud stated that for some time he had wanted to fly and wished to be an air gunner but would agree to the RCAF's selection of whatever trade it felt was suitable for him.[19]

At the depot (on Toronto's Canadian National Exhibition grounds), the boys slept in double-decker bunks situated in cattle stalls that "stretched from end to end of this sea of a building. Here, a blue kit bag beside your bunk, you endured the orientation from civvy to military life."[20] Bud, like all other new recruits, including the boys he would eventually serve with, regardless of their trade, was stuck with needles and given vaccinations, took aptitude tests, was issued a uniform, and began basic training, which included exercise drills such as marching and taking commands.

Despite the petty thievery, the fights, and the ill-fitting uniforms that required tailors to insert a zipper fly and cloth wedges inside the pant seams so they would fit over boots, most recruits survived the depot experience.[21] Bud achieved an overall good assessment as well as being noted for his good bearing and deportment.[22] He left the depot as Air Gunner, Aircraftman Second Class. Given leave over Christmas, Bud spent it with family and friends. It was the last Christmas he would have at home.

On January 6, 1943, he began training at No. 8 Manning Depot in Souris, Manitoba. Here, in Pre-aircrew Education, he took courses and wrote examinations in science, mathematics, signals, and aircraft recognition. At the end of the course the commanding officer recommended he be trained as an air gunner.[23]

Bud started work in March at No. 17 Service Flying Training School in Souris. Already, Jim, who was training as a pilot, and Bud were going their separate ways. Bud, being a likeable and good-natured chap, made new friends with others on the course, but he also looked forward to getting back to Brampton. He found the training tedious, even with practice in Anson and Harvard aircraft. In a letter to his sister Evelyne, he commented, "If I can live this place out, I guess I can come through anything. I don't think I'd mind *too much*, getting shot or something like that, but I sure hate this slow death."[24] Having to go through long bouts of training frustrated many young men eager to get on with flying or the task of fighting the enemy.

Bud completed his training in Manitoba in early May, then headed to No. 2 Air Gunners Ground Training School in Trenton, Ontario. Located in what is today part of Canadian Forces Base Trenton, the school graduated 1,900 air gunner trainees over the course of the war.[25] Bud wrote tests in a variety of subjects, including navigation, night vision, signals, guns, and anti-gas. He also took part in physical training, drills (likely learning how to pull his gun apart and put it back together quickly in any circumstances),[26] maintenance of machine guns, and training in small arms (portable firearms such as light machine guns, rifles, and pistols). Although deemed unsuitable for training as a gunner instructor, he received a grade of 75 percent in stage one of the course. The instructor considered him to be a hard-working, average gunner with good discipline and fair practical knowledge.[27] Promoted to Air Gunner, Leading Aircraftman, Bud headed back west to complete the next stage of the course.

His Canadian training finished with No. 3 Bombing and Gunnery School in Macdonald, Manitoba, where he did flight training in Battle and Norseman aircraft. The equipment he used included the Vickers Gas-Operated and Browning guns, as well as Bristol, Fraser-Nash, and Boulton-Paul turrets. The training consisted of armaments, aircraft recognition, drill, signals, turret manipulation, and shooting from air-to-ground[28] and in air-to-air situations.[29] He achieved a final grade of 77.8 percent with a position of 79 out of 129 students. His training report graded him an average gunner, neat, accommodating, and reliable, noting that he could grasp a situation quickly, knew his trade, and would make a capable crew member.[30]

He wrote his sister a quick letter on YMCA stationery as he prepared to head home. He was already planning to celebrate: "I've got a *small* favour to ask. Do you think you could pick me up a crock of liquire [*sic*] or a jug of Jungle juice sometime before Sunday. You see I'll get into Toronto Sunday night or Monday sometime and I'd like a crock on hand. At least I mean I'll get into Toronto if I graduate. I don't know for sure yet, but I'm not worrying about that too much."[31] He did not need to concern himself—celebrating would be the order of the day. At the end of the course the RCAF awarded Bud his air gunner's badge and promoted him to sergeant. Bud happily headed home on embarkation leave in late July 1943.

Bud's brother Ken, thirteen at the time, still remembers Bud visiting and being visited by family and friends from both Canada and the United States during that short summer leave. He admired him in uniform: "He looked so neat, trim and nothing out of place . . . I remember his last day at home and I could not go when he was driven to Toronto Union Station because there was not room in the car."[32] Little did he know that this would be the last time he would see his brother.

Mid-Upper Gunner—Robert (Bob) Hudson

Despite the lack of personal information in Bob's service record, with his sister Pat's help I was able to picture an active, accident-prone, mischievous, good-natured, bright lad, a progressive, independent thinker, who was helpful around home and eager to serve his country. Based on the first photograph of him that I saw, however, he would forever be the boy with the big ear-to-ear grin. He beamed in every photograph.

Bob was born September 5, 1924, in Sileby, Leicester, England, to Walter Henry Hudson, a farrier and blacksmith, also born in Sileby, and Madeline Hudson (née Camp), born in Sutton-in-Ashfield, Nottinghamshire. Bob was the third child and son in a family of six children.

When not attending Sileby Infants School or studying, Bob could be found playing exuberantly outside, sometimes to his own detriment. In the mind of a schoolboy, a blacksmith's yard, filled with tools and a collection of farm implements awaiting repair, was a perfect place to play hide-and-seek. On more than one occasion, however, in his excitement to find a better hiding place, he leapt up and hit his head on the protruding part of a machine. His sister thought that he "hit his head twice in the same place, needing stitches," after just such a game, which left him with a scar on his forehead where his hair never grew back, but his brother Peter believes it was the pan Bob pulled from the stove that caused that scar.

Come autumn, when the hay was being harvested, Bob and other children in the area commonly played around the fields where the men were working. Somehow, in his frolicking about, Bob managed to break his leg as he swung on the field gate.[33] Despite his injuries, Bob, a good-natured boy, always seemed to have a smile on his face, which his mother described as a "three-inch grin."[34] Nothing seemed to keep him down for long.

Later, Bob went to senior school. "No records or year book were kept in those days," Pat told me, "but . . . he was a keen scholar and did well at sports."[35] He achieved a grade of A1 for his annual school certificate when he was twelve and was also *victor ludorum* for sports, gaining first in Junior Boys 80 yards, Junior Boys 150 yards, and Relay.[36]

With both their grandfather and father employed as blacksmiths and farriers, Bob and his siblings were very much involved with horses. In November 1936 he received a certificate from the Pony Club for passing the D grade test. His older brother Peter won countless trophies for his horsemanship, but Bob enjoyed just having a go. He was inspired by jockey Gordon Richards, a champion for years, and made a scrapbook from brown paper in which he pasted newspaper clippings and pictures of the famous rider.[37]

Bob's father had joined the Leicestershire Yeomanry as a farrier in 1911 and served in the First World War. After the war he continued to serve with the Yeomanry despite suffering regularly from chest problems contracted during his wartime service in France. He passed away in January 1937 at only forty-one years of age. The Yeomanry honoured him with a military funeral, which Bob and his older brothers attended.[38] Even at the tender age of thirteen, he stood up to the challenge of being a man. "Bob was a loving son and brother, and after Dad died he would help out around the home, even cooking breakfasts," his sister recalled.[39]

Bob's childhood was behind him. He left senior school at fourteen and attended night school instead, working by day. He even learned shorthand, which was unusual for a boy. When war broke out he had just turned fifteen, much too young to enlist, but his two older brothers were soon called up.[40] Clarence (Cag) joined the Army's Royal Corps of Signals in 1939, serving in Northern Ireland, North Africa, and Italy, while Peter joined the RAF as a radio mechanic in 1940 at age eighteen, serving in Corsica, Italy, and Egypt.[41] Young Bob remained behind, now the man of the house.

Like many youth of the time, Bob was fascinated by planes and joined a local branch of the Air Training Corps with the hope of later joining the air force. He couldn't wait to be old enough to do his bit. In 1941 his mother remarried, and with all set right at home, Bob volunteered his services to the RAF and waited for his turn to be called up. Meanwhile, he kept busy working for a company that originally made tennis courts but had diversified to building airport runways after the outbreak of war.[42]

The RAF finally called Bob up for service as he neared his nineteenth birthday. He signed his enlistment papers on June 14, 1943, at B & Ham/No. 1 Aircrew Reception Centre, London, becoming an Aircraftman Second Class. He went through the battery of inoculations and received his uniform and required kit, such as a shaving, sewing, and physical training kit, before learning to clean his gear, follow instructions, perform rigorous drills, and pass inspections, just as the boys in Canada did.

With the basics learned, Bob moved to No. 14 Initial Training Wing, Bridlington, in early July, serving under "F" Flight in No. 4 Squadron, and probably living in one of the requisitioned houses on the seafront. The beach played a significant role, giving the new recruits a large area where they could perform drills, such as marching in the sand, and do some initial target practice. Lectures in various halls, as well as work carried out in their billets, covered subjects like Morse code and aircraft recognition.[43]

After passing his course, Bob went home for a week's holiday before starting turret training at No. 1 Elementary Air Gunner School in Bridgnorth, Shropshire, in early August. The course introduced the theory behind how the turret and its guns worked, giving Bob the background knowledge he would need when he was fending off a night fighter. He learned about the parts of the guns and how to look for faults— an important skill, considering that when he was in the air, it would be up to him alone to fix any problems. Instructors taught him how to take the guns apart and put them back together, and he studied how to use his guns effectively, learning how to calculate the curve of fire (deflection) for a moving target,[44] how to determine the amount of bullet drop over the distance to the target, and how to harmonize his guns.[45]

By the end of the month he had moved to No. 1 Air Gunners School in Pembrey, Carmarthenshire, Wales, as part of "A" Squadron 83 Course. Here, Bob put his knowledge to the test, practising turret manipulation and shooting skills. Gunners took turns firing guns at moving targets on the ground and in the air. The latter work proved especially difficult, as the gunners were also moving, firing at a drogue being towed behind a plane. The lecturers assessed Bob's shooting accuracy by using a cine camera that recorded each gunner's aim.[46] Bob eagerly wrote to his brother Cag, "I shall soon be dashing about in those big bombers, I hope! I've only got 4 weeks to go before I get my stripes and brevvy."[47] Bob had nothing to worry about. He completed the course successfully and received his wings, passing out of the school as a temporary sergeant on October 16, 1943.

» Farm Lads Wanting to Be Pilots

Out of the seven boys, four are known to have requested the position of pilot. Of course, for every seven men in a Lancaster bomber, only one could be the pilot, and there were six other positions to be filled. This posed a problem for training from the beginning. Some recruits were diverted from pilot training at an early stage due to one issue or another (perhaps physical problems or an obvious lack of aptitude), while others began pilot training only to be disappointed later as the natural attrition of training showed they were more suited for other roles within the aircraft. It was not an easy road for Bill and Norm, two farm lads who were both intent on piloting a plane. Slightly older than the gunner boys, they shared similar farming backgrounds and came together in training to be pilots, but their training ultimately took them in different directions.

Air Bomber—William (Bill) Taylor

The excellent work already done by the authors of the two books from Saskatchewan, plus the family's own fond memories, revealed a young man of vigour who was good-natured, responsible, inventive, industrious, and conscientious. Most of all, however, I found Bill's story endearing. He demonstrated an unwavering drive and determination to serve his country despite his struggles. And in the end he found his true calling.

Bill was born April 20, 1920, on his parents' farm, east of Carnduff, in the Carievale-Nottingham District of Saskatchewan. He was the second-youngest of nine children born to Harry Herbert Taylor, from Warwickshire, England (who came to Canada via St. Louis, Missouri, to homestead in 1901), and Mary (Minnie) Ann Taylor (née Quail), born in Belfast, Ireland. Bill's early education, from Grades 1 to 10, took place at Thunder Creek School, in the typical one-room schoolhouse for students of all ages and grades. During those years he got up to the usual boyish shenanigans of the time. His siblings have fond memories of him making stilts with his brother, which they used to walk to school; of Bill wrestling with his other siblings daily in the kitchen, to the dismay of his older sister who was trying to cook breakfast among the mayhem; and of his particular love for riding horses.[48]

His active lifestyle kept him fit and healthy. He enjoyed a number of sports including softball, swimming, horseback riding, and cycling, along with the occasional bout of baseball, football, curling, and skating when he wasn't wrestling in the house. However, he was also interested in somewhat less vigorous activities such as mechanics and gardening.[49]

From an early age, Bill learned to share in the work and knew his responsibilities when it came to chores. During the Depression, with so many mouths to feed, all family members had to pull their weight.[50] Bill did his part. As he grew older, to help make money for the family, he took advantage of a government scheme to reduce the number of crows on the prairies. The birds were pests, and the government offered "two cents an egg (more if it was a live bird)" to people who would raid crows' nests in the spring. On one occasion, after Bill had collected a number of eggs and deposited them in the presumed safety of his hat, he galloped home on his horse, June, causing the eggs to break. No money was made that day, but the family had a good chuckle when Bill came home with "egg on his face" and running down his cheeks.[51] In another attempt to make money, he bought young roosters from a hatchery. Although he did okay, according to his sister Dorothy, he had neither the facilities in place for such an undertaking nor the experience required to make it fully successful.[52]

In those days, many people left school at a young age and went to work, especially in rural areas where higher education was not easily accessible. After Grade 10, Bill went to work on several neighbouring farms. His cousin Charlie Taylor employed him from 1937 to 1938, but then he was let go because there was no crop to harvest. Until 1940, he worked for Jim Murray in Melita, Manitoba, doing seasonal harvesting work.[53]

Between 1938 and 1940, talk of war and news of what was happening overseas spread around the small rural communities. Bill listened attentively, and the BCATP airfields that were beginning to pop up all over Western Canada awoke in him the desire to become a pilot. Excitement soon met disappointment. The air force required young men with a Grade 12 education, but Bill only had his Grade 10.

When his sister Edna was hired to teach at Oakley School, Bill seized the chance to further his education so he could meet the requirements for enlisting in the RCAF. Given permission to attend the school along with another lad, he took his Grade 11 through correspondence under the supervision of his sister.[54] To finish Grade 12, however, Bill needed to attend Carievale High School, much too far for a daily commute. Luckily, a neighbour, whose son was a friend of Bill's, had moved within three kilometres of the town, and he suggested Bill board with them for the school year. Bill eagerly accepted the offer. While living with the family, he helped out with chores when he was not studying, and used a bicycle to get back and forth to school.[55]

Now eligible to enlist, Bill initially signed up for the army until he could get a discharge from the army and re-enlist in the RCAF. During the enlistment process he received a glowing reference from his high school principal:

> I have no hesitation in stating that William Taylor was very
> industrious and conscientious in his work at school. He
> never hesitated in partaking of any activity at school and was
> always willing to give a lending hand. His association and
> co-operation with the rest of the students was of the very best.
> I may also add that his moral conduct was above reproach.[56]

When Bill went through a medical for the RCAF, despite his rambunctious childhood, the doctor noted that he had no identifying body marks or scars. At the time he was described as 150 pounds, five foot eight inches tall, with hazel eyes, a medium complexion, and dark brown hair. The examiner gave him a clean bill of health and, although he considered the boy somewhat excitable, concluded that he would make fair aircrew material and that his excitability would lessen with training.[57]

On February 4, 1942, Bill finally signed the attestation declaration at No. 5 Recruiting Centre, RCAF Regina, Saskatchewan, becoming an Aircraftman Second Class. The selection board recommended him as pilot or observer, with the possibility of being suitable for a commission. Board members deemed him a "good, clean-cut type of farm lad. Keen to be any position Air Crew. Nice manner and should do well. Mentally alert."[58]

Now enlisted with the RCAF, Bill focused on becoming a pilot. He entered No. 2 Manning Depot in Brandon, Manitoba, in mid-March for basic training. On his forms, he admitted he did not want to return to farming after the war despite feeling competent to run a farm, having had six years' experience as a labourer in mixed farming. Instead, he wanted to become a commercial pilot.[59] He had set his heart on flying.

In early May he was at No. 10 Service Flying Training School in Dauphin, Manitoba, and a month later at No. 7 Initial Training School (ITS) in Saskatoon, Saskatchewan. Not long after entering this unit, Bill underwent another medical. In this short time he had gained ten pounds and grown two inches in height.[60] He was, after all, still a growing lad and was likely gaining muscle from all the drills he had done.

New recruits had a great deal to absorb at the ITS, and Bill started to experience problems. The number of students (over 150 men in Bill's course), the incredible speed at which training took place, and the lesson format used by the ITS and subsequent schools likely left little time or leeway to adapt the training program for those experiencing learning difficulties. At the end of the course, Bill failed his navigation component.[61]

However, he had demonstrated ability and was transferred for further instruction to continue his pilot training. He passed, achieving a respectable 77.9 percent and a decent position in his class, coming thirty-five out of seventy-three students. The instructor regarded Bill as a slow learner but possessing a good spirit.[62] He was promoted to Leading Aircraftman.

Bill carried on to No. 19 Elementary Flying Training School in Virden, Manitoba, in mid-September. It was likely here that he had his first solo flight, an eventful one. He "had difficulty bringing the plane down. Wind kept bouncing it back up. He decided that he would land the plane if it were the last thing he would ever do, so through determination and patience he eventually landed safely."[63]

At Virden, he worked on reading cockpit instruments (dials, gauges, etc.) and did Link training in a simulator before taking to the air in a Tiger Moth aircraft, doing dual and solo flights during the day and at night.[64] He continued with instruction in navigation, airmanship, armament, aircraft recognition, and signals, obtaining 75.42 percent and a position of twenty-three out of thirty-eight students.[65] At first it seemed that he had overcome his earlier struggles, having obtained an average grade in flying aptitude, including natural skill, skill in landing, airmanship, cockpit drill, instrument flying, night flying, and aerobatics. The final comment by an intuitive chief supervisory officer suggested an explanation for Bill's problems—and indicated they might not be over: "Not possessed of natural ability. A slow thinker and somewhat difficult to teach. Has shown improvement however as time increased . . . Unique pupil and his marks indicate exactly what his trouble was. He could not learn from a book no matter how hard he worked. He will improve in Navigation with more plotting."[66]

Regardless of his difficulties, Bill remained a determined young man with a dream. But that dream came to an end at No. 11 Service Flying Training School, in Yorkton, Saskatchewan, on December 9. Determination was not enough. Bill had failed his course in general flying, and there would be no further opportunities. The fates would now play their hand.

According to the Ceased Training Certificate received by the Composite Training School at Trenton, Ontario, Bill had, on a number of occasions, struggled to take in or retain information within a course. Although his instructor considered him a hard worker who demonstrated a nice attitude, he also felt that he was "miscast as a pilot and more suited in temperament to become a Navigator or Bomber."[67]

This was not an uncommon experience. Steve Fortescue, a tail gunner in 630 and later 57 Squadron, remembered training in Canada and failing his wings test, describing it as "one of my life's low points."[68] During the war, many men found themselves disappointed by the reality that they would not become a pilot, but their new job, whatever it was, would be every bit as important as flying the plane. Flight Officer (Flt. Off.) Douglas Hudson, DFC, who served in the RAF Volunteer Reserve, did not even get a chance to become a pilot. Instead, he was assigned to navigation duties. He emphasized the importance of each person within the aircraft, noting, "Everybody is important to each other . . . It is teamwork that counts."[69]

Bill reported for duty at the Composite Training School in Trenton on December 13 and awaited his next assignment. Perhaps he was upset because his hopes of becoming a pilot had been dashed. Perhaps he was bored while waiting for his new duty to be selected, or overwhelmed by the differences between Eastern Canada and his prairie home, or homesick. Whatever the reason, Bill absented himself from the Reselection Centre without leave for a day and a half. For this he was confined to barracks and forfeited two days' pay.[70]

On December 22 the reselection board finally made its decision. While Bill and the others were "lined up to receive orders where they were to be sent for further training, the young fellow ahead of William was assigned to the West, and William mumbled 'Oh that wouldn't be my luck.' The boy ahead of him turned and asked if it would be worth five dollars for him to have their destination changed as he would much rather stay in the East. Bill jumped at the chance, and the change was made. This allowed William to remain in his beloved West and be closer to home and family."[71] Although he probably felt a little melancholic over the loss of his dream and the uncertainty of his new role, he was at least headed back to Saskatchewan.

The selection board, noting that Bill was of "average intelligence, conscientious, [of] good disposition and . . . a willing student," had decided that he could "do well as an Air Bomber provided he can get some encouragement."[72] After an illness requiring hospitalization, Bill took the first steps in becoming a bomber, training at No. 5 Bombing and Gunnery School in Dafoe, Saskatchewan, in late January. He flew in Anson aircraft doing day and night bombing, and used a

Bolingbroke aircraft for gunnery practice. As well as flying tests, there were also examinations in bombing, gunnery, aircraft recognition, and signals. In his exams he achieved 70.6 percent overall, with a position of twenty-two out of fifty-nine students and demonstrated above-average work in his bombing component. In general, he was seen as a "conscientious type—not brilliant but keen to be in aircrew. Should make a satisfactory air bomber."[73]

At No. 1 Central Navigation School in Rivers, Manitoba, in mid-April, Bill started the second part of his air bomber training: flying in Anson aircraft and studying a full range of subjects, including air work in navigation, bombing, and photography, as well as signals, reconnaissance, and aircraft recognition. In all, he flew just over thirty hours by day and just over twelve hours by night, earning a grade of 76.3 percent and a position of twelve out of twenty students. Bill presented a neat log and sketches and possessed good map reading skills. He was quiet, neat, and a hard worker. Assessed as an average air bomber, suitable for commissioned rank,[74] Bill had found his niche.

His final assessment presented a similar calibre of work. His grade in air observer school was 76.3 percent, and in bombing and in gunnery school 70.6 percent. Overall he averaged 72.4 percent, achieving a position of eleven out of twenty students. His instructor again noted that he was a hard-working, quiet type, and recommended him for commission.[75]

On May 28, Bill received his air bomber's badge and was promoted to the rank of sergeant before beginning his pre-embarkation leave. The leave seemed terribly short for the Taylor household. "There was a spell of crying when William was sent to England and he said his goodbyes to his family in Carnduff, including a sister who was about to give birth."[76] Before his niece or nephew was born, Bill headed for Nova Scotia.

Pilot—Norman (Norm) Andrew Lumgair

The service records, along with the personal stories and photographs Charlie provided, presented Norm as a true farm lad. Confident in a profession he had grown up with, he was energetic and a bit rough around the edges but considerate, and he had a soft spot for those in his care. Quiet at times, he was pleasant as well as co-operative. He struck me as a young man who preferred action over words. He liked to get on with things, to be hands-on.

Norm was born April 12, 1922, at the Freemasons Hospital in Morden, Manitoba. He was the youngest of four living children born to Robert Wallace Lumgair, born in Forfarshire, Scotland, and Hannah Louisa Lumgair (née Ching), born in Darlingford, Manitoba. Norm grew up near Thornhill, Manitoba, where he started his primary education at Orange Hill School in 1928, and later attended Wellington School in Thornhill, a two-room school with Grades 1 through 6 taught downstairs and Grades 7 to 11 taught upstairs. No school bus picked children up back then. Instead, Norm and his brothers either walked the two and a half kilometres to school or rode on horseback. It was the same if they wanted to visit friends on the weekends. Classmate Roger Ptosnick recalls playing various sports, including ball, skating, and skiing, and also enjoying sleighing with Norm in those days. Norm played hockey and continued to skate and ski as he grew older. While still going to school in 1937, Norm, now old enough to take on more responsibility, worked as a farm labourer for his father.[77]

In his late teens Norm became fond of the girls, and they were equally fond of the grey-eyed, brown-haired lad. Rumour has it Norm and his elder brother, Robert, were mischief-makers. One schoolmate, Lydia Andrew (née Bollenbach), called him a "tease." According to Robert, Norm liked to dress well. He would often wear a bow tie and spent ages pressing his gabardine trousers before he went out. When he was old enough to drive, he and his cousin Alice borrowed the family car one evening so they could attend a dance. They had a good time dancing with their respective partners. However, on the way home he got the car stuck in the mud and they had to walk home for help. It was dark, and Alice "slipped in the mud and fell. . . She was waiting for a hand up but heard Norm say, 'You can pick yourself up, I fell down too.'"[78] His fondness had not yet developed into chivalry, not even for his cousin; he was, after all, still a teenager.

When Norm finished school in 1939, his eldest brother, Wallace, hired him for a year to do odd jobs, including woodcutting.[79] Wallace has fond memories of a youthful Norm working with another hired hand. They spent a good deal of time patiently training a young horse during the winter. When spring came, they hitched the young horse to a wagon alongside a reliable old mare, and all went well. Seeing this, Wallace joked "that they should back the horses into a long narrow shed and pull out the seed drill. They did. The seed drill took up most of the width of the shed. Wallace felt the operation was a total success due to the mutual respect between men and horses."[80]

Wallace's son David (Norm's nephew), who was seven or eight at the time, recalls Norm eating with the family, which included David's sister Louise, who was two or three years old. "Uncle Norm [was] pouring cream on Louise's chocolate cake when he was here. If I remember correctly, Mother was concerned because of his generous servings to Louise."[81] Apparently Norm's fondness extended even to the little ladies.

Now eighteen, and with the farming season over, Norm applied to join the RCAF on December 6, 1940. However, due to his "dry skin" (a condition that may have required medication and impaired efficiency as a result), the medical officer considered him physically unfit and promptly turned him down. Norm went back to work for his father.[82] When not busy farming, he enjoyed dabbling in fretwork, carving ornamental designs in wood, but his mind was never far from serving his country. In 1942, when his brother Robert was nearing the end of his RCAF training in Canada as a wireless operator and air gunner,[83] Norm again attempted to enlist. During the interview, he stated he wished to be either a pilot or an air gunner, although his preference was for pilot. The interviewer assessed his education, ability to learn, and personal background as "satisfactory" and recommended him for pilot training.[84] Although Norm volunteered as a pilot, he had every intention of returning to farming after the war. He felt competent to run a mixed farm, although if the opportunity presented itself, he had ambitions to work as a grain buyer.[85]

The medical officer described Norm as five foot eight and 150 pounds, possessing an athletic build. He had a half-inch scar on his chin. The membrane of his left ear had a healed perforation, probably from a childhood problem with bilateral aural paracentesis, which had required an operation,[86] but this would not pose an issue for flying duties. Although he still had what the doctor called "advanced fish skin" or "ichthyosis of joint areas"[87]—the same malady that caused his application to be turned down nearly a year and a half earlier—he was deemed fit for aircrew.[88]

With a clean bill of health, Norm signed his attestation papers on February 26, at the Winnipeg Recruiting Centre as an Aircraftman

Second Class and then waited for his call-up. Three weeks later he entered No. 2 Manning Depot in Brandon, Manitoba, to begin his basic training. Larry had already been through the depot in mid-1941, and Bill had arrived just two days earlier than Norm, but whether they became acquainted over the months of training is unknown. However, both Bill and Norm commenced and finished basic training at the same time.

On May 9, Norm, like Bill, moved to No. 10 Service Flying Training School in Dauphin, Manitoba. By May 29, however, Norm began to feel unwell and was admitted to the station hospital with an elevated temperature. The physical exam divulged no clear finding. The doctor's diagnosis was pyrexia (fever) of "unknown origin" that "cleared up without treatment."[89] Discharged from the hospital in early June and feeling much better, he headed for Saskatchewan with the rest of the recruits.

At No. 7 Initial Training School in Saskatoon, Norm again ended up on the same course as Bill, learning basic flying theory. His medical showed he too had put on some muscle and weighed in at 160 pounds. The practitioner thought Norm "may have some trouble with G.S. [ground school]." Despite being pleasant and co-operative, he seemed "somewhat nervous fidgety and blushes when spoken to"[90]—he hadn't found his balance and confidence in this new world that was so different from farming. At the end of his studies, Norm passed the course with a grade of 66.5 percent and was rated 133 out of 150 students, receiving the rank of Leading Aircraftman. The officer in charge considered him a "farm boy, just average type, fair student. Should do better with hard work."[91]

At the end of August he started his first proper flying training at No. 6 Elementary Flying Training School in Prince Albert, Saskatchewan. He once again took ill, however, and ended up at the station hospital from late September to early October. When he returned to his studies, he put in a good effort. He did very well in instrument flying and was considered an above-average instrument pilot, obtaining a grade of 87 percent. Overall, he received a grade of 67.9 percent, similar to that for his previous training, and a position of thirty-four out of thirty-seven students.[92]

In the air he trained in a Tiger Moth aircraft. It was here where he excelled, achieving 75 percent and a position of four out of thirty-five students. His flying aptitude was average, with an above-average understanding in airmanship. Norm took to practical flying. The officer commented that he was a "good average pilot" and made "good substantial progress throughout the course." However, he still had work to do as he required "more practice in cross wind take-offs and landings and in precautionary landings."[93]

He entered No. 4 Service Flying Training School in Saskatoon in early November and continued with more in-depth pilot training in the Cessna Crane. He continued to be marked as having average flying aptitude, achieving 69 percent and a position of thirty-seven out of fifty-six students. Norm's general studies improved from his previous courses, and he finished with 72.3 percent and a position of fifty-six out of fifty-eight in the class. The chief instructor noted he needed "practice on landings and turns." However, he was "generally sound and should develop." The commanding officer recognized his efforts in his written work, stating that Norm "worked hard in Ground School— is rather quiet and slow thinker but is dependable."[94]

Having passed his course, he received a rank of temporary sergeant and his flying badge on March 5, 1943. The following day he went on pre-embarkation leave, going home to visit family before he prepared to go overseas to join his brother Robert in the skies over Germany.[95]

» Husbands and Fathers

Out of the seven men, only two were husbands and fathers. Representing the older recruits, Larry and George had several more years' experience in the world of work and life. They had married, had children, and made a life for themselves and their families. They added steadiness and a deepened sense of responsibility to the mix, and their reliable and more settled nature made them ideal candidates for the arduous tasks of wireless operator and navigator.

Wireless Operator—William Lawrence (Larry) Doran

From the beginning, Larry proved my weakness. The experience of placing my hand on his fingerprints in his service records forged a special place for him in my heart. Because he was older than the rest, his story was longer, and the fibres in that broader tapestry carried a more intricate weave and a depth that captivated me. He proved to be a motivated, energetic, highly intelligent, confident, good-natured, and well-liked individual who marched to the beat of his own drum.

Larry was born September 2, 1914, in Vancouver, BC. He was the eldest of six children born to civil engineer William John Doran, born in Bansha, Tipperary, Ireland, and Jessie Hearst Doran (née Skidmore), born in Motherwell, Scotland. His parents moved to Canada separately around the early 1900s and later met at Grand Forks, BC, marrying there on September 27, 1913.

Blue-eyed, brown-haired Larry had an unusual childhood. As an engineer, his father worked on various railway and bridge construction jobs, which required the family to travel frequently. During Larry's early years the family moved back and forth between BC and Manitoba, following his father along the rail line built from Winnipeg to Hudson Bay. When Larry reached school age, however, they settled in BC, limiting moves to within the province. For a period up to 1921, the family lived in Quesnel, BC, taking up residence in a caboose while his father was involved in construction of the Pacific Great Eastern Railway.

These job-related moves required Larry to "pick up his education in many different towns in BC,"[96] so little is known about his formative school years. He likely attended the local village schools dotted along the expanding railway. However, the family continued to grow, and eventually Vancouver became home base. This allowed Larry to spend Grades 5 to 7 (1925–1927) at Lord Tennyson Elementary School before starting Grade 8 at Kitsilano Junior–Senior High School.

During the late 1920s and early 1930s, the older Doran children often spent time in the care of a housekeeper while the younger children and Larry's mother visited or stayed with their father on construction jobs.[97] This forced Larry to develop his independence early in life. He kept busy over these years. At some point he became part of the Meraloma Club, where he played basketball—not surprising considering he was probably tall for his age, growing to be a thin, five-foot-eleven lad.[98]

In Grade 11, his final year at Kitsilano, he was enrolled in class seven of the high school graduates. Essentially now the man of the house while his father, mother, and youngest sister remained in Williams Lake, he began taking on more adult pursuits. It is believed Larry served as an air cadet at what is now Vancouver International Airport. An industrious teen, he also worked in the office and circulation department of the *Vancouver Sun*, a local daily newspaper at the time, which continues to run today as one of the city's major news-papers. The paper had a keen affection for the well-presented young man. Beside his picture in the school's annual is the message "Larry swam into Vancouver in 1914 and has been improving in swimming ever since. A very good business man, says the Vancouver Sun, and it knows it. He'll own it yet."[99]

Larry's final education took place at King Edward (Technical) High School. While still at school he began work with the Vancouver Sewer Board as a labourer. He was seventeen and still in his junior matriculation year when he left school, continuing his work with the Vancouver Sewer Board and later finding employment with the Foundation Company of Canada as a labourer and sandhog, working underground or underwater on excavation projects in the city, such as bridge and construction work. Working as a sandhog prepared him for what would later be his lengthiest occupation before enlistment: gold mining.

Larry started work as a miner at Bralorne Gold Mines on May 12, 1934. He may have moved to Bralorne, BC, after reading a pamphlet that circulated in Vancouver in 1933. The pamphlet promoted stocks in gold mining in the Bridge River Valley, three hundred kilome-tres north of Vancouver, and claimed fortunes would be made in the area.[100] Considering the poor economy of the time, Bralorne and other mines in the area attracted hundreds of miners and businesses that supported them and their families with general services and goods. For Larry, Bralorne Gold Mines offered a stable, long-term job, but his life was not without its share of ups and downs.

At some point early in his time in Bralorne, Larry met Grace Violet Jones. Love blossomed between the two young people, and on October 26, 1935, Larry and Grace married. Larry became actively immersed in the community that was now his permanent home. In 1937, there came a happy addition to the family, when Larry and Grace's first child, William Hugh, was born. For the next few years, life was busy for Larry and his little family. In November 1938, the Bralorne Community Club published a profile of this popular and active man, noting that "his cheery greeting and ready good nature have made everyone proud to call him 'friend.'"[101] Outside work and his involvement in community organizations, he engaged in extensive fishing and seasonal hunting.

He enjoyed playing baseball as well as curling and skating, but his main interests leaned more toward reading, photography, politics, and journalism.

Over the years he worked his way through many mining positions, and his broad and lengthy experience taught him a great deal about mining as well as the hazards of the job. In his final job at Bralorne, as a mucking machine operator, he worked the machine that moved the rock and earth loosened by drilling, digging, or blasting. This work was dangerous because of the operator's close proximity to fine dust particles that, when breathed in, could cause silicosis, an irreversible lung disease. When the Bralorne Co-operative Committee, precursor to the miners' union, established a silicosis sub-committee, Larry was named second-in-command of the committee "and in that capacity toured the province to appraise other miners and affiliated tradesmen of the need for greater compensation" to workers suffering the detrimental effects of silicosis.[102] Larry's work on the committee was a great help to those stricken by the disease, and it was an impressive feat considering he was only in his early twenties.

On the cold winter morning of February 28, 1941, Larry got up as usual and drove into town to work at the mine. Not long after starting work he received news his house had burned to the ground, taking all of his family's possessions and the life of his and Grace's four-year-old son. The fire appeared to have spread from the wood-burning cookstove.[103] Sadly, this tragedy drove a wedge between the couple, and it would eventually end their marriage.

Larry left Bralorne Mines in late April and began the war enlistment process, signing his attestation papers on May 21, 1941, at the RCAF Recruiting Centre in Vancouver. His letters of reference affirmed his good character; the general manager of Bralorne Mines commended him as a "good reliable workman" who "has taken an active part in community life and is a good citizen,"[104] while the North American Life Assurance Company stated he was "always found to be trustworthy and honest of purpose."[105]

Clean and refined in appearance, tastefully dressed in a conservative manner, and older than the average enlistee, Larry stood out. He was a healthy, slender man, weighing 151 pounds. He smoked a pipe and enjoyed the occasional drink of alcohol. The interviewer remarked that he possessed a pleasant, confidently mature personality and demonstrated quick, organized, and accurate intelligence. Larry was anxious to serve as a pilot, despite still being married at the time, and was "keen and willing, though a little critical in his attitude," but in the interviewer's estimation he "should turn out well after training."[106]

His medical examination established two unrelated issues. He had enlarged tonsils, which had caused problems in the past and would continue to cause difficulties. His eye test was of more concern. The practitioner concluded he had poor ocular balance, or esophoria, which causes the eye to turn inward. The doctor described him as alert, co-operative, relaxed, and a "good candidate for aircrew," but his position would have to be something other than pilot.[107]

Larry entered No. 2 Manning Depot in Brandon, Manitoba, as Aircraftman Second Class to begin basic training. While there he completed an occupational history form that shed light on his plans for the future. He did not intend to return to mining on discharge and thought he would rather find employment in journalism.[108] Whatever his reasons, Larry was starting a new life that would take a very different direction from his previous underground work.

Later he travelled to No. 4 Service Flying Training School in Saskatoon, Saskatchewan, followed by more intensive study at No. 4 Initial Training School (ITS) in Edmonton, Alberta, where superiors decided Larry would train as a wireless operator and air gunner. During his time at the ITS, Larry underwent another medical. The doctor remarked that his septic tonsils should be "removed at the first opportunity,"[109] but in the meantime Larry continued his studies. His examination results averaged 82 percent, putting him 56 in a class of 146 airmen. The instructors duly acknowledged him as a "tough hard working type" with a "good service spirit."[110] Promoted to Leading Aircraftman, he headed to No. 3 Manning Depot in Edmonton and waited for the next part of his training to begin. It is likely during this time that he met Marjorie Coughlan, who would become his second wife.

Larry began the first part of his wireless training at No. 2 Wireless School in Calgary, Alberta, in mid-September. For the first month things went as planned, but then Larry suffered two back-to-back bouts of tonsillitis, which left him in the care of the school's station hospital until early November. Larry had to transfer to another course because of all the time he had lost in hospital. His training continued until early January 1942, when he complained to an aural surgeon about his continual sore throats. He was admitted to Calgary's Colonel Belcher Hospital the following morning to have a tonsillectomy. The doctor removed his tonsils along with a non-malignant papilloma found on his palate. Larry was later discharged from hospital a full eleven pounds lighter and was excused from duty for a few days.[111]

Finally fit and well, he took his first marked flight on January 22, as a passenger in a Norseman aircraft. In ground training (which covered theory, radio equipment, Morse code, procedure, signals organization, armament, drill, and physical training) he achieved a 79 percent average overall and came 18 in a class of 120 students. During late March he once again took to the skies in a Norseman and a Tiger Moth, practising his newly acquired skills in operating radio equipment. At the end of his training the instructor graded Larry as an above-average student.[112]

The second part of the course, armament training, took place at No. 8 Bombing and Gunnery School in Lethbridge, Alberta, in late April. Larry was authorized to wear his wireless operator's badge and began lessons as an air gunner. He trained in a Fairey Battle aircraft, doing gunnery practice similar to Bud and Bob, and earned a 74.1 percent average and a rank of nine in a class of twenty-six students. The chief instructor remarked that he was "diligent and industrious showing quite a thorough knowledge of his armament work," while the commanding officer added that he was a "straightforward and likeable" sort with "good results in air firing work."[113] Larry's achievements placed him in the top 20 percent of the class upon graduation, which earned him merit from the Board of Officers and a recommendation that he be appointed to commissioned rank after service in the field.[114] He was authorized to wear his air gunner's badge and was promoted to sergeant.

In early June he headed to No. 2 Air Observer School in Edmonton. This was his last school in Canada, but he remained here for nearly a year, beginning his duty as a wireless operator flying in Anson aircraft. The summer consisted of short day and night flights around Edmonton and as far south as Lethbridge, Alberta.[115] In the autumn he continued his duties as a navigator and wireless operator, flying day and night runs around Alberta and as far as Regina, Saskatchewan.[116]

A personal assessment report described Larry as self-assured, quick, clear, and concise, a good operator and excellent instructor. He demonstrated initiative, and was diligent, efficient, organized, and highly reliable. His co-operative and helpful attitude also entailed good leadership, and his superiors believed that his personal qualities and the value of his services justified appointment to commissioned rank. They recommended him for accelerated promotion, and at the end of November he was promoted to Acting Flight Sergeant.[117]

Also that autumn, now officially divorced from his first wife, Larry married Marjorie Evelyne Coughlan on October 17, 1942, at McDougall United Church in Edmonton. He ended the month by writing and editing an article for *The Observer*, a monthly newspaper published by the unit.

After a short stint of flying that continued right up until the early hours of December 24, Larry went on four days of Christmas leave. He returned straight after, spending the early part of January 1943 doing exercises in "loop swing," a process of calibrating a loop antenna or a magnetic compass used to pinpoint the aircraft's location. It wasn't until the middle of the month that he received a proper annual leave, when he spent as much time as possible with his new bride. Larry wore his heart on his sleeve when it came to Marjorie; returning to duty, and knowing he would soon have to leave her, he wrote his final will and testament, bequeathing unto "My Beloved Wife . . . *My Entire Estate*."[118]

For the remaining months he spent time as a wireless operator and navigator, and then took his remaining seven days' annual leave; it would do him no good overseas. At the end of April the unit requested that Larry be promoted once again, this time to Warrant Officer Second Class. His petitioner noted that "since coming to this station he has been very active in work he has undertaken both in the Signals Section and in Station work generally. His work in the former is well above average and any instructional work he has done in all respects has been good."[119]

Larry went on embarkation leave for much of May. While he was away, another personal assessment noted that his confidence had increased, he demonstrated excellent ideas, and he promoted harmony and good will among his associates. His superior stated he had "done exceptionally well in instructional work he has undertaken on our unit as well as carrying out all other work assigned with the best of results." The commanding officer considered him a "good operator and an excellent instructor," recommended him for ordinary promotion, and felt Larry warranted commissioned rank.[120] The RCAF duly appointed Larry Warrant Officer Second Class on May 25, 1943, just before he headed to Nova Scotia for embarkation.

Navigator—George Parker

The father of two represented the educated, caring, responsible older recruit. George was thoughtful, dutiful, mature, confident, hardworking, and pleasant. A loving family man, he went to war to protect his family and made the ultimate sacrifice.

George was born October 20, 1915, in Forest Heights, BC. He was the youngest of three children born to coal mine owner Levi Parker, who had been born in Newhall, Derbyshire, England, and Mary Ann Parker (née Harris), born in Pontypridd, Wales. His parents married in Wales and later moved to Western Canada, where the family lived in and around Edmonton.

Blue-eyed, brown-haired George spent his primary education years in Edmonton and Cardiff, Alberta, then went to Morinville High School, where he obtained his Grade 12 diploma. Patricia Ann Goodman, later to become George's wife, went to the same high school. When George completed his secondary schooling, he headed to university in Calgary to complete his professional first-class teaching certificate. Patricia trained to be a nurse.

George began his teaching career in the Pibroch School District. However, he remained close to home for the 1936–37 school year so he could spend time with his mother, who later died from uremia. It was a sad time, but the sadness was tempered on May 11, 1937, when George and Patricia were married by Reverend J.K. Ketchen at Immaculate Conception Rectory.

In September George returned to teaching in the Pibroch School District for another year. Then he began working for himself as a truck operator in Edmonton, driving a coal truck for his father's mine. The job likely paid better than teaching, and it allowed George to remain closer to his family.[121]

When war broke out in 1939, George, eager to do his duty, made his first attempt to enlist. However, the RCAF rejected his application.

Recruitment in those early years focused on young, single men with healthy physiques and sharp eyes. Fresh from the Depression, plenty of unemployed men were eager to join up and do their part. Married men in their mid-twenties, especially those awaiting the birth of their first child, were not initially expected to sign up. They had other obligations to attend to.

George continued to drive a coal truck, and in June 1940, he and his wife welcomed their first child, a little girl they named Mary Gail, in memory of his mother. His little family grew again in February 1942, when they were blessed with a second child, Levi George.

By this time, things were not going well overseas. The recruits who had been swept up to defend their country in the first days of the conflict could not fill the needs of the war machine, and many had died in those early years, so the air force took all the new recruits it could get. When George again attempted to enlist at the age of twenty-six, he came prepared with personal references from trusted sources, including the school trustee at Pibroch, a storekeeper in Cardiff, and both a banker and barrister from Morinville. Even though George now had a wife and two children, the RCAF accepted his application. He signed his attestation papers on June 20, 1942, in the Ramsay Building at No. 3 Recruiting Centre in Edmonton and was given the rank of Pilot or Observer, Aircraftman Second Class.

George went through the usual battery of medical exams. He had acquired two scars: one on his forehead as well as a semicircular one above his right ankle. He, like so many others, was interested in becoming a pilot. However, during his medical examination it became clear he was unlikely to realize this preference due to a visual deficiency in his left eye.

Even though George had continued to play a number of sports as an adult, including baseball, hockey, golf, skating, and curling,[122] his initial medical reported that he had a sedentary physique. Considering his enjoyment of cigarettes, his years as a truck driver, and the tasty, home-cooked meals his wife prepared for him, it may be no surprise that he carried 165 pounds on his five-foot-seven frame.

The selection board, however, considered him to be fit, robust, and strong, with a good bearing and manner. He was described as a well-matured, confident, and intelligent type who "knows his own mind."[123] They considered George acceptable for a commission and recommended him for aircrew.

At some point after enlisting he bought property at 9847 151 Street in Edmonton. Married servicemen had more than just themselves to consider: the house would give George's young family a stable home in his absence and would be an asset in the event that something went wrong.

George reported for duty to No. 3 Manning Depot in Edmonton on June 30, 1942, and the air force kept him in Edmonton for much of his training, so for at least some of the time he remained close to his family. Near the end of his first month of basic training, the RCAF issued him with a standard pair of glasses.[124]

George later travelled to No. 7 Initial Training School in Saskatoon, where he began the first part of the course in mid-September. His interviewer considered him to be a pleasant, sincere, and earnest man with a good attitude and motives. [125] When he went through his second medical, the doctor noted that his left eye had worsened. Despite this, George still wanted to become a pilot or take any aircrew position.

George performed well on the course, receiving a total mark of 87.5 percent and a position of 43 out of 112 students. The RCAF duly promoted him to Leading Aircraftman. His hopes of becoming a pilot were over, likely due to his eyesight, but he would continue as a navigator. His instructor noted that he was a "mature, energetic, resourceful airman. Self confident, has character and initiative. Has acquitted himself well at this Unit."[126]

George entered No. 2 Air Observer School in Edmonton in late November. By this time, Larry Doran had already been at the school for over five months and had been married for one month. Larry and George probably met during their four months together at the school, and it is likely around this time their wives were introduced to each other. Patricia Parker and Marjorie Doran remained lifelong friends, and the Parker children grew up calling Marjorie their aunt.

George began the second part of training for air navigators, which involved day and night flying in an Anson as first and second navigator. While at the school, he enjoyed the camaraderie of his classmates and was described as "popular in classroom with a pleasant personality."[127] George and his fellow students later posed for an informal photo taken during the winter of 1942–43.

That winter the courses included air work, navigation and photography, magnetism and compasses, instruments (likely reading direction-finding aids and using a sextant), signals, maps and charts, meteorology, reconnaissance, aircraft recognition, and armament. George obtained an overall mark of 69.8 percent and was ranked eleven out of twenty-three students. Despite acquiring a decent position in class, he was considered unsuitable as an instructor but suitable for commissioned rank. In navigation he had "worked hard and put forth good effort at everything. A bit inaccurate at times but improving fast."[128] Promoted to sergeant, he received his air navigation badge.

Things began happening fast. Two days later George commenced his embarkation leave, spending those last weeks with family. Photographs of these special last moments captured a happy family man, proud to do his duty.

» True Servicemen

Unlike the rest of the volunteer recruits gathered and trained after the outbreak of war, Jock was a representative of the small number of true servicemen who had enlisted in the RAF, not just for the duration of the war, but as a full-time job.

To my surprise, even with so little information, I found myself forming a mental image of Jock. He was responsible, sensible, and dutiful, with the ability to adapt and bravely serve his country. I would always remember him as the young man who made a choice to take that extra step. He had already done his part to serve his country for many years, but he stepped up to face almost certain death when his country needed him most.

Jock was the only crew member who had joined the air force before war broke out. One of the original servicemen looking to have a career in the air force, he did not originally serve with the intent of flying a plane; rather, his first role was to maintain the aircraft for others to fly. He became a flight engineer more than a year after the new four-engined heavy bombers began arriving from the aircraft factories in 1942, in need of skilled men to control the engines, manage fuel consumption, and perform other jobs, allowing the pilot to focus on flying the plane.

Flight Engineer—Douglas (Jock) Cruickshank

Jock was born May 9, 1921, in Consett, County Durham, England. He was the middle child and eldest son of five children born to William Cruickshank and Eleanor Cruickshank (née Douglas). When he was still a young boy, Jock's family moved to 12 Coronation Road in Harrogate, and Jock attended Oatlands Primary School and later Christ Church Secondary School for boys. Sadly, nothing more is known about the early years of Jock's life.

When he finished his formal education, Jock took a job at Glovers Garage, also known as Appleyards, located on Leeds Road. The garage was situated behind the family home, making it a convenient employment location for a lad just starting out. For a short time he trained as a mechanic. Soon, however, Jock decided to enlist in the RAF. Germany had already annexed Austria and would soon invade Czechoslovakia, but Britain had not yet declared war. None of Jock's surviving family knows whether he decided to join the RAF out of interest in mechanical work or due to the rumblings of war.

Jock enlisted at Sub-depot Dishforth on September 20, 1938, and was given the classification Aircraftman Second Class. He was only seventeen years old. Here he underwent basic training that was likely similar to what all the others experienced. However, there may not have been as many new recruits all jumbled together as there would be once war broke out.

After completing the basics, Jock went to No. 5 Wing, Halton (Buckinghamshire), No. 1 School of Technical Training, in early December. This school was part of the Aircraft Apprentice Scheme introduced in 1920. It specialized in training skilled mechanics for aircraft maintenance. Apprentices normally required three years of service before graduating.[129] However, during the war years this was shortened to two years to address the need for men in service. Halton also schooled adult entrant tradesman in short, specialized engineering courses in the years leading up to and during the war, supplying many of the RAF's maintenance crews.[130] Jock may have been enrolled either as a fitter (engine mechanic), a rigger (airframe mechanic), or in some sort of maintenance capacity.

After successfully graduating from the school, he moved to No. 1 Wing, Hednesford (Staffordshire), No. 6 School of Technical Training, in April 1939. During this period the school was teaching electricians, instrument makers, and armourers. However, given his short stay, Jock probably trained in airframe maintenance. While he was in Hednesford, things were heating up in Germany. Blackouts began in Britain, and on September 3, Britain declared war on Germany.

Now part of the war machine, Jock was sent to 240 Squadron at Invergordon in Scotland in early October 1939. This was an operational flying boat squadron that flew the Saro London II. At the time, the RAF tasked the squadron to do North Sea patrols.[131] It is believed Jock trained in his trade at the station, working on the patrol planes.

After only a month with the squadron, he moved to the School of General Reconnaissance on Thorney Island, Hampshire, which taught navigation and reconnaissance to Coastal Command crews. While he was at the school, rationing began at the start of 1940. The unit moved to Hooton Park in Cheshire in June, and to Squires Gate, Blackpool, the following month.[132] Jock spent nearly a year at the school and was promoted twice during this period. His first promotion occurred on July 1, when he became an Aircraftman First Class. Within a matter of days, the Germans began bombing raids on Britain, escalating these attacks over the following months. On October 1, Jock was promoted to Leading Aircraftman, a move that marked the end of his training.

Although Jock had been away at one school or another for two years, and despite more than a year of war, his brother Gordon remembers that the family home was a "very happy one where, whenever possible, the family would get together."[133] This changed when the School of General Reconnaissance transferred to South Africa, a posting that would make it impossible for Jock to visit family and friends during leaves. He and the rest of the personnel boarded a ship, possibly part of the Winston Convoy (WS3), on October 6, 1940. It was a long trip but an exciting one. South Africa was the land of milk and honey, where rationing and blackouts did not exist, and when Jock disembarked at Cape Town in late October, he found himself in a bright, sunny place full of friendly, social people, a far cry from the current situation at home.

On October 29, Jock settled into No. 61 Air School at Station George, located near the southern coastline of South Africa, approximately halfway between Port Elizabeth and Cape Town. Today the original Second World War airfield is the site of P.W. Botha Airport. The base opened in April 1941 to train crewmen in navigation and included military reconnaissance in both ship and aircraft recognition. While working at the station, Jock was demoted to Aircraftman First Class from April 16 to October 1, 1942, then promoted back to Leading Aircraftman. The reason for this change in rank is unknown,[134] but whatever the grounds, he continued to work at the station for a further nine months before the RAF's need for flight engineers changed the direction of his life once again.

By July 1943, the increasing number of four-engined bombers being produced to bomb the Reich meant the RAF had a shortage of flight engineers, all or most of whom came from other engineering and mechanical trades in the RAF. Jock, like many others who had spent time in Africa, probably welcomed the chance to return home and join the direct fight against the Axis. Jock might have volunteered, or the RAF may have requested he remuster as a flight engineer. In any event, he likely boarded convoy WS31 on its return journey from Cape Town in July.

In Britain, perhaps after a few days of home leave to visit the family he had not seen in years, he entered No. 18 Operational Training Unit, RAF Finningley, in mid-August. Jock may have worked in his original trade here or may have been held at the unit until he got into the flight engineer course at No. 4 School of Technical Training, RAF St. Athan, in South Wales, near Cardiff, in early October. All flight engineers who trained in Britain, which was most of them, were trained at St. Athan. Instruction included Short Stirlings, Catalina Flying Boats, Liberators, Handley Page Halifaxes, and Avro Lancasters. In the case of the Lancaster course, instructors lectured flight engineers on aircraft systems and construction, emergency repairs, pre-flight checks, controls, takeoff and landing drills, and efficient engine handling.[135] These were vital tasks when flying long distances over Germany, especially given that the bombers were often damaged or experienced engine failures, serious weather variables, and many changes in route. Without careful control of fuel consumption, the plane and crew would not get home.

In early November, Jock spent a week at a Lancaster assembly factory in Woodford, near Stockport, on a "makers course." During this visit, Jock listened to lectures and watched demonstrations regarding the Lancaster bomber. Then he returned to No. 4 School of Technical Training and completed his lessons, leaving the school with his engineer's brevet and a promotion to temporary sergeant. This was an early Christmas present that he no doubt celebrated during the holiday season with his family. However, training was not over yet. There was one last step before flying in a squadron, so he headed for No. 1679 Conversion Unit on December 11 to meet the crew with which he was to fly.

8

The World by Mid-1943

D uring the boys' years of training, the war progressed rapidly. Germany invaded Denmark, Norway, France, Belgium, Luxembourg, and the Netherlands and then began bombing Britain. Initially the air raids centred on British radar stations, dockyards, factories, and RAF airfields, destroying a significant amount of Britain's air defence infrastructure. These were followed by raids on London and several other cities, including Belfast, Bristol, Cardiff, Glasgow, Liverpool, Manchester, and Southampton. Britain was struggling to prepare for an expected invasion.

However, when Germany's focus turned to blitzing the British population, the RAF got a much-needed reprieve. Britain worked to rebuild its airfields, aircraft, and aircrew, and the RAF began small aerial bombing raids against Germany, though it took time to build up its full strength. Germany continued the Blitz until early May 1941, with sporadic bombing thereafter, and British citizens demanded retaliation.

Those early years saw an unsustainable loss of both aircraft and servicemen for the Allies. Initially the RAF was ill-equipped; planes like the Fairey Battles, Blenheims, Whitleys, Hampdens, and Wellingtons were not powerful or agile enough, and their technology was unequal to that used by their German counterparts in the first years of the war. The British aircraft flew in daylight raids and were only able to carry small bomb loads. These negatives outweighed any positive outcomes of their attacks on the German superpower. The Allies needed to adapt; they needed to develop their aircraft to meet the demands of war, increase both the number of aircraft and crewmen, and build capacity for night bombing in order to "hide" the bombers from German view and protect them as much as possible before each attack.

New heavy bombers, the Stirling, Manchester, and Halifax, arrived in 1941, but there were still severe losses. The Lancaster joined the heavy bomber fleet in early 1942, offering increased bomb load, speed, and altitude. New technology that made it easier for bomber crews to find and identify targets more accurately was beginning to be developed. It wasn't until early 1943 that Bomber Command was able to focus its bombing operations on Germany, attacking the industrial belt in the Battle of the Ruhr.

Canada, strongly allied with Britain, had by now formed several Canadian squadrons under Bomber Command. Its first was 405 Squadron at Driffield, Yorkshire, established on April 23, 1941, followed on June 24 by 408 Squadron, which initially fell under 5 RAF Group, at Lindeholme, Yorkshire. As more Canadian squadrons were established, Yorkshire became home for many of them until the end of the war.

In the early years, 408 Squadron was just a number, remaining under British command and flying Handley Page Hampdens, mainly doing mining sorties—dropping mines in strategic locations in waterways as a means of defence or protection from enemy ships. By the end of 1942 it was flying Halifaxes, and on January 1, 1943, it joined 6 Group, run by the RCAF, which gave it a more distinctly Canadian identity.[1] Around this time, King George VI formally approved the squadron's "Goose" badge. The formation-flying Canada goose, a sturdy powerhouse as sure and true as the seasons, was a worthy choice as the mascot for a bomber squadron. As J.G. Armstrong wrote, "[The goose] is at home in Canada, England and Scotland. Its speed and powers of flight are indicative of the operational functions of the Sqn."[2] The squadron's motto, "For Freedom," perfectly summed up their reason to fly.

Linton-on-Ouse became 408 Squadron's home on August 12, 1943, and remained so until the end of the war. Shared with 426 Thunderbird Squadron, Linton could be called the place of hope on wings.

The Lancaster Mk II arrived at the squadron forthwith, and although this was not 408 Squadron's final major change of heavy bomber, it was the most loved. The Lancaster was the stronghold of planes, neither heavenly nor nature bound. The plane's sleek and powerful lines made it a beast of war, carrying the battle to the foe. Everything was in place and the war was now in full swing.

above left—Aircraftman Second Class, Robert (Bud) George Alfred Burt, ca. late 1942. COURTESY OF BURT FAMILY

above right—Bud Burt in his Lorne Scots uniform, ca. 1941 or 1942. COURTESY OF BURT FAMILY

below—Bud Burt, far right, with fellow trainees. The location is presumed to be No. 3 Bombing and Gunnery School in Macdonald, Manitoba, 1943. COURTESY OF BURT FAMILY

above—Sergeant Robert (Bud) George Alfred Burt, 1943. COURTESY OF BURT FAMILY

below—Sergeant Aubrey Elmer McLennan, Pat Hudson, and Leading Aircraftman Arthur Goodley, ca. 1944. The Hudsons opened their home to the two airmen during the war. COURTESY OF HUDSON FAMILY

right—Air Gunner Sergeant Robert (Bud) George Alfred Burt, 1943.
COURTESY OF BURT FAMILY

below—Last days at home before embarkation. Bud Burt with his parents, Myrtle and Robert Burt, 1943.
COURTESY OF BURT FAMILY

above left—Peter and Bob Hudson with their ponies, ca. 1936. COURTESY OF HUDSON FAMILY

above right—Sergeant Robert (Bob) Henry Hudson, aged nineteen, 1943.
COURTESY OF HUDSON FAMILY

below right—Bill Taylor, with his nephew Ross Reid, during training in Canada, headed to No. 1 Central Navigation School, Rivers, Manitoba, likely 1943.
COURTESY OF TAYLOR FAMILY

below left—Leading Aircraftman William (Bill) Taylor, 1942. COURTESY OF TAYLOR FAMILY

above left—Harvest time on the Lumgair farm, ca. 1939: Robert Lumgair, John Kendall, and Norman (Norm) Lumgair. Only Robert returned from the war. COURTESY OF LUMGAIR FAMILY

above right—Sergeant Norman Lumgair, 1943. COURTESY OF LUMGAIR FAMILY

below left—Doran family, Larry at bottom right, July 1918. COURTESY OF DORAN FAMILY

below right—Larry and Grace Doran with their son, William Hugh Doran, Bralorne, BC, March 1938. COURTESY OF DORAN FAMILY

left—Leading Aircraftman William
Lawrence (Larry) Doran, 1941.
COURTESY OF DORAN FAMILY

below—Fred and Kay (née Doran)
Vanstone, Wally Doran, and Larry
and Marjorie Doran, likely during
Larry's embarkation leave, 1943.
COURTESY OF DORAN FAMILY

right—George and Pat Parker with
children George and Gail, ca. 1943.
COURTESY OF PARKER FAMILY

below—George Parker with his siblings
Jack and Winifred, 1943.
COURTESY OF PARKER FAMILY

above left—Sergeant George Parker, 1943.
COURTESY OF PARKER FAMILY

above right—Douglas (Jock) Cruickshank in Claremont, Cape Town, South Africa, February 1942. COURTESY OF CRUICKSHANK FAMILY

below left—Norm Lumgair with his uncle, John Lumgair, ca. 1944. COURTESY OF LUMGAIR FAMILY

below right—Robert and Norm Lumgair, likely together on leave, ca. 1944.
COURTESY OF LUMGAIR FAMILY

Norm Lumgair, Larry Doran, George Parker, and Bill Taylor, likely at No. 22 OTU, August 1943. COURTESY OF PARKER FAMILY

Bill Taylor, Norm Lumgair, Wally Richmond, George Parker, and Larry Doran, likely at No. 1666 or 1679 HCU, 1943. COURTESY OF TAYLOR FAMILY

PART 3

HAVE WE MET BEFORE?

$=$ **9** $=$

Moving On, Moving Forward,
but Never Quite Forgotten

Talking with families, friends, and others who had a connection to the boys made me realize that things were never the same for them after March 15, 1944. However, life has a way of pushing us forward whether we wish it to or not. Time passes and the living carry on.

Both Marjorie Doran and Pat Parker remarried, in 1947 and late April 1949, respectively. According to Pat's daughter, her mother married a "wonderful man," whom she and her brother called "Dad." Although "there were a lot of bad times," she says, especially on Remembrance Days, as the years passed by, "it got easier but [he was] not forgotten."[1]

In contrast, Bud's mother never fully recovered from the shock of losing a son. Only a few years after the final letter from the Casualties Branch, she died. Bud's father carried on alone, but perhaps the strain of seeing another March 15 come and go was too much. He died of a heart attack almost exactly twenty-five years after his son, on March 16, 1969.

After the final letters from the RCAF, reporting that the headstones had been placed on the graves and the graves registered, the story ended as far as most people were concerned. The boys became names, memories, and stories remembered by those who had once known and loved them. The families did their bit to keep the information alive.

However, the older generation—the parents, siblings, and those closest to the boys—also faded, and the stories became as blurred as some of the aging photographs that held the boys' images. Memories of forgotten times bubbled to the surface and sometimes created a sticky web to untangle when vague recollections of shared moments with their loved one mixed with other events and merged into stories of their own.

Members of the next generation—nieces, nephews, and cousins—were in most cases either too young to remember those lost or not born until after the war, but they held on to the stories and pictures passed down by family, and they too made an effort to remember. Decades passed.

In the broad scheme of history, the boys were now only numbers—seven among hundreds of thousands who were casualties of war, names on memorials and cenotaphs. The 408 Goose Squadron flew 4,610 sorties between its creation in 1941 and its dismantlement after the war ended in 1945, dropping a total bomb load of 11,340 tons. In this squadron alone, 933 personnel did not return, either taken as POWs or counted among the missing or killed.[2] Although 408 Squadron suffered the most losses (shared with 419 "Moose" Squadron) among the Canadian squadrons[3] (understandable, perhaps, as it was the second-longest-running Canadian squadron during the war), and accounted for 10 percent of the 9,919 casualties the RCAF endured,[4] this was a vanishingly small number compared to the 55,573 deaths sustained by Bomber Command aircrews.[5] These numbers are hard to comprehend, but if we add to them the total air force, army, and navy personnel, not to mention the civilians, killed worldwide during the conflict, the boys come up as a minuscule loss, like the particles in the air, present but unseen.

The historical aspects of war had always bored me, seeming a little too sterile and faceless. The famous had their time in the spotlight of history books and cinema, but who were all these dead young men, the mind-boggling numbers behind the famous few? What had happened to them, what was their story, and where could that story be found? Someone had to know, and someone should be able to stand up and speak equally for those men, the men who never came home.

But who was I to ask? When I began my research, I often saw the underlying question "Why you?" in the eyes of people I spoke to, if they did not say it aloud. One person in particular repeatedly called me a "distant relative," as many others may have done quietly, as an aside. I cringed every time I heard the phrase and struggled to answer in a few words, to make people understand how it had become important for me to know their whole story. I did not feel distant to Bud, let alone the other crew members. My father never forgot Bud, he never let me forget Bud, and now that I knew some of the boys' personal histories, I could not let it rest. I needed to complete the story, and my distant blood should make no difference. They died for blood and non-blood alike, and if they could sacrifice for me, distant relative or not, so I could enjoy my life, then I could take a few years out of my privileged existence to sacrifice for them and keep them alive the only way I knew how.

I had spent a year of my free time researching the boys' lives, piecing together their individual travels through time, and I doubted there was anyone more bound to all seven boys. Although individual members of the families, such as John Hudson and Ken Burt, as well as others involved in the story, like the Steydli family, had achieved incredible understanding and communication in a time of no or limited Internet access, significant distances, and the added challenge of the language barrier, no one had taken all the pieces and tried to put the puzzle together for all seven boys. They had a right to be formally and equally remembered among the many. That was now my goal.

But even I sometimes asked myself why I, who had never known them, was not allowed to forget? What was I supposed to be finding out? From my childhood, Bud lay in wait, a small speck of light in the back of my brain that refused to go away. He surfaced from my subconscious now and again, over the years. Or, rather, he bounced around my brain, disappearing and reappearing at will. His will, not mine. I kept wanting to know more about him. He died just short of his twentieth birthday—what could he possibly have done in life in that time? Hell, what had I done in that amount of time? But neither Bud nor his crew mates seemed insignificant to me, despite their ages.

I had to know the truth. For me, their personal truth mattered. That's what I searched for—their truth or as close as I could possibly come to it.

Months earlier, Michael and I had visited the Australian War Memorial, hoping the people there might be able to help me with my research. Unfortunately for me, but appropriately, the Memorial focuses on Australians, and the staff and volunteers were unable to provide answers to a number of my questions. However, one volunteer suggested I place a short note with my contact details in the pigeonhole belonging to Edward Fleming, a Second World War Lancaster pilot who volunteered at the museum. When months passed with no reply, I assumed Mr. Fleming did not wish to talk about his own experiences during the war. I could fully understand this, and although I was disappointed, I continued to search the last recesses of electronic sources available to me. Then I received a call. It turned out the reason for Mr. Fleming's silence was that he did not often check his pigeonhole. We made plans to meet.

I got up early the morning of the interview, arriving at the War Memorial with over thirty minutes to spare. Seated outside in the shade, I flicked through my notes, checking to make sure I had not missed listing a question I wanted to ask. What would it be like, talking to a Second World War Lancaster pilot? Aware of the differences in age, gender, and, likely, perspective, I wished Michael were with me.

Five minutes before we'd agreed to meet, I walked around to the front of the building and began climbing the stairs, jostled by the already growing number of eager visitors. I looked up to see a red polo-shirted volunteer standing in the morning sun on the top landing, off to one side. We caught each other's eye immediately and smiled at one another as I closed the distance, knowing straightaway we had each found the person we were looking for despite the vast number of people shuffling into the Memorial. Making our way through the crowds, he obtained a pass for me and we went into the back rooms where we could talk with fewer distractions.

We sat angled, side by side, at a table, with my notebook and a few of my research materials for reference spread out before us. After sharing our general stories as an introduction, I gathered as much information as I could jot down in the time available while he provided clear, simple answers to my various questions. I wanted to know his impressions when he disembarked in Britain, what it was like to pilot a Lancaster, whether there was much interaction between aircrew and ground crews, what typical daily life was like for a crew, and typical procedures on base. I knew the answers would not be the same for everyone who went overseas, but it would give me a platform from which to gather a general understanding about life overseas.

His confident, easygoing manner drew me in. I marvelled that he too had disembarked at Greenock, just like my boys. Not surprisingly, he enjoyed flying the Lancaster, but I was surprised to learn how crews formed up and that their differences in rank sometimes caused problems. Having been on a squadron during the war, he was able to fill me in on the routines of a working squadron and training terms such as "bullseye," "fighter affiliation," and "circuits and bumps," three terms that appeared frequently in the boys' log books but which were still a bit foggy in my mind. Mr. Fleming was a wealth of information, and I did not want to finish talking with him. With all my questions answered for the time being, though, and with his volunteer work about to begin, we wrapped up the interview. I shook his hand and thanked him for his help.

Once home, I wondered about his own life. I wished I could learn more about his time in Britain, see pictures of him in uniform, and get a better understanding of his own experiences. I wondered if someone had recorded his story. He had told me he felt he had little to offer me, but in that regard he was mistaken. His comments verified information, made it clearer, but that did not explain the feeling he left me with. He gave me a glimpse of the psyche of a young man in the 1940s, the sense of excitement, the absolute naïveté, and even the downright stupidity of the situations they found themselves in, and the incredible sense of the invincibility of youth. He smiled grandly as he related snippets of his own time in the Royal Australian Air Force. What struck me most was the still evident personality of that young lad on his way to war, the bright-eyed look, the beaming smile, the eager anticipation to see the world, find adventure, and actively do something. The human spirit.

My boys' eagerness to apply now made sense. Perhaps the older among them had a more realistic view of the situation, but it didn't stop them. Larry and George had families, so maybe a sense of duty held some sway, especially for George with two small children to protect. Some of the younger boys, however, seemed to apply without any serious contemplation. Bud had joined the air force on the flip of a coin. Bill had extended his education just to get a chance to pilot a plane. Their goal was to fly. Air force posters played on this: they would make their family proud, do their duty, and be part of the team! It is unlikely that flying conjured images of danger as the thought of fighting in the trenches had done for their fathers in the First World War. Flight, to a trainee, equalled excitement, not its potential end state of spiralling to their death. When reality set in, training was done and they were initiated into squadron life with the knowledge that thirty operations over enemy territory awaited them. By then they lived for the moment because they never knew if they would survive to see another day.

I could imagine a more youthful version of Mr. Fleming under the spell of freedom from home and the expectation of what was to come. It was not dread, as one might assume, but exhilaration. A sense of vitality juxtaposed with the finality of death, the two opposing forces precariously balanced on the tightrope of war, and yet the blaze and energy of youth refused to topple. With a twinkle in his eyes, and smiling from ear to ear, he had remarked, as we finished our chat, that while waiting to return to Australia he had "fallen madly in love."[6] Obviously life and the forces of nature lived on regardless of war.

His situation was very different from that of my boys. He didn't do bombing runs. Based with 550 Squadron in North Killingholme during the later years of the war, he and his crew were assigned to head out prior to main bombing raids and drop "window," bundled strips of foil cut to a length that would disrupt the enemy's radar. The Axis relied on radar, with its electronic echoes, to locate incoming bombers and direct the Axis fighters sent to fend them off. Window created confusing, false electronic echoes, making it seem as though bombers were in one place when they were somewhere else instead. By dropping window, Mr. Fleming and his crew lured night fighters away from the bomber stream and helped reduce the risk of attack.

I was feeling my interest slide into this man's history, but I would have to push that aside. I had the story of my crew to write. I didn't have the time or resources to do two stories at once, although I wished I could. My life was beginning to take on a greater complexity than I had ever imagined.

After writing up my notes and musing over our conversation, I carried on with my research, but the interview had lit a flame of dissatisfaction with the work I had done so far. It was not enough. I was too far away from the action of war. I could watch more films, documentaries, and the like, read more books, and continue to talk with the families, but it still would not be enough. I had to be where they had been, walk where they had walked, and taste the realities of their death. My heart was set. Michael, back from overseas, had asked me what we should do for our second wedding anniversary, and now I had an answer.

"Honey, I know what I want for our anniversary," I said tentatively one evening after he had returned from work, excitement held inward in case I got a direct no. Dammit, no was not an option; I had to go. He had to agree. If not, would I be willing to go it alone?

"Hmmm, what's that then?" came the relaxed and unsuspecting question. He was probably expecting a request for a theatre show, or perhaps a second Steiff teddy bear. He had promised me a bear as a wedding gift, but I had not yet found the exact one I wanted. Here I was about to blindside him with something a bit more hefty on the pricing scale.

"I want to go for a ride in a Lancaster bomber," I blurted.

"Right," came the somewhat confused and hesitant reply. Well, it wasn't a no.

"I thought we could go to the UK and do a taxi ride in the Lancaster *Just Jane*," I added, showing him the website.[7] God, I was asking a lot of my new husband, to just blindly follow me to the other side of the world so I could get a glimpse into the life of the crew. This was supposed to be an anniversary gift after all. My plans included bringing seven other men along. And that's not all I had in mind. I wanted to visit the places the boys had been, then go to France and see the graves. These didn't hold quite the same interest for Michael as a ride in a Lancaster bomber, however, so this was about getting our mutual anniversary gift and then scheduling my research around that in the short time we would have overseas.

In the end I got my wish. We would have ten days in total, six in England and four in France. I made plans to meet Bob Hudson's family for at least the first two days of our time in England, and the Steydli family, eager to make our acquaintance, emailed us as soon as they knew of our trip in hopes of catching me before I booked a B&B. They graciously offered to put us up for our time in France. We accepted, and over the next few months I mapped out our itinerary to include a number of places and people I desired to visit, determined to make every day count.

= 10 =

To England

H alifax, Nova Scotia was an important port during the war years, the terminus for convoys to Britain. All servicemen, whether they were headed for overseas duty or working on the ships that carried others there, came through Halifax, flooding the little city. This often played to the advantage of merchants, who had a captive audience and could charge "extortionate prices" for everything.[1] However, with few changes made to the facilities in the area, the servicemen were an annoyance for many of the local population who remained in Halifax. While some men were only there a short time, others waited up to a month before boarding ship, and one can only imagine what havoc so many young men created over the six years as they waited restlessly to be on their way to war.

My five Canadian boys arrived at different times, depending on their profession and training end dates. Norm, the pilot, reached Halifax's No. 1 Y Depot first, in late March 1943. A week later he embarked for Britain. Navigator George arrived soon after, from Edmonton, and embarked four days later.

Larry, the wireless operator, arrived in late May, just seven months after his second marriage. He was still at the depot when Bill, the air bomber from Saskatchewan, showed up in mid-June, and even though the city was inundated with men ready for overseas duty, it is possible these two boys met during this time. They left the depot on the same day and probably embarked for Britain on the same ship.

Bud, the last to arrive, made his way to the depot by train, as the others had done. En route, he sent a postcard to his sister: "Well here I am again. I just got off the boat. We came across the bay of Fundy. Give my regards to everyone . . . Will write as soon as I can."[2] By late August, he too was on his way to Britain.

The crossing varied in duration from convoy to convoy due to ship speed, route, and other factors, taking anywhere from six to nine days. Some of the boys may have crossed the Atlantic on the *Queen Elizabeth*, a converted passenger liner, which was used to transport servicemen from the BCATP to Britain. During their ocean voyage the men slept all over the ship. They played cards, sang, and joked, but danger lurked on and below the dark waters of the Atlantic Ocean. Some men never made it to the war, their ships sunk by German ships and submarines. Keeping a lookout for anything unusual could save their lives.

The boys disembarked at Greenock, Scotland, on the south bank of the River Clyde. During the war, numerous shipyards were located there, which made it an excellent base for ships of war as well as a good assembly point for convoys coming across the Atlantic. Laurie Woods, a bomb aimer with 460 Squadron who was later awarded the Distinguished Flying Cross, crossed the Atlantic from New York in July 1943 and recalled having a "marvellous view of the shipping in the Clyde, including a goodly number of warships of different types." There were also "little white thatched cottages all along the northern shoreline with the gently sloping green hills in the background providing a wonderful first visit of Scotland."[3]

My Australian veteran, Edward Fleming, remembered reaching Greenock after travelling around the southern tip of Africa. In his memory, the bright green fields stood out under the grey, cold, drizzling sky. The men coming out in small motorboats to collect the new servicemen on the ships wore singlets, to his astonishment. How could they handle such cold weather in nothing but a singlet, while the men disembarking remained fully dressed and freezing?[4] The men in the boats took the boys from their ships to the Princes Pier Railway Station—a beautiful old building, built in 1893, overlooking the Firth of Clyde—where they boarded a train.[5]

Sharing seats with civilians, the troops travelled approximately seven hours to Bournemouth, in the south of England (the trains were slowed to reduce danger in case the track had been damaged by bombing),[6] and arrived in the city the day after stepping off the ships. Having nothing to do but chat or look out the window of the train—a must for any traveller in a new country—and with two hours of extra daylight thanks to the implementation of daylight saving time, they were able to see the "hives of activity" that seemed to be everywhere. However, when night fell, "everywhere the country was blacked out." The blackout and food rationing became the norm for Allied forces, previously unused to such restrictions.[7]

Each of the boys registered and was taken directly to No. 3 Personnel Reception Centre (PRC), Bournemouth, essentially a processing unit. For most Canadians and Australians, among many other allies, this represented the induction to life overseas, although not all went to this particular location. The RCAF took over large hotels to accommodate the newly arrived airmen, who settled into their assigned rooms and waited here on the south coast until they received postings to various training units.

Like most new visitors to Britain, the boys spent time enjoying what they could of the sights and a very different type of life to the one they had back home. Countless aircrew shifted about, and a few locals or older vacationers braved the brisk sea air, even though the seaside promenade was "closed and huge rolls of barbed wire stretched along the sea front."[8] For many young men, the novelty soon waned and boredom set in, with little to do for weeks on end but wait for assignment to a flying unit. Most felt a good deal of homesickness along with an equal amount of excitement tinged with anxiety.

Norm received no leave during this period. Finally, in mid-May, after a month at Bournemouth, he began some more intensive pilot training at No. 15 (Pilot) Advanced Flying Unit (AFU) and its various satellite airfields. In Canada, the skies had been clear and the training focused on teaching young men to fly. Now Norm learned Standard Beam Approach (SBA), a blind landing aid that helped a pilot position the bomber for landing in bad weather, and other methods of dealing with the varied weather conditions of northern Europe. He also learned how to fly larger aircraft and how to fly in formation with other aircraft. All of these skills would be necessary for flying as part of a bomber squadron in Britain.

This probably didn't keep Norm busy enough, and he may have taken part in some crazy antics. On July 25, he sprained his right wrist and elbow after falling off his bicycle. According to J. Douglas Harvey's recollection in *Boys, Bombs and Brussels Sprouts*, a memoir of his early days in the British training scheme, sometimes aircrew would "run races on the main highway." They cycled down a hill and grabbed hold of trucks moving at forty kilometres per hour (slowed to such speeds as a precautionary safety measure under blackout conditions). The outcome: their "rides ended in the ditch, a pile of broken spokes and bent and twisted wheels and handle bars, as the truck rounded a curve or swerved to miss strayed farm animals. A lot of bruises, torn uniforms, and chipped teeth later, we would wend our happy way back to base."[9] Whether Norm's injuries were the result of such youthful antics or just an unfortunate fall, he complained of pain and extreme tenderness in both elbows and wrists while at the local district hospital in Newbury. An x-ray showed no break, but the doctor did find "limitations of flexor and extension of elbows and wrists." He instructed Norm to do flex exercises on his arm for ten minutes every hour, and discharged him on August 2 as fit for full flying duties.[10]

Despite his injuries, Norm continued to fly. In his SBA training he was described as an "above average pupil with no faults,"[11] and in his final report the instructor noted that he was "fairly well up to standard and if he can develop himself a little he should make a satisfactory captain."[12]

Unlike Norm, George went on private leave for the first week of May after spending only twelve days at Bournemouth. He likely visited his uncle in Newhall, Derby, or spent the time roaming the local area. Once back from leave he continued to wait for a posting but, also unlike Norm, he stayed out of trouble. Upon waking up each morning, George put pen to paper. Each evening, whatever the duties of the day, he returned to his letter writing, finishing his thoughts off before sealing the envelope and sending his love to his wife. He did this every day he spent apart from his loved ones.

On June 11 he began a pre-advanced flight unit course at 16 Elementary Flying Training School in Burnaston, South Derbyshire, and then went on to another at No. 29 Elementary Flying Training School in Clyffe Pypard, Wiltshire. At both schools he flew in Tiger

Moths and worked to improve his map reading and his ability to determine position and speed in an aircraft. Coincidentally, the South Derbyshire school couldn't have been any closer to his uncle's farm in Newhall, and George likely spent much of his free time visiting his relatives. This would have kept some of the homesickness at bay and helped him settle into the routine of overseas duty.

When he moved to No. 2 (Observer) AFU in Haresfield, Gloucestershire, in late July, George flew in Anson aircraft, mostly as first navigator, plotting the plane's course on various practice runs along the southwest coast of England, as well as over the Irish Sea and along the northeast coast of Ireland.[13] His time in the air increased to an average of three hours at a stretch. He finished this course in late August.

Meanwhile, Bill and Larry spent much of July and August at No. 3 PRC in Bournemouth, waiting for their next training school. They may have run into each other here, perhaps being billeted in the same room or talking with one another before moving on independently to their next units.

Bill, the bomber, began his overseas training in mid-July at No. 6 (Observer) AFU in Moreton Valence, Haresfield, flying in Anson aircraft and learning to perform several tasks at once. He would eventually man the front gun turret in the Lancaster, so he had to fine-tune his ability to recognize different aircraft, sight and fire his guns, read maps (to help with navigation), and use signals communications. However, he mainly practised the very difficult task of bombing in the typically inclement weather of northern Europe, day or night. Training included simulation night bombing using infrared. Bill was considered an all-round average bomber and noted as a hard worker in the air but lacking concentration in map reading.[14]

Larry left No. 3 PRC just after Bill, entering the advanced wireless training unit at No. 4 (Observer) AFU in West Freugh, Scotland. Flying in an Anson aircraft, Larry developed his skills on a Marconi transmitter/receiver, an important piece of equipment that provided "long-range, high-frequency (HF) radio communications and navigation facilities." The radio portion allowed for transmission by voice or by Morse code to the rest of the squadron or to the base on the ground. The Marconi equipment also carried a direction-finding facility, "which used a rotatable loop antenna to determine the aircraft position."[15] Larry had to fully understand and be able to use the equipment as well as recognize and correct any faults if they occurred during a bombing run. He achieved a Morse speed of twenty words per minute and an Aldis lamp speed of eight words per minute (using flashes of light to communicate by Morse code). The instructor considered him to have exceptional aptitude as a navigator, and he was definitely suitable as a wireless operator/air gunner instructor. Overall, Larry was seen as a "capable air operator, very keen, well disciplined," who would make a good non-commissioned officer, above the usual standard.[16] When he finished his course in mid-August, Larry immediately went on a week's leave.

Bud sent a postcard to his mother as soon as he arrived at No. 3 PRC, assuring her he was "safe and sound." He gave her his address and told her he would write a "lengthy letter" later.[17] Lucky to have five days' leave in mid-September, he visited London and made the most of his time there, probably seeing the sights—Trafalgar Square, Westminster Abbey, the Tower of London, St. Paul's Cathedral, and Buckingham Palace—between attending shows. Returning to Bournemouth, he was assigned directly to No. 22 Operational Training Unit (OTU) in Wellesbourne, Mountford. The rest of the Canadian boys had already arrived there and were preparing to crew up.

11

Becoming a Crew

B ill, Norm, Larry, and George arrived at No. 22 OTU in August 1943, followed by Bud in late September, and all began training on the same course. No. 22 was a pre-heavy bomber conversion unit, where the separate aircrew trades used a medium bomber, the five-man Wellington aircraft, and would eventually form the initial five of a seven-man crew.[1] Upon entry to the unit, each crewman had his own trade to attend to, doing different tests and practical work. They also practised flying in groups with various trade members. This gave them a chance to get to know other crew trades and form a camaraderie with various individuals over the weeks of the course.

Bill averaged 66 percent between ground and air work in bombing, map reading, gunnery, and ship and aircraft recognition. Added to the mix was photography. He would be required to take a photograph over the target as the bombs were dropped to help verify the damage done. Emergency crew drills were also added, as bomb aimers were positioned over the main escape hatch of the bomber and were expected to begin emergency procedures in the event the crew had to jump from the aircraft. Bill's instructor considered him an average bomber, "slow but thorough and conscientious,"[2] who actively applied himself. Dependable and confident in his ideas, Bill provided good leadership, co-operated with others, and participated in station activities, all ideal characteristics for aircrew.[3]

Larry continued to improve his skills in Marconi equipment, both in the classroom and in the aircraft, achieving an overall average of 76.5 percent. The instructors also noted, when separately assessing qualities of character and leadership, that he was exceptionally quick to understand and forceful at getting his ideas across, and his competence gained the confidence of others. He was vigorous and enthusiastic in all he undertook and able to provide good leadership to those around him.[4] He earned a mark of 80 percent on this portion of the assessment, and was recommended for a commission.[5]

On September 23, Larry, having "almost completed all this advanced training," and despite "keeping very busy flying," managed to jot a one-page letter to his mother and sister Eileen. He had received three letters from them within a month, and he remarked that they should "keep up the good work." Updating them on his present situation he noted, "Another month–a couple of weeks' leave and then it starts. I think I'd give a week's pay right now for a good steak with half a dozen eggs on top of it. Those are the only things I miss greatly over here. Marj keeps me well supplied with all the little extras that go to make life worth living."[6]

George took tests as first and second navigator, using the data from the same loop antenna Larry used, as well as a sextant and GEE (radio pulses on a display), to plot the location of the aircraft on prepared charts/maps, earning above-average marks in the latter. His instructor remarked that he had "done some good work whilst at this Unit. A steady and reliable type. Should do well on a squadron."[7] He had confidence in himself, understood his tasks, and expressed himself clearly. A dependable airman, he displayed initiative and was willing to work with others and to participate in station activities.[8] George was promoted to Flight Sergeant on September 19, 1943.

On the ground, Norm worked on airmanship, navigation, and signals, earning an overall mark of 79 percent. In flying tests, which included instrument and night flying, his mark was 67 percent. Overall, he was seen as "an average pilot. . . a very quiet type who could use a little more drive, but he is steady enough, and will be able to cope quite well with larger aircraft."[9]

Bud furthered his gunnery knowledge, learned the components of various gun turrets, practised identifying different types of aircraft and estimating the distance from one aircraft to another, and gained practical experience in sighting a target and firing. In the aircraft, he practised using the FN20 turret and the Browning .303 gun, along with a cine-camera gun that allowed the instructor to assess his accuracy. He achieved accuracy of 75 percent and was deemed "a good keen gunner, [who] carries out any job with vigour and can be relied upon to cope with most jobs. Average ability as fighting controller; made very good progress in this after a slow start. Cine films—needs more practice when shooting in combat manoeuvres. Good for turret manipulation and range estimation but poor for deflection (amount). Recommended for a commission."[10]

That November, Bud received a letter from his former employer at Hewetson Shoe Factory, updating him on the news around the factory and passing along their wishes to have him home, as well as some Christmas cheer. "Within the next week or so you may expect a pound note as a little present from the firm. These will be forwarded as Postal Notes through the post office. We hope you have been receiving your quota of cigarettes quarterly through the Canteen. Everyone joins in wishing you a very happy Christmas and the very best for the coming year."[11]

Early November was also when a final decision on crewing-up was made. At this time, the first five members of the crew—pilot, navigator, wireless operator, bomb aimer, and one gunner—came together. It was an informal affair. The men had spent the previous eight or nine weeks flying with various combinations of tradesmen. Now they formed crews on the basis of how they got along on those short flights, even though they had been given little chance to get a feel for working with a range of individual personalities, and often had only a basic understanding of what their prospective crew mates were like.

The decisions made now could be good or bad. Choose the right crew mates and a good working relationship resulted. Usually the crews spent a great deal of time together, in and out of the aircraft. Ideally, when they went on operations, the crews would act as a well-oiled machine, working together as a single unit and looking out for each other as brothers, not strangers. If they survived the war, their friendships often lasted a lifetime.

Pick the wrong crew mates, however, and tensions could be high, often the result of clashing personalities or a mismatched rank distribution. This could be dangerous, even deadly. In *None but the Brave*, his book on Bomber Command, David L. Bashow notes that "since both the American and the British hierarchies felt that the pilot was the logical aircraft captain and crew commander, the British inconsistency of rank with respect to crew positions often led to awkward situations and additional stress if a junior pilot was attempting to discipline or coordinate senior crew members."[12] When I spoke to Edward Fleming in Australia more than six decades later, he confessed that some crews were poorly matched because members did not have the chance to get to know each other very well, making a blind decision to crew up with the nearest men to hand, regardless of whether the pilot had leadership skills or the crew had the maturity to accept a lower-ranking pilot's authority in the aircraft.[13] At least a few individuals felt a twinge of jealousy over rank or crew trade, but perhaps the most common problem involved the use of alcohol before takeoff. If one crew member was drunk, the others were less able to trust that man's trade abilities, and the lack of confidence affected the crew's operational abilities, potentially threatening their lives. It is surprising that such crews ever survived the war.

Ready or not, Norm, George, Larry, and Bill were instructed to crew up, which meant finding one of each of the trades to make a crew. The boys found each other. As early as September 13, 1943, Bill and Larry flew in the same aircraft while the pilot practised doing "circuits and bumps" (repeated square flight paths around the airfield, increasing altitude on each turn, before descending on the final turn of the square for a touchdown on the runway, then immediately taking off again without stopping). Six days later, Norm piloted the plane doing the same exercise, and the next day George joined them for local practice in bombing. From then on, more often than not, they flew together, so it is no surprise they picked each other during the crew-up. Wally Richmond, an RAF gunner, rounded out the five, flying with the boys during this time.

At first, Bud was not part of this crew. He had come in later than the initial group and first flew with Norm and George on October 20 as a mid-upper gunner. He met Bill three days later on a night flight with Norm and George, doing a cross-country exercise. Bud's meetings with various members of the crew settled him for the mid-upper gunner position in what would be their operational plane, the Lancaster, leaving the more experienced tail gunner position for Wally Richmond.

In early November the crew took leave while Bud continued to fly, gaining experience as both tail and mid-upper gunner. He too then went on leave. But his lot had officially been cast. Scrawled on the top right corner of his report was the note "Lumgair's crew."

Although RAF Sergeant Bob Hudson came to the unit from No. 1 Air Gunners School in Wales on October 19, he did not fly with the Canadian boys. He may not have even met the boys except in passing. His initial flight occurred nearly a month after his arrival, and he flew mainly as a mid-upper gunner. Like Bud, he practised day and night flying, as tail and mid-upper gunner, with various crews.

In mid-November, fresh from leave, Norm, Larry, Bill, and George moved to No. 61 Base, their last training unit before they were assigned to a squadron. They underwent two weeks of ground defence training at 6 Group Battle School in Dalton Thirsk. This course gave them the basic knowledge needed to escape, evade capture, and survive if they were shot down and managed to parachute out of their aircraft over enemy territory. They practised shooting a Sten gun and a light machine gun, and learned field survival techniques and map reading before going out for a practice exercise in which they used their newly acquired skills to make their way back to the base without being captured. When they had completed this training to the satisfaction of their instructors, the crew, including Bud, had a two-week holiday.

Six days into the course, Larry was awarded the rank of Warrant Officer First Class when the commission recommended at No. 22 OTU came through. This made him the highest-ranked member of the crew.

Meanwhile, Jock Cruickshank entered 1679 Heavy Conversion Unit (HCU), one of the No. 61 Base units, on December 11, although he did not join the crew for at least another month. And Bob arrived at the base right before Christmas, after he had completed his gunner training at No. 22 OTU. Bob had big plans for his Christmas leave. He was going home to see his family, but that wasn't the only thing on his mind. He planned to ask his girlfriend, Mavis Barker, to marry him.

Just before the end of his holiday, Bud wrote his parents a quick postcard, sending his love to all and letting them know he was fine.[14] He also wrote a poem to his sweetheart, Audrey Harris, expressing his hopes and feelings as training neared its end and operations over Germany loomed ahead.

> This little poem, I just had to write;
> To let you know that things are all right,
> That my thoughts are of you, wherever I roam,
> Whether it's over Berlin, or over old Rome.
>
> And though things look stormy, cloudy or bright,
> My thoughts and my prayers are with you every night,
> Though God has willed that we drift far apart,
> I feel we are closer, both in spirit and heart.
>
> The dark clouds are lifting, and things now look bright,
> It won't be long now, till we have things right;
> So here's to the future, the past has gone by,
> The future I've dreamed of for both you and I.
>
> So chins up, old girl, things really look bright,
> Though I know I shan't be home, today or tonight;
> But tomorrow is coming, and we'll win the darn war,
> Then we'll pick up again, where we left off before.
>
> Say hello to your mother, your family and mine,
> Give them my regards and tell them I'm fine;
> In closing, there's yet one thing I'd like to do,
> And that is to convey just how much I love you.
>
> Well, dear, I'll write "finish" to this poem or rhyme,
> My eyes are complaining, it's past my bed-time;
> Hereafter I'll stick to my turrets and my guns,
> And leave things like this to poets and their sons.
>
> So good night, my dear, pleasant dreams, pleasant rest,
> And may I add, "Merry Christmas and all of the best";
> And I hope that, God has willed it to be,
> To protect and to keep you safely for me.[15]

Upon returning from holiday, the Canadian boys and Wally Richmond continued their training at No. 1666 and No. 1679 HCU at Wombleton, as crew 36 on course 6. At these heavy conversion units, crew members honed the skills they had learned on the twin-engined Wellington from No. 22 OTU and applied the knowledge to the heavier four-engined Halifax and Lancaster bombers.

As they were on duty, they spent their Christmas in the local area. George became ill in late December and missed out on training. He had a head cold for several days along with a cough, followed by severe chills and a headache, then "went to bed in his billet and during the night . . . developed a severe pain to the right of the nipple. The pain is made worse by deep breathing or coughing." In the morning "he noticed his sputum was rusty and blood streaked." He headed for the base medical facility and was transferred to RAF Hospital North Allerton, Yorkshire, on January 2, 1944, where he was admitted with atypical pneumonia in the right middle lobe.[16]

The rest of the boys remained at No. 1666 HCU, flying mostly Halifax aircraft, with the exception of Larry who also flew two flights in a Lancaster. At the beginning of the course the boys often worked separately from each other or with only a few of their crew mates. Norm practised flying circuits and bumps, Bill practised dropping bombs on targets, and together they tried to develop the close working relationship they would need for bombing runs, where the bomb aimer directed the pilot over the target. Bud and Wally, meanwhile, practised shooting moving targets from their turrets, George practised map reading and plotting flight paths, and Larry took to the skies to hone his skills on the Marconi equipment. By mid-month, Jock, the RAF flight engineer, had officially joined the crew, but in a letter home Bill mentioned that they hadn't "seen much of him yet,"[17] as he still had his own training to attend to. Jock would have been hard-pressed, learning to put out engine fires, understand the finer details of reading gauges, and monitor fuel consumption so the crew could make it back to base after a bombing run.

By January 10, the same day Bob was taken on strength at the base, George's health showed a marked improvement, but it wasn't until January 18 that he was finally discharged from the hospital. Bill mentioned his crew mate's health in a letter home. "I was telling you in my last letter that George was in the hospital. Well he got out a couple of days ago but was given ten days sick leave so is now away at his uncle's place. He says he is feeling alright now but he seems to be pretty weak." Bill, too, had a slight touch of the flu and admitted there was "certainly a lot of it around" the unit.[18]

Considering the cramped Nissen hut accommodation, it is no surprise the boys got sick. They slept twelve to a hut, six to a side, in iron cots. An ineffective small iron stove in the centre of the hut blocked the aisle and gave very little heat but a good deal of smoke. The Nissen hut itself was essentially a half-cylinder of corrugated iron arching over a concrete floor, with two wooden end walls that featured two small windows and a door at one end. Cement and iron are not warming, and the dampness and cold of the 1943–44 winter meant the men spent their nights inside what amounted to a cold, moist cave. J. Douglas Harvey later remembered that "putting on clothes in the morning, if you had had the courage to remove them the night before, was like putting on a wet bathing suit, only much colder."[19]

Like George, Bud ended up going to RCAF Wombleton's medical facility. On January 21 he complained of a sore throat, severe headache, vomiting, and occasional pains running down his fingers and legs. With a temperature of 102 degrees Celsius, red throat, and a septic left tonsil, he was diagnosed with acute tonsillitis.[20] He missed seeing the movie *How Green Was My Valley*, which was played at the station for the servicemen the following day.[21] Instead, he spent four days under treatment.

In late January, Bud and George returned to flying duties, and by January 29 the crew (Norm, Bill, Jock, George, Larry, Bud, and Wally) had begun flying together in Lancaster aircraft, doing circuits day and night, and practising cross-country flights, map reading, and bombing by night.

The boys went out as a group to get to know one another better one evening between January 27 and 30, but when they returned to base, Wally Richmond, the tail gunner, stepped out of the taxi and fell, breaking his ankle. For Wally, fate dealt cruelty unequally with kindness. As he mended in hospital, he learned that "his mother had been killed in an explosion of a load of bombs."[22] And by the time he returned to duty and entered 408 Squadron, his original crew mates, the boys of EQ-P, had gone missing after their March 15-16 mission. Spared the fate of his mates, he served as a tail gunner with another crew and survived the war.

With Wally out of commission, the crew needed a last-minute replacement before they could move on to a squadron, but the replacement did not appear overnight. An unidentified gunner stepped in for a practice flight on February 2, 1944, when the boys took off from the base at 1800 hours in Lancaster DS-626 J. They flew at 6,000 metres— and at a temperature of minus twenty-five degrees Celsius—simulating a bombing run, but over friendly territory. Heading out from base, George read his maps and plotted their course to the bombing target. Bud scanned the night sky vigilantly from his turret, looking for night fighters, and Norm practised evasive corkscrew manoeuvres while a friendly fighter pretended to attack. Reaching their target, Bill released his bombs, and George plotted their route back to base, landing at 0007. The instructor noted George's plotting and log work were very good, but he had not used the sextant and SBA to plot the plane's location, had used some incorrect symbols, and had not accounted for flight time between his last plotting point over the town of Goole and the base.[23]

Bob joined the crew at No. 61 base the next night for his first and only training flight with the crew. Bud, the slightly more experienced gunner, moved to the tail gunner position, leaving the mid-upper gunner position for Bob.[24] They took off for a bullseye exercise at 2029, again flying at 6,000 metres and at a temperature of minus twenty-four degrees Celsius. They spent about the same amount of time in the air as the night before, covering much of England and landing back at base at 0055. George's plotting and tracking proved well done, but he needed to watch his "ETA [estimated time of arrival] a little more carefully," along with his use of plotting symbols.[25]

With this flight completed, the boys prepared to move on to a squadron. Their final individual reports showed they were ready for squadron flying duties and for the stresses of bomber operations over Germany. Norm was described as "a cool confident pilot who appears to be very level headed. Has fair crew control and will listen to and carry out orders."[26] He fit the standard of bomber pilots, described by Lancaster historian Leo McKinstry as "a special breed of men, whose job required fortitude, authority, calmness, patience, technical awareness and aerobatic skill."[27] George demonstrated the required qualities of a navigator, even though he had entirely missed training at No. 1666 HCU. He studied hard to catch up, and his instructors continued to remark on his work ethic. His plotting skills were good, and the evaluator noted that he "works very hard in the air and makes very good use of his aids—should do very well on operations."[28] Bill's bombing leader deemed him an "average air bomber" who "should prove an asset to his crew."[29] Larry was reported to have good ability in Morse and general knowledge of Lancaster and Halifax aircraft,[30] and Bud also showed steady progress. His instructor commented he worked hard and demonstrated a marked improvement.[31]

The boys, including their two newest crew members, Jock and Bob, were now ready for squadron life under the badge of the Goose.

12

408 Squadron

"The start of a new month, a month closer to victory."[1]

The boys arrived at Linton-on-Ouse, home of two Canadian squadrons, 426 Thunderbird and 408 Goose, on February 5, 1944. A number of purpose-built buildings, including hangars, an air control tower, offices, instructional rooms, a mess, and housing, dotted the flat terrain. However, the number of ground and aircrew working from the base meant much of the accommodation was farther afield.

The boys, all non-commissioned airmen, had neither the best nor the worst of the situation. Most staff, commissioned officers, and ground crews took up residence in the camouflaged H-shaped brick buildings on the base or in other readymade accommodation, only moments from their Lancasters and a short sprint from training rooms and the mess. The boys billeted at Beningbrough Hall, about four kilometres away. This was a huge step up from the damp Nissen huts but not nearly as convenient as being on base.

The government had requisitioned the hall from its owner, Lady Chesterfield, for use by those stationed at Linton-on-Ouse during the war. She remained on the property, moving out of the hall and into Home Farm, a much smaller building. On more than one occasion she complained about damage done by the airmen. This included not only the trampling of a vegetable garden,[2] but also the use of inside staircases as raceways for those afoot or on bicycles, who wished to see who could get to the downstairs bar the quickest. The great staircase is unused today, its delicate condition likely in part the result of the battering it received during these racing sessions—although it cannot only be attributed to wartime abuse. Under the ownership of Lieutenant-Colonel Lewis Dawnay in 1892 (before Lady Chesterfield's time), there were reports of "'tobogganing' down the main staircase."[3] It seems the stairs at Beningbrough were destined for the racing games of the young or the young at heart.

In more than one room, evidence remains of the servicemen's ill-treatment of the house. There are cigarette burns on the waist-high coping to the right of the door leading from the closet (used as the darts room during the war) to the dressing room (at the time the bar room) on the ground floor. In the adjoining room, the drawing room (then the social area), the words "Olie loves Gypsy" are carved just above the fireplace, memorializing a British girl and her love for a Canadian airman. Throughout the years, doorknobs disappeared, most likely removed as keepsakes.[4] Today, many look upon these damages with a smile, attributing them to the craziness of the time, but it must have been stressful for Lady Chesterfield to be moved out of her own home, to see her belongings packed away before the airmen arrived, and then to watch as what amounted to young hooligans treat her home as a barracks.[5]

The men used the ground floor for socializing and the two floors above as sleeping quarters. The saloon room, the largest of the sleeping quarters on the first floor, was originally designed for large gatherings such as "county balls, formal banquets, family parties and other occasions that needed space and a sprung floor."[6] During the war the walls likely remained the peacock blue colour painted by the Chesterfields, but the room was stripped bare and now contained nothing more than exposed wood floors and a three-metre-long aisle with iron cots along each wall. As there was nowhere to keep their kit, duffle bags acted as bedside cupboards. The mattress consisted of wire springs, covered by three canvas squares, which made for little comfort.

The hall had two redeeming qualities, however: first, it was located near the pub, the Alice Hawthorn, situated on the opposite bank of the River Ouse in Nun Monkton. The waterway posed little problem for the crews billeted at the hall. They simply walked to the river bank and, for a fee, the land-owner on the far bank would row the crews back and forth to enjoy a drink.

The second redeeming quality was the bathtub adjoining the sleeping quarters inside the hall. J. Douglas Harvey, a pilot with 408 Squadron, recalls, "There was only one bathroom for twenty-five men. Ah, but the bathtub. A huge seven foot crater! The only time I was ever warm in an English winter was when immersed to the chin in that tub. Government regulations prohibited the use of more than five inches of hot water. The frozen young Canadians said, 'Balls,' and plunged in to their necks."[7] It is no surprise, then, that "it was like Grand Central Station when anyone took a bath with people going to and fro all the time."[8]

Bud, coming from the starkness of the Nissen huts and not privy to the even more luxurious accommodations of the commissioned officers on base, obviously agreed with the sentiment when he wrote to his sister Evelyne: "Well this situation is pretty good. We sleep in a huge country estate. It's really lovely. However we have C.O.s instead of butlers and there's no Chamber maids unfortunately. Outside of that it's okay. The whole house is centrally heated plus a fireplace in each room. Also our own private bath. No it's not heaven I'm in, but a likely substitute. I guess they're just getting us prepared for it. I hope my crime sheet isn't here or they'll move me to the cellar to shovel coal."[9]

Bill concurred, telling his brother, "This seems to be a pretty good station we are on. We are billeted in an old manor house and it happens to be steam heated which is certainly quite a change and besides that it is nice to have a bathroom outside your door with plenty of hot water."[10]

Obviously the accommodations were appreciated, if not for the locality then at least for the central heating and the hot water they could soak in after a cold winter's flying practice, a seven-hour flight over Germany, or a long walk or bike ride back from the station. Those billeted at the hall found the four kilometres separating them from the base frustrating at times. The bus that transported the men back and forth to the base ran infrequently, and its schedule did not always coincide with bombing runs or practice flights. At the end of a raid, if they did not mind the wait, they could catch a ride back to the hall in the back box of a truck. For most, however, it was either ride a bicycle or "walk in the rain or walk in the mud or walk in those clammy thirty degree [Fahrenheit] temperatures that are colder than any arctic weather."[11] Whatever the reason, the cold, dreary winter of 1943–44 in Yorkshire and the bathtub at Beningbrough Hall had a lasting impact on many of the aircrew billeted there over the war years.

On the base, the boys found themselves in the centre of the whirlwind. Terrible weather, the demand for record-breaking numbers of aircraft in flight, and significant losses in terms of both planes and lives plagued the squadron. In Canada's 6 Group, "between August 1943 and March 1944, the group's Avro *Lancaster II* loss rate averaged 5 percent per operation, producing a concomitant 21 percent survival rate."[12] Bud and his crew mates joined the fight at the worst time, during the "Berlin raids, which occurred from November 1943 to March 1944," where the "individual crew odds of survival were much less than for those who commenced operations later in 1944."[13] To put it in the starkest perspective: "The bomber offensive of 1942–43 and the first months of 1944 was the Second World War's equivalent of the First World War's Somme and Passchendaele [battles in which hundreds of thousands of men were killed]."[14] The boys would practise manoeuvres over the English countryside, endure the ups and downs of waiting for their turn in the war-torn skies over Germany, and fly near the end of the Battle of Berlin, through the nights of Big Week and beyond, but they, being part of the other 79 percent, would never make it home.

The first few days of squadron life consisted mostly of settling in, with no flying for the sprog (new) crew. The moon was in its bright phase, known to squadrons as a "moon period," making bombers highly visible to night fighters. This, mixed with unfavourable weather, meant bombing operations were off for the time being, so the squadron put on a variety of training and exercise drills, with the boys taking part in inspections and a lecture on Visual Monica, a radar in the bomber that warned the crew of approaching enemy night fighters.

On February 8, the boys waited on the ground for their first training flight on the squadron while other crews took to the sky, each member practising his own skills within the aircraft. They made use of their newly acquired Monica training, trying to evade friendly fighters as though they were the enemy. They bombed in designated areas and took radio communications from base before landing. The boys finally got their chance to fly that evening.[15] They left at 1849 hours in EQ-Q,[16] one of a group of six aircraft, on a bullseye exercise. A technical failure caused one plane to return early, but the rest carried on successfully,[17] returning five hours later.

The next day, 408 Squadron crews took part in another extensive flying training course before receiving six Lancaster IIs from 432 "Leaside" Squadron, which was converting to Halifax IIIs.[18] In all, 408 Squadron absorbed eleven Lancaster IIs over the next few days, while 426 Squadron received eight Lancasters. These were battle-worn planes that had flown between three and thirteen operations each.[19] While some planes flew in and out of Linton on practice runs, others landed to roost in their new home. The boys departed at 1848 hours in EQ-R for a night training flight across the countryside with two other aircraft.[20] Although one crew was diverted to RAF Station Compston, all successfully completed the task in just over three hours, with the boys and the other crew landing back at base.[21]

Five days into squadron life, snow and rain again grounded the crews. They attended ground training and lectures on wireless communications and new equipment.[22] Throughout the latter half of the war several new pieces of equipment were produced to help crews find their target or alert them to approaching night fighters. For the crews, there was always something new to learn. Afterward, Bud wrote to his mother, letting her know he still had a light cold and enlightening her about his recent experience in the air:

I froze my face the other night. Both cheeks. Boy do I ever look lovely. I've got two big brown welts down both cheeks. Then I went to the hospital to get some salve and it makes it look twice as bad. As you know we fly pretty high. Well at the altitude we fly at it's damn cold. I have heated clothing etc., but that doesn't cover my face. You've probably seen pictures where aircrew wear an oxygen mask which covers their nose and mouth. Well my outlet valve froze up, due to the condensation of my breath. Well there is only one place for the air to get out then and that's up along the bridge of my nose. Well it gets out okay, then condenses in the cold air and the moisture falls on my cheeks, and then freezes. All in all very uncomfortable. How'd you like to sit for about 6 or 7 hours in 28-35 below zero with ice forming on your cheeks and eye-lashes. Also there is no cover. All the back of my turret is open so when I turn onto the beams (90 degrees from dead astern) I have the slipstream to contend with too. It's about 120-150 m.p.h. wind. Well I've overcome most of that now. I wrap a scarf around my face, stuff cotton-batten between my scarf and face. Put on my helmet and mask, then goggles so nearly all my face is covered. Then I've still got my mask to contend with. As my breath condenses the water can't get out as an oxygen mask fits real tight, so you can draw the oxygen in. Well about every half hour or hour I have to empty about a cup of water. Well when I take my mask off the cold air freezes the moisture on my face where the mask was. Also there's a thin film of ice that forms in the mask. Then the fun begins all over again and I put the mask on and wait for my breath to thaw out the ice that's formed. Sounds like a full time job eh? Well that's just a small part of it. Also as height varies I have to keep blowing my ears out to keep the air in my head at the same pressure as the atmospheric pressure outside. Then in my spare time I keep the turret moving so the anti-freeze doesn't get sluggish. Take fixed watch for occults,[23] and a hundred other odd jobs I have to do. Lots of fun eh? Just thought I'd give you the bare outlines.[24]

Life as a tail gunner evidently had its share of downsides.

On February 11 the squadron took advantage of better weather and no bombing duties to give the crews an extensive flying training course. The day played out its typical routine of flying around the skies with the boys practising their skills, while at night the crew again took to the sky, departing at 1857 in EQ-W on another bullseye exercise with four other crews, returning nearly five and a half hours later.[25]

The following morning the base again stood down from operations. Bud, still smarting from frostbite, began to feel the twinges of an illness coming on, but he got up as normal and headed to base with the rest of the boys for more lectures and more training.[26] All the boys except Larry left the station in EQ-W at 1430 hours as one of the crews assigned to a two-hour fighter affiliation (in which they practised defensive manoeuvres, such as corkscrews, against friendly fighters) and bombing exercise.[27] Larry flew at the same time with

Flt. Off. Harvey in EQ-S, practising with Visual Monica.[28] Later that evening, other crews took part in a training flight across the countryside.

On Sunday, February 13, it looked as though Norm might get his first chance at operational flying as a dickey pilot when Bomber Command called on the squadron to carry out operations. Dickey flights gave a new pilot the opportunity to experience an operational bombing raid with a seasoned pilot and crew before taking on the challenge alone with his own crew. Only moderate ground training took place, with seventeen crews preparing themselves and their aircraft for the night ahead. However, "just about an hour and twenty minutes before takeoff, the whole detail was scrubbed, apparently owing to the weather closing in."[29] A sense of disappointment balanced with relief greeted the news.

Monday proved to be just as frustrating, as lingering fog pinned the squadron down for much of the day. Heavy ground training was a refreshing change from the previous week's air exercises. Operational crews—crewmen versed in fighting over enemy territory—engaged in parachute and dinghy drills. Non-operational crews, whose pilots had not yet taken their dickey flight (such as the boys), sat in on a lecture about intelligence and tactics. All bomb aimers, like Bill, trained in GEE and Link. Wireless operators, including Larry, took intense Morse training, while air gunners, such as Bud and Bob, got off easy with light training in shooting practice.[30] This was just as well for Bud, as he was feeling the full effects of an illness setting in and was not in any shape to fly.

At some point during the day, the fog cleared enough for a crew from 432 Squadron to ferry Lancaster II LL637 over to 408 Squadron.[31] It was a couple of days before she was ready to fly again, as she had to have her old code removed, to be replaced with EQ-P. The boys now had their bird.

~~ **13** ~~

EQ-P: Birth of a Dragon

he Lancaster is forever synonymous with the RAF and the Allied air forces of the Second World War. This plane, loved by those who flew her and loathed by those who experienced her wrath, was considered a "mighty broadsword"; a dragon "shrouded in darkness," breathing "menace and aggression"; a "pulverizing weapon of attack" whose "sole purpose was destruction." Oddly, few examples of the great beast remain today, but it continues to conjure up "pictures of bleak Lincolnshire bases in the depths of winter, with icy winds sweeping across concrete runways, or streams of black aircraft, weaving their anxious way through the German night, then suddenly plunging into the turmoil of bright searchlights and exploding flak shells."[1]

Originally, the Lancaster started out as another aircraft, the unreliable Manchester. The "addition of two engines turned a dangerous mediocrity into a world-beater."[2] Other notable changes included lengthened wings and a tail variation. This new version, labelled the Lancaster Mark (Mk) I, developed into a full-blown war machine. The sky over Europe during the Second World War would never look or sound quite the same, with the ominous black belly and the roar of power passing overhead.

There were several versions of the Lancaster made over the war years, with changes made to improve the aircraft and provide room to accommodate larger bombs. The Mk I, III, and X versions were similar, and all had engines that were variants of the Rolls-Royce Merlin. The Mk II was the only Lancaster powered by four Hercules VI or Hercules XVI engines.[3] Merlin engines were used in numerous types of aircraft, including the Halifax, Mosquito, and Spitfire, and the significant demand caused a shortage. The Hercules served as a stopgap, but in the end only 301 of the Mk II version were produced, due to the shortage of Merlins.[4]

Use of the Hercules engines made some difference to the performance of the aircraft, of course. The more powerful Hercules engines, which would later be an asset to the Halifax III, consumed more fuel in the Lancaster Mk II. The Hercules also made the aircraft slightly less easy to handle, with a lower maximum speed than its predecessor. However, the Mk II was superior in low-altitude flying as well as during takeoff and ascent,[5] which would have been important when taking off fully loaded or when returning to base with bombs still hung up in the bomb bay, an all-too-common occurrence.

Two other main differences on many of the Mk IIs—a larger bomb bay and a ventral (belly) gun turret—were intended to improve the aircraft's bombing and defence capabilities. The stepped protrusion at the front of the bulged bomb bay in the belly of the plane varied, becoming larger over the period the Mk IIs were built, and was also used in various other models of the Lancaster. It was designed to allow the aircraft to carry a larger bomb load. Despite this advance, which worked well in the other marks, the Mk II commonly carried a lighter bomb load.

The ventral turret was added to defend the vulnerable underbelly of the aircraft from German attacks from below, but in reality it was of little use. The turret moved too slowly to be of any real advantage, and gunners found it difficult to sight enemy aircraft through its periscope. As well, having a third turret required an extra gunner to be added to the crew. In the end, many of the turrets were removed to reduce weight, maximize bomb load, and possibly reduce landing problems. Some squadrons installed H2S, a mapping radar that helped with navigation and target identification, in its place, although this was not likely added to EQ-P, as 408 Squadron was still using the radio navigation system GEE or GEE-H.

Regardless of mark, many pilots have professed their love of flying the Lancaster. Not only were the planes beautiful to behold, but they were a joy to fly, powerful yet responsive and manoeuvrable. She could still function on three or even two of her four engines,[6] and her abilities gave confidence to those who flew her. Even when one or more engines had failed and her body had been riddled with flak and night fighter rounds, the Lancaster often brought her crew home. "It was this resilience, allied to its power and beauty, that inspired such devotion towards the Lancaster from airmen, ground crews and the public," Lancaster historian Leo McKinstry has written. "Rarely in history has a weapon of mass destruction been so cherished."[7]

LL637 was one of 450 Lancasters built by Armstrong Whitworth in the serial range LL617 to LM296. She was built with Hercules XVI engines, one of only one hundred of this particular power plant, which were delivered between October 1943 and March 1944.[8] On January 6, 1944, LL637 arrived at RCAF 432 "Leaside" Squadron, at East Moor, Yorkshire.[9] While there, the plane was coded QO-Z and assigned to Flt. Off. Earle K. Reid.[10] While Bud Burt and his mates were finishing their training at No. 22 OTU, QO-Z took part in several training flights and three major raids. On January 25, 1944, Reid and his crew carried out a night cross-country exercise in the aircraft before QO-Z made her maiden voyage over enemy territory. She was involved in three major raids as part of the Battle of Berlin, on January 27–28, January 28–29, and January 30–31.[11]

In early February, unable to bomb due to the weather, QO-Z flew on various training runs. The seventh of February heralded a distinct change when the arrival of two Halifax Mk IIIs began the squadron's conversion from Lancasters to Halifaxes. QO-Z's last training flight with the 432 Squadron crew took place the following day as part of a night cross-country bombing exercise.

On February 14, Flt. Off. Reid and four of his crew, Sergeant (Sgt.) May, Flight Sergeant (Flt. Sgt.) McDonald, Sgt. Clarkson, and Sgt. Barr, along with another crewman, Flt. Sgt. Butrewitz, ferried QO-Z to Linton and returned to base in a Halifax with 1st Lieutenant (Lt.) Lubold.[12] Now one of many Lancasters moved to 408 Goose Squadron, LL637 was duly recoded EQ-P and began a new chapter in her story.

EQ-P would have carried the stepped, bulged bomb bay but is unlikely to have had the ventral turret. Regardless, EQ-P consistently carried only seven crew members on her flights with 408 Squadron. The crew's positions, listed in order from the nose to the tail of the aircraft, were bomb aimer, pilot, flight engineer, navigator, wireless operator, mid-upper gunner, and tail gunner.

The bomb aimer, Bill, was positioned at the very front of the aircraft, below the cockpit, within a Perspex blister. On the way to and from the bomb site he took on jobs as required, including aiding the navigator with course directions and manning the front gun turret above the blister. However, he seldom shot at night fighters from this position, as they normally attacked from behind or below the aircraft. The bomb aimer also had training in piloting the aircraft and was a skilled map reader. His main responsibility was during the bomb run, when he was essentially in charge of the plane. He would lie flat on his belly, staring into the eye of the fiery blasts below, and guide the aircraft over the target by giving the pilot simple but imperative commands—"steady, left, steady," and so on. Once over the target, he would release the bombs and take a photograph. At that point he would return to his vigil in the front turret, helping the navigator and keeping a lookout for night fighters.

The pilot, Norm, sat above and behind the bomb aimer on the left side of the plane. Whatever his rank, it was his duty to make sure the crew worked as a team in the aircraft. He spent his entire time flying the aircraft to the target and back to base. A simple description, but this was not an easy job. Even getting a fully loaded bomber off the ground was a difficult task, especially when the visibility was poor, as it often was. Once in the air, the pilot had to be immediately ready, at the command of his gunners, to throw around a fully loaded or empty bomber to avoid night fighters. This was done in the dark of night, often after the aircraft had already suffered some damage, and with the awareness that there were several other bombers above, below, and beside them that they could easily collide with. Over the target, the pilot had to be almost nerveless as he kept the bomber steady in the midst of the searchlights, night fighters, and flak-filled skies while listening to the bomb aimer's instructions. The flight home was no better, with the constant threat of attack, and the landing frequently as dangerous as takeoff—or even flying over the target—especially if the aircraft had been damaged during its operation or carried bombs hung up in the bomb bay.

The flight engineer, Jock, sat beside the pilot on a jump seat that could be flipped up to allow the bomb aimer to pass by to the nose of the aircraft. On both takeoff and landing, the engineer assisted the pilot with the throttles. While travelling to and from the target, the crew would take the aircraft on different routes in order to confuse the

German radar system as well as to follow the safest path to the target. With only enough fuel to get to the target and back, it was crucial that the flight engineer constantly monitor fuel, oil, and pressure gauges to ensure the highest efficiency. The crew relied on his expertise to keep their often flak- and night fighter-damaged bird in the air.

In a curtained-off area behind the pilot, facing to the port or left side, was the navigator, George. He spent every moment keeping the Lancaster on its route to the target and then home. The navigator's role "required a clear mind and a high degree of mathematical ability. When electronic instruments failed or had been blown up, the navigator had to rely on dead reckoning or guidance by the stars, something that required both imagination and precision."[13] He worked at a table with charts and instruments lit only by an Anglepoise lamp (hence the curtain separating him from the pilot, whose night vision would have been disrupted by lamplight). His responsibility was to monitor electronic navigational equipment and wind speed to keep the aircraft on time for its bomb drop. He acquired a fix on position every six minutes, using the GEE or GEE-H radio receiver to pick up electronic pulses emitted from England.[14] Considering changes in wind speed and direction, as well as other factors, the navigator would recalculate times and route changes that the pilot would follow.

Slightly farther down the fuselage, in front of the main spar and facing forward on the left of the aircraft, sat Larry, the wireless operator. He was in the warmest part of the aircraft, with the astrodome above him. This crew member, who took care of all radio operations, was the link between the aircraft and the outside world. He spent his time straining to hear the Morse code group broadcasts, three per hour, through the static that filled his headphones. These transmissions were vital, as they contained important messages for the crew, including the order to return to base. In a serious situation, the wireless operator could tune the radio to an emergency frequency to find the way back to base. He would be the first to hear a voice from the station on return, which would let the pilot know when he could land. When not doing his own job, the wireless operator spent much of his time in the astrodome. With his knowledge of navigation equipment, he assisted the navigator by taking star shots. He also kept a lookout for night fighters, and was trained in first aid, gunnery, and the electrical system of the aircraft.[15]

In the middle of the cold, unheated section of the fuselage, Bob, the mid-upper gunner, sat with his head and shoulders inside the Perspex of the mid-upper turret and his legs dangling from a sling-like seat. Bud, the tail gunner, meanwhile, sat in the isolated and also unheated turret at the back of the plane, separated from the rest of the crew by distance and doors, and usually subject to frigid temperatures because the middle Perspex panel had been removed so he could see clearly. These men spent every moment moving their guns, both to scan the skies for night fighters and to prevent the weapons from freezing. Their job was to defend the plane and to warn the pilot to take evasive action. If they saw a fighter, they would order the pilot to "corkscrew port [or starboard] now!"

The dangers of the gunner positions were many. For one, it was not unheard of for oxygen lines to be damaged, and oxygen deprivation caused some gunners (as well as other crew members) to collapse, leaving the plane vulnerable to attack and the crew in danger of death. Frostbite, on the face or any other body part exposed to the elements, was almost a normal consequence of the job. If one touched the metal of the aircraft with unprotected flesh, frostbite resulted and could lead to the loss of fingers.[16] With nothing to do but scan the sky continuously for seven or more hours, the gunners had a monotonous job, but they still had to keep their brain and eyes alert for the smallest change in the endless black canvas—except over the target, where it was as light as day thanks to the searchlights, bomb blasts, and fires. Finally, the tail gunner was often the victim of fighter attacks and bomb drop accidents that sheared the turret off the plane.[17]

The Lancaster was built specifically for bombing, so the crew and its comfort were afterthoughts. Bomb capacity was what counted, and the plane ended up as "a flying bomb bay"[18] with nothing more than closet space, often frigid, for the crew. Most disheartening was the lack of space and the minimal, tiny exits, which made the Lancaster a death trap. The Halifax, for example, had a larger interior and did not have the Lancaster's internal main spar. This made movement within the aircraft, especially when crewmen had their flight gear on, much easier.[19] Although the Lancaster had three possible parachute hatches and three non-parachute hatches, in locations similar to those in other bombers, the percentage of men who actually escaped these planes in emergency situations was small when compared to the statistics for other bombers. The belly of the Lancaster, like that of any bomber, was used to hold bombs, so this vast area could not be used for escapes. The few areas from which one could safely leave the aircraft were less than ideal given the confines of the plane, especially when it was under duress from fighter attack, flak, major damage, or collisions that caused fires or made the plane spin, holding the crew tight to the fuselage, unable to move.

The best parachute hatch, to "be used by all members of the crew if time is available," was in the floor of the bomb aimer's area, in the nose of the plane.[20] While the pilot attempted to keep the plane steady in the air—an amazing feat in itself when the Lancaster was damaged to the point of going down—the other six men had to move forward in their bulky clothing, often in dark, cramped conditions, and find their way to the bomb aimer's area, where they would jump out the hatch, one at a time.

The second parachute exit was the main entrance door at the side, but it was to "be used as a parachute exit only in extreme emergency,"[21] as there was a good chance of men being injured or killed by colliding with the tail end of the plane when they jumped out. This exit, too, required the men to move through most of the fuselage as they went toward the back end of the aircraft.

The third parachute exit, in the tail gunner's turret, was really only meant for the tail gunner, and it too had serious issues. If the hydraulic line was damaged in an attack or the turret mechanism jammed, which was often the case, the turret became an inescapable capsule.[22]

To make matters worse, the parachute escape hatches were smaller than those in previous bombers, such as the Halifax—twenty-two inches in the Lancaster versus twenty-four in the Halifax. Although a difference of two inches seems minor, the statistics say otherwise: "25 per cent of Halifax crews who were shot down survived, compared to just 15 per cent of Lancaster crews."[23] The larger interior and escape hatches of the Halifax were the difference between life and death for many crewmen. Perhaps the Lancaster's designers believed the improved speed and heavier bomb load of the dragon meant she could complete her task more quickly and thoroughly and did not need elaborate escape routes, but the statistics show that the dragon was by no means invincible.

≈ 14 ≈

Berlin: A Dickey Flight

O n the morning of Tuesday, February 15, 1944, Norm Lumgair
again found his name listed as a second or "dickey" pilot for the
night's raid. He was assigned to Lancaster Mk II DS726, EQ-Y,
with a crew led by Flight Lieutenant (Flt. Lt.) W.B. Stewart,
a seasoned pilot fully accustomed to the rigours of flying over enemy
territory. Eight other new squadron pilots were also dispersed among
the crews listed to fly. Norm was probably able to suppress his excitement and nervousness as he settled into the day's busy routine, only to
feel them rise again at the briefing when he heard the dreaded word,
Berlin. He braced himself to fly over the "Big City" and get his first
taste of a real bombing operation.

This was the fifteenth of what were eventually sixteen attacks in
the Battle of Berlin, a bombing campaign launched by Air Marshall
Arthur Harris, commander-in-chief of Bomber Command, on the eve
of November 18, 1943, and extended to the morning of March 25, 1944.
The point of the campaign was to crush Germany's power by destroying both its economy and the morale of its population. Instead, German
resistance continued despite the bombardment, while bomber crews'
apprehension grew with each raid as hundreds of aircraft and thousands of men were downed by the city's heavy defences.

The force of 891 aircraft sent on the February 15 raid was the largest
number dispatched at one time for the Berlin operations. Of this total,

561 aircraft were Lancasters, 61 more Lancasters than previously sent on a mission. An additional 314 Halifaxes and 16 Mosquitos rounded out the participating aircraft.[1]

Linton-on-Ouse readied a total of thirty-two Lancasters, seventeen from 408 Squadron. Most of the men in 408 and 426 Squadrons prepared for the operation—checking aircraft for any problems, going to the briefing, plotting the route, bombing up (loading an aircraft with bombs), and so on—so there was no ground training on the agenda. With their pilot scheduled to fly with the crew of EQ-Y, Norm's mates in EQ-P were grounded and likely had time to themselves.

During the downtime, Bud visited the medical unit and was admitted to RAF Hospital Cranwell. He was originally diagnosed with urethritis at Linton-on-Ouse, but the station subsequently stroked this classification out and replaced it with "urethritis V." or VD.[2] He was under hospital treatment for nearly two weeks.[3]

That evening, the first 408 Squadron aircraft started its journey at 1720 hours. The crew Norm was accompanying—pilot W.B. Stewart; RCAF members Flt. Off. G.E. Mallory, Flt. Off. W.C. Burns, Flt. Sgt. R.D. Ochsner, and Flt. Sgt. H.F. Murphy; and RAF members Sgt. J. Bray and Sgt. H. Varley—left at 1726 hours as part of the third wave of bombers, carrying 60 four-pound "X" type, sixteen 30-pound, and 540 four-pound incendiaries, and one 4,000-pound high-capacity cookie bomb.[4]

Operations over enemy territory were planned to the last detail. Bomber routes were perpetually changed, and new equipment was constantly being developed to outwit German radar controllers and help get the bombers to the target without interference from night fighters. On February 15, even though "German controllers were able to plot the bomber stream soon after it left the English coast," and the twenty-four Lancasters that carried out a diversionary raid on Frankfurt-on-Oder "failed to draw any fighters" away from the incoming bomber stream, the bombers had a relatively easy run to the target. Bomber Command had instructed the pilots to turn north toward Denmark, keeping the smaller-engined night fighters, with their lower fuel capacity, from reaching them for at least part of the inbound flight.[5] It was a good tactic.

Berlin, the heart of the Reich, was by now used to repeated attacks. The inhabitants went about their daily lives, resilient in the face of destruction, continuing to live and work among the rubble that had once been a residence, shop, or factory. The city was heavily fortified, with a high concentration of flak guns, searchlights, and night fighter defences. However, even the best defences can fall into disarray, and on this night, the defences over the target were unusual.

Previously, the night fighters had dropped flares of their own—not to illuminate the target, but to highlight the bombers in order to attack them. However, when the Pathfinders (the Allied aircraft that marked the bombers' route and target with flares) dropped their first markers on February 15, the response came from German flak guns rather than night fighters. The bombers assumed the "flak was so violent" because the "Germans' main fighter force was late getting on the job."[6] What they didn't know was that German controllers had "ordered the fighters not to fly over Berlin, leaving the target area free for the flak."[7] This left many bombers free to drop their loads without the added pressure of attacks from the air. Later, scattered fighter flares appeared in the sky as many night fighters decided to ignore the commands to leave the target open for flak, but even in the last stages of the raid, many crews bombed without any opposition from fighters.[8]

The 408 Squadron Lancasters were dispersed among the bomber stream, flying at an altitude of 5,100–7,300 metres.[9] Still hidden in darkness, Norm and the crew of EQ-Y flew toward the glowing light ahead. Norm would have been carefully watching Stewart's every move, aware he'd be following the same routines soon in EQ-P. What he learned now, in these vital moments, would be foremost on his mind when he next flew in charge of his own crew. From his front-row seat, high in the air, he would have seen Berlin as nothing more than an orange glow, as burning incendiaries illuminated the heavy clouds. January to early February 1944 brought the worst weather of the war, with the "skies clear enough for visual bombing" only once in six weeks.[10] To make matters worse, "the gloomy conditions of cloud cover and darkness increased the chances for mid-air collisions or navigation errors."[11] Tonight, they would have to bomb blind, relying on navigation equipment and the accuracy of the Pathfinders' sky marker flares to find the drop zone. The light winds were in their favour, allowing the marker flares to remain relatively close to the target.

Lancasters from their own and numerous other squadrons were all around them, flying in front, beside, behind, below, and above, usually unseen until the last moments before bombing. All followed the same procedures as they prepared to bomb the city: while gunners watched for approaching night fighters in the sky, lit by searchlights and the glow of incendiary bombs already burning the buildings below, bomb aimers lay on their stomachs, looking through their bomb sights and giving commands of "left, right, steady" to the pilot, positioning the bomber directly in line with the target. Around them, heavy flak blasted away.

Over the target, however, the experience of each squadron, and, in fact, of each bomber, varied dramatically, depending on where they were situated in the bomber stream and whether they were unlucky enough to be hit by flak or exposed by night fighter flares and searchlights and subsequently shot at by the smaller aircraft. Each operation was a dangerous game of chance. While some fared well and experienced few issues, others found themselves fighting for their lives.

The 408 Squadron crews of Smith, Harvey, and Sutherland flew in just minutes ahead of Stewart. Smith and Sutherland had an uneventful flight and bombed without problems, but it was another story for Harvey. "The oxygen in the rear turret failed," the air positioning indicator became unserviceable, and just after the crew dropped their bombs, the heavy flak "knocked the perspex out of the nose."[12]

At 2126, the Stewart crew, with Norm on board, released their bomb load over the target from 6,700 metres. The eight men saw few fighters on their journey, experiencing a quiet trip. They had lost the use of Monica, the electronic tail warning system used to alert bomber crews of approaching night fighters, but this was likely in part the reason their trip was so quiet. The signals emitted by Monica to help the bombers were being received and used by the Germans to locate and avoid detection by the bombers.

Despite the flak and poor weather, all of the 408 Squadron crews returned safely. Only three landed at base; the rest were diverted because of poor landing conditions at the station. The Stewart crew landed at 0053 at Burn aerodrome along with two other 408 Squadron crews.[13] Unfortunately, forty-three aircraft from other squadrons failed to return.[14]

The huge contingent of bombers dropped a record 2,642 tons of bombs on the city during an attack that lasted thirty minutes.[15] The heavy cloud cover made it difficult for the 408 Squadron crews to accurately assess the bombing. The red-orange glow reflecting on the clouds, the only visible indicator of the attack, suggested there were fires raging below. The following morning a newspaper commented on the full extent of the damage "done in the already hard-hit capital, mostly in the industrial outer belt including the Wittenau, Lichtenberg and Marienfelde districts" of the city. Communication in the city was disrupted, and in the Schoenberg area "not a house was left standing." Hitler's Chancellery once again received damage, and the "Charlottenburg and Grunewald sections also had been bombed."[16] Later reports noted that bombs hit some significant war industries in the Siemensstadt area.[17]

The following morning the squadron again readied for operational duties. The boys of Norm's crew, with Norm now officially initiated in combat flight, hurriedly gulped their breakfast before getting out to EQ-P. They primed her and themselves for their maiden voyage, but by mid-afternoon the weather had closed in, and at 1510 Bomber Command cancelled the operation.[18]

It proved a reprieve for Norm, who was likely tired from the previous night's operation, and for Bud, still in hospital, who didn't want to miss an operation with his crew. With the release of tension and time off, many men would have caught a ride into York or paid for a paddle across the River Ouse to the Alice Hawthorn pub for a drink. Others found alternate methods of allaying stress. Bob wrote to both his elder brothers, telling them that his girlfriend had accepted his proposal and he was now engaged. In signing off, he remarked to Cag that he had yet to fly on an op but hoped, by the time the letter reached his brother, to have a few to his credit. He joked about the future and the obvious pounding of the Big City, saying, "See you in what's left of Berlin, eh!"[19]

The next morning, eleven crews began readying themselves for the night ahead, but plans changed and then changed again. An hour and a half into the task, inexperienced crews like Norm's were taken off the flight list. At 1600 hours the six remaining crews stopped preparations as Bomber Command scrubbed the raid. The next day was the same: fourteen crews prepared their planes, attended the briefing, and waited for takeoff with stomachs and minds churning. Then, at the last minute, the operation was scrubbed again.[20]

Veteran crews struggled with conflicting emotions. They wanted to go and get their ops in, but at the same time they knew that each flight might be their last. New crews wondered what they were in for as they saw experienced crews begin to unravel in the daily routine of call to ops, preparation, briefing, and scrubbed runs. Lieutenant-Colonel (later retired) David L. Bashow noted that "cancellations, especially *late* cancellations," had a disastrous effect on morale.[21] Dr. D. Stafford-Clark, a medical officer with Bomber Command, wrote, "No one who saw the mask of age which mantled the faces of these young men after a period of continued standing by, punctuated by inevitable false alarms, is likely to forget it. Their pallor, the hollows in their cheeks, and beneath their eyes, and the utter fatigue with which they lolled listlessly in chairs about their Mess, were eloquent of the exhaustion and frustration which they felt. In ten hours they seemed to have aged as many years."[22]

$$\equiv 15 \equiv$$

Operation 1: Leipzig

n Yorkshire, the morning of February 19, 1944, dawned bleak but dry with a chill wind.[1] The "stomach turning words, 'You're on, tonight,'"[2] gripped the crews. Everyone got down to work. Preparations, by now automatic after so many calls to ops, left time for their minds to wander. *Is tonight the night? Will it be like what I've been told? Will I be here tomorrow morning?*

The commanding officers, intelligence officers, and meteorologists (Met men) in various squadrons across England organized themselves to brief the crews for the raid. A last-minute phone call from Bomber Command changed a prebrief scheduled for 1100 hours at 78 RAF Squadron to 1700, with the main brief planned for 2130.[3] The same change likely happened at all the bomber squadron bases across England. Everyone went about their business as ordered, but the questions remained in the back of their minds: *Why the change in briefing? What's going on?*

It was not uncommon for nerves to get the better of those destined to fly, and last-minute changes to routine unsettled even the most seasoned of crews. By the time the main brief occurred, tension had worked its way to the surface like infection in a wound, escalating over the hours until the men were sky-bound. Early signs ranged from a poor taste in jokes, twitching, and uncontrollable shaking, growing in pitch and tempo as day turned into night.[4]

On February 19, more orders came down the pipeline than usual. Although at this point crews didn't know where they would be heading, they had a good idea it was a distant target. All unnecessary weight was stripped from the plane, including the external armour plating and a certain amount of ammunition,[5] so they could fly farther on the same amount of fuel. The longer they spent in the air, the greater the chance they'd encounter a night fighter, and now they'd have less ammunition and armour plating with which to defend themselves. Anxiety increased, but the men carried out their duties in preparation for the long night ahead.

The main brief finally came. The commanding officer (CO) began by noting the target on a wall map. Tonight the bombers would pay a call on the city of Leipzig, about 193 kilometres southwest of Berlin. A thick red ribbon marked the long path of the bombers from the base to the target.[6] An elongated route was planned to avoid heavily guarded areas as well as to confuse the enemy as to the final destination. The flight would take them "east over Holland and the Zuider Zee [sic], south of Bremen, north of Hanover, and between Berlin and Magdeburg, then south to Leipzig."[7] The crews were to attack the industrial city's fighter-plane production works, such as the Erla Maschinewerk aircraft factory that produced Messerschmitt Bf 109 fighters at three plants (Heiterblick, Abtnaundorf, and Mockau).[8] Bomb loads for 408 Squadron planes consisted of fifty 4-pound "X"-type, sixteen 30-pound, and 550 four-pound incendiaries, and one 4,000-pound cookie.[9] The CO continued, discussing gas loads and route-specific special tactics.[10]

The intelligence officer informed the crews of fighter bases, flak gun emplacements, and searchlight batteries close to the designated bomber route.[11] They needed to stay tight to the route. If they went astray, they would find themselves over numerous danger zones before they even got to the target. That night the Pathfinders were to mark the target with green flares and red stars,[12] and they would be dropping one bundle of window per minute along the route, with an increase to two bundles per minute when they were eighty kilometres from Leipzig, and the same pattern on the homeward journey. The attack was expected to last twenty-one minutes.[13]

The Met man took over, telling the crews they were likely to be dealing with winds of up to 160 kilometres per hour, ice-forming clouds, and a full cloud cover obscuring the city.[14] Ground crews busily sprayed a de-icing liquid onto the propellers and windscreen of each bomber, and spread a paste on the wings' leading edges, but these precautions were generally ineffective and did little to protect the bomber or reassure the crews.[15]

In the last hours before the flight, those scheduled to fly ate their pre-op supper—what they dubbed the "last supper"—consisting of real eggs and bacon in place of the powdered eggs or other usual bland fare. For those staying behind, the typical meal consisted of boiled or fried Brussels sprouts, potatoes, and mutton.[16] Then the crews headed to the crew room to suit up, donning their flight gear. After the men collected their parachutes from the parachute shed, their last stop on base, they climbed into trucks and rolled out to the aircraft dotting the perimeter of the airfield.

When they hopped out at their own Lancaster, tension built to fever pitch. Some remained silent with stomachs knotted; others chain-smoked or checked compulsively to ensure they had brought their talisman or lucky charm. The men sat or stood outside their respective aircraft, glancing toward the control tower, hoping for a white flare, denoting a cancelled operation, or a green one giving the go-ahead.[17] With the weather report not looking so good, surely there would be another white flare tonight. In those last moments, when their nerves became too much, the men heaved, ejecting the "last supper." Or they emptied their strained bladders.[18]

When the green light showed, nerves slowly dissipated, overshadowed by the focus needed to prepare the aircraft for takeoff.[19] Each crew member handled specific responsibilities, and the rest of the crew relied on him to do it properly. The seven men were now part of the bomber, a human-metal beast requiring coordination and teamwork if it was to achieve its purpose. If someone failed to do his job now, it could be the first and last time.

When Norm took the controls of EQ-P on his initial operation in charge of his own crew, Bud lay in hospital, replaced by Sgt. W.R. Clapham (believed to have survived the war), but George, Bill, Larry, Jock, and Bob were in their usual places. With all checks completed, the squadron's "operational aircraft lined up at both sides of the runway."[20] Norm, like all the other pilots, watched the control van, situated out the left-hand side of his Lancaster, for the green light from the Aldis lamp that would clear him for takeoff. Ground crews stood, waving their best wishes from the sidelines to the departing airmen. "The pilot and flight engineer increased engine power to the point where the tail lifted off the ground."[21] Jock, sitting on the jump seat next to Norm, helped hold the throttles wide open for takeoff. The rest of the crew waited. Norm released the brakes, and as EQ-P reached takeoff speed, the next aircraft pulled into position behind them.[22] The boys lifted up into the cloudy darkness, bracing themselves for the unknown.

This operation essentially marked the beginning of the RAF and American joint operations known as Big Week. However, the Americans initially hesitated as there was a threat of snow, cancelling the mission and then rescheduling it as planned for the following morning after receiving a forecast for better weather over the target.[23] The RAF decided to press on regardless.

Big Week, also known as Operation Argument, took a different approach from the typical area bombing that bomber crews performed. The US Strategic Air Forces, in conjunction with the RAF, launched a strategic bombing campaign made up of a number of missions that directly attacked the German aircraft industry, including component and assembly plants, and airfields.[24] While the Americans attacked by day, the RAF raided by night, bombarding the area in hopes of hampering if not obliterating production.

Bomber Command detailed 921 aircraft to take part; 98 were sent on diversions and support operations while the remaining 823 aircraft were sent to Leipzig. Of the 561 Lancasters involved in the Leipzig raid,[25] thirty-one came from the base at Linton-on-Ouse, with eighteen from 408 Squadron. EQ-P, flying as part of the second wave, brought up the rear, likely the second-last or last to take off at 0009, with all planes from the squadron up by 0010. They plotted a course toward the North Sea, heading for the Dutch coast.

The German night fighter force was not fooled on this night. It took an unusual approach, splitting itself in two. A portion of the fighters headed to Kiel Bay in northern Germany, where forty-nine Allied aircraft (four Pathfinder Halifaxes and forty-five Stirlings) were dropping sea mines from a low altitude into the bay below prior to the main raid. Such diversionary and support operations were common on most bombing runs, helping to draw away or scatter night fighters so they were not concentrated on the bomber stream headed for the main target. However, those fighters sent to Kiel on this night quickly rejoined the rest of the fighter force, greeting the main bomber stream as it crossed the Dutch coast.[26]

Radar controllers were able to tell night fighters the general direction of the bomber stream and used radar assembly beacons to indicate where the fighters should assemble for further instructions. The bombers' route on February 19, detailed during briefing, took them straight over the German assembly beacon "M." Rather than waiting near the likely target area as they normally did, the night fighters massed near this beacon, with the main concentration of fighters swarming south of Bremen.[27] The result was disastrous. Fully loaded bombers plummeted from the sky in flames or exploded in a brief blast of bright light. There was nothing to be done for the unfortunates. The boys flew on.

A new and highly effective technique known as *Schräge Musik*, or Jazz Music, in which night fighters attacked the bombers from below with upward-firing guns, further confounded the Allied crews. They "felt the shells tearing through the airframe or saw the wings bursting into flames before they were even aware that a fighter was underneath."[28] According to squadron leader Peter Russell, who wrote *Flying in Defiance of the Reich*, "A short burst between the fuselage and an engine nacelle or between the two engines . . . put the bomber immediately into a spin. Even if the cannon did not sever the main spar, the petrol flowed across the red-hot cut made by the cannon shot and the Lancaster burned fiercely. They were, after all, built of an alloy of aluminium and magnesium, and burned liked [sic] paper. In those circumstances, no one ever got out."[29] Although crews knew that such attacks were possible, they remained vulnerable to them as they had no way to see fighters approaching from underneath. The first of these attacks came in late January 1944, and the RAF reckoned that 3.2 percent of downed aircraft were lost to *Schräge Musik*. In February the number escalated to 11.4 percent, and it continued to rise over the next few months, accounting for 13.3 percent of aircraft losses in April, at its height. Use of the technique decreased after that, but this was too late for those at Leipzig—where the area between Bremen and Leipzig alone accounted for twenty Allied aircraft on the night of February 19–20, all considered to be fighter kills[30]—or for the many who died through the winter and early spring of 1944.

As EQ-P and the others continued on their way to Leipzig, they faced icing and variable wind speeds well beyond expectations. Air gunners had to fire their guns intermittently to keep them from freezing up. The unlucky souls left with iced guns fell through the air like ducks in a shooting gallery. For some gunners, just breathing posed a problem when the oxygen tubes, which supplied them with air due to the minimal oxygen available at the high altitudes they were flying, filled with condensation and froze. Other crews struggled to keep the bird from freezing on the inside, while ice formed on the wings, air intakes, and tail before falling off at will.[31]

The winds fluctuated, reaching up to 130 mph,[32] so bombers arrived over the target area much earlier than expected. Many attempted to rectify the problem, delaying their arrival by doing "doglegs" or zigzagging—in effect lengthening the journey to accommodate the tail winds—but this significantly increased the chance of colliding with other Allied aircraft attempting the same manoeuvre.[33] According to Warrant Officer (W. Off.) J. Douglas. Harvey of 408 Squadron, "With our primitive navigation instruments and the lack of reliable winds, the navigator's job was made extremely difficult. The weather on that raid was foul, with terrible high winds that blew many bombers off course and over heavily defended cities."[34]

The bombers that made it to the target early were at increased danger as they circled the fighter-, searchlight-, and flak-ridden area at an altitude of 5,700–7,600 metres,[35] waiting for the Pathfinders to arrive and mark the target. The delay led to four collisions and the loss of twenty Lancasters to flak. When the Pathfinders arrived, cloud cover required the use of sky-markers,[36] which were easily blown off the reference point by high winds.

EQ-P, despite attempts to slow its journey, arrived earlier than expected, although the Pathfinders' green flares and red stars were visible as it approached. Where the flares clustered, Bill released his bomb load from 6,400 metres at 0359, but because they were early, they were unable to see the results.[37] EQ-P was one of the first bombers over the target as "British and Canadian Lancasters and Halifaxes . . . opened the offensive at 4 a.m. Sunday with more than 2,300 long tons of bombs."[38] In all, the Canadian squadrons dropped 422,000 pounds of incendiaries and 112,000 pounds of explosives that night.[39] Although early bombing was deemed accurate, later bombing was scattered.[40] By then the markers had blown too far off their original position.

After dropping their load, the bombers headed out of the cauldron of danger, escaping the flak, searchlights, and fighters. "The route home was almost due west, in an attempt to stay south of the Ruhr Valley and north of the Rhine Valley."[41] The heavy winds and cold conditions continued to plague EQ-P on the homeward journey as the windscreen iced up, making it difficult to see.[42]

During debrief, the "airmen reported the glow from large fires could be seen long after their aircraft left the armament and aircraft building centre. They said, however, that heavy clouds prevented a good view of the damage done. Their main comment was on the heavy fighter opposition. W. Off. Jim Houston of Carleton Place, Ontario, reported his aircraft was attacked eleven times," while according to Flt. Lt. Cliff Murphy, the "Germans seemed to be concentrating on shooting out our markers."[43]

That same morning, February 20, the Americans flew over Leipzig and began their strategic bombing. From the southern part of the city, remnants of the RAF attack remained evident. Smoke billowed up from the bombed area still burning below.[44] On the ground, the Erla aircraft factory's Heiterblick plant was seriously damaged, while damage to the Mockau assembly shops was moderate. However, "the Erla complex was left more or less intact, with final capacity that could be restored by simple repairs within a month. Most of the press and machine capacity, however, and much of the capacity for preliminary work on fuselages and for sub-assembly and erection of control surfaces was destroyed."[45] Photographic evidence from the joint RAF/US Army Air Force operation revealed damage to the Paunsdorf workshop's roof and the railway sidings. Later evidence showed various railway tracks damaged, along with hundreds of buildings.[46]

According to a newspaper, photographic reconnaissance revealed "damage to the plants at Leipzig, Brunswick and Bernburg. . . The two principal Messerschmitt 109 fighter assembly buildings at Leipzig-Mockau were damaged and a parts plant at Leipzig-Heiterblick was set aflame. . . 'major damage' was done to the Nazi fighter plants. . . most concentrated around Leipzig. The Messerschmitt plant at Brunswick was well fired and the Junkers plant at Bernburg heavily damaged by direct hits."[47]

There was loss and damage on the Allied side as well. All told, on the night of February 19–20, between engine failure, fighter damage, crew sickness, and icing, sixty operational aircraft aborted bombing.[48] Two of 408 Squadron's Lancasters did not reach the target. One was unable to maintain height after the failure of the starboard outer engine, while the crew of another experienced oxygen failure. Flak damaged the port fuselage and wing of Flt. Lt. W.B. Stewart's aircraft, which Norm had flown in only days before, but the crew was able to bomb the target and return unharmed.[49] EQ-P, on its first operation with its new crew, landed at 0706. Eight more bombers descended in the cold morning light, and their aircrews headed for debrief while ground crews and traffic control waited for the others to reappear. They waited in vain.

When the hour for arrival passed with no sign of the remaining crews, there was no hope of return, because the aircraft would have had no more fuel. 408 Squadron had been dealt a significant blow. Like 35, 77, 103, and 166 Squadrons, 408 Squadron lost four bombers and twenty-eight crewmen, twenty-one of whom died.[50] Only 514 Squadron lost more lives, with twenty-two crewmen, including a dickey pilot, perishing when three planes went down.[51]

408 Squadron duly boxed and removed the missing aircrews' belongings. They were all essentially new crews, flying on their first to fourth operation. Still in the first phase of "attitudes towards survival," as described by pilot Harold Davis of 101 Squadron, everything was still new to them, and "you're scared all the time. You don't know what's coming and you're still learning."[52] New crews or not, this raid turned out to be the second-most costly of the war in terms of Bomber Command's loss of bombers and aircrew. Out of 921 aircraft involved in the sorties that night, seventy-nine had been lost,[53] including eighteen Canadian bombers.[54]

EQ-P rested on the grass, having braved all that Germany could throw at her and returned unscathed. If nothing else, the crew's confidence in her and in Norm's abilities must have been bolstered. The night had been long and the boys were tired. When they and the others returned to their rooms, twenty-eight beds remained empty. The boys had just come through what must have seemed like hell on earth. The next morning, still shaken, they received word they were on again for the coming night.

16

Three More Operations: Stuttgart, Schweinfurt, and Augsburg

T hat night the crew of EQ-P returned to the skies over Germany. This time they headed for Stuttgart, a "city of 500,000 population, and one of Germany's biggest manufacturing centres," with "Daimler-Benz auto works making engines for Messerschmitt fighters and Heinkels, the Bosch works specializing in ignition equipment for all kinds of engines, and plants making tanks, trucks and submarine parts." Stuttgart was also a main railroad junction on the route to Italy.[1]

Of the 598 aircraft on this raid, 460 were Lancasters, 126 Halifaxes, and 12 Mosquitos.[2] Linton-on-Ouse sent twenty-five Lancasters on the operation, twelve from 408 Squadron. Due to technical failures, two did not leave the base. Another experienced icing of the main windscreen but continued on. EQ-P, the second-last to take off, left base at 2348 hours as part of the second wave.

After the previous night's disaster, Bomber Command employed modified tactics, varying route marking and diversions each night. The bomber stream was routed to the south, away from the assembly beacons.[3] Diversionary ploys also successfully diverted German fighters to Munich and along the North Sea two hours before the main raid swept inland.[4] This gave the bombers a much-needed reprieve from night fighter attacks on the way to the target. The result was a calmer night.

En route a few 408 Squadron crews encountered strong winds that forced them to lose time. Flt. Sgt. N. Sutherland's crew was caught in the slipstream of another Lancaster. "The rear gunner fired a short burst at us, but no damage was sustained."[5]

Reaching the target, the bombers flew above the city at altitudes of between 5,700 and 7,300 metres.[6] For the most part the target was covered by clouds, and the attack scattered. Flt. Sgt. N. Sutherland and his crew were able to release only incendiaries directly over the target when their plane's electrical circuitry faltered, leaving them to release their 4,000-pound bomb manually.[7] EQ-P reported good visibility over the target, and at 0406 Bill dropped fifty 4-pound "X"-type, twenty-four 30-pound and four hundred 4-pound incendiaries, and one 4,000-pound cookie from 7,000 metres.[8] Many crews reported seeing numerous fires and bomb bursts. According to a newspaper article, "R.A.F. and R.C.A.F. bombers had set the war centre of Stuttgart afire with 2,240 tons of high explosives and incendiaries . . . the concentration of fires was seen through the clouds so light that it was the first really good view of a German city in several weeks."[9]

Most of the squadron's crews encountered no particular difficulties. Only one brought back incendiaries hung up in the bomb bay. And even though Flt. Off. E.M.C. Franklin's crew experienced heavy flak that inflicted small holes in the starboard wing of their Lancaster, they successfully bombed the target and returned safely to base. All the 408 Squadron bombers returned, with Norm landing EQ-P, the second-last bomber to arrive, at 0737 hours.[10]

Local reports noted damage to regional buildings, including parliament, "the state picture gallery, the state archives, the state theatre and two old churches" in the centre of the city. The bombing of the industrial area at Stuttgart resulted in significant damage to the Bosch factory, "which produced dynamos, injection pumps and magnetos and was considered to be one of the most important factories in Germany."[11] The bombers had effectively delayed the manufacture of war parts.

Upon returning to base, the boys got a day's reprieve. No operations were scheduled for February 21, and ground training was kept low-key because the crews were tired after being on operations two nights in a row.[12] The boys gladly took to their beds after a relaxed evening at the Alice Hawthorn or Betty's, local bars. At this point they and their shattered nerves deserved the treat. Later news from the day reported, "When the heavy [American] bombers finished their day's work, it was estimated unofficially that more than 5,000 Allied bombers had been over Germany within 36 hours and had dropped nearly 8,000 tons of bombs on targets vital to Germany's aerial defense."[13]

On February 22 the squadron was readying the maximum number of bombers, seventeen, for operations, but Bomber Command called the raid off at 1800 hours.[14] The next day no operations were called for, and fog and a low ceiling made flying practice impossible. Some ground training took place, but it was minimal.[15]

At some point on February 22, Larry found time to write a letter to his wife, Marjorie. He mentioned that the "back wheel of his bicycle had fell apart in the morning. A shop promised to have a new one in by the afternoon if possible."[16] And Bud, who was still recuperating, passed some hours answering his little brother's letter. Ken had been learning Morse code with the Cub Scouts back home and had "struggled long and hard composing a letter to Bud completely in Morse code." Satisfied with his efforts, he had sent it to his brother overseas, and Bud now took the time to respond in kind.[17]

On Thursday, February 24, the squadron received instructions to ready the maximum number of bombers for night operations. Their target on this night, Schweinfurt. A total of thirty-five aircraft from 426 and 408 Squadrons were detailed to take part. Eighteen crews from 408 Squadron prepared for the night ahead, though one Lancaster and crew were scrubbed when no replacement could be found for a wireless operator.[18] The crew of EQ-P had no such problem. Sgt G.A. Reid filled in for Bud.

This operation, like those to Leipzig and Stuttgart, was part of Big Week. Bombing began during the day, carried out by 266 American B-17s, and Bomber Command followed up with night operations involving 734 aircraft, 554 of them Lancasters. Their focus was the ball-bearing factories.[19]

Bomber Command implemented a new tactic that entailed splitting the bomber force into two separate groups with a two-hour interval between them. The first group of 392 aircraft left the base two hours before the second group of 342 aircraft.[20] EQ-P flew in the earlier group as part of the second wave from the squadron. It was the first of six Lancasters to depart at 1822 hours carrying four hundred and fifty 4-pound and thirty-two 30-pound incendiaries and one 4,000-pound cookie.[21]

On reaching the target, crews dropped their bombs from altitudes of 5,100–7,900 metres.[22] "Large fires took hold rapidly and the light from them illuminated the entire area . . . Schweinfurt resembled 'a ploughed field studded with diamonds.'" According to one bomb aimer, "One hundred and fifty to 200 searchlights ringed the target and what seemed to be thousands of incendiaries criss-crossed it with lanes of light . . . The attack was wonderfully concentrated."[23]

Over the target the crew of EQ-P encountered good visibility despite the smoke haze. Bill released the bombs at an altitude of 6,400 metres at 2321. Then the crew headed home, reaching the base at 0233 hours and experiencing little difficulty until landing, when icing posed some problems.

Other Goose Squadron Lancasters had a more eventful night. One "arrived half an hour late over the target and staged a one-plane attack."[24] Flt. Off. H.R. Chekaluck of 408 Squadron was wounded after flak damaged his aircraft and hit him in the leg and arm, but he continued to fly. A number of the 408 Lancasters struggled with unusable equipment, including their Monica radar and their air positioning indicator, Mk XIV bombsight. As they returned from the raid, three crews from the second group had to dodge flak over London when they encountered an enemy raid. Many of the Squadron's aircraft, seven in all, diverted to other bases; among them was Flt. Off. Chekaluck's Lancaster, which landed at Hampstead Norris due to his wounds.[25] Nearly half of the squadron brought back incendiaries hung up in the bomb bay. In all, the Canadian contingent dropped 251,000 pounds of incendiaries and 136,000 pounds of explosives over Schweinfurt.[26]

Two 408 Squadron crews failed to return,[27] the sprog crew of Flt. Sgt. A. Keiller and the experienced crew of Pilot Officer H. Sherlock.[28]

The results for the night proved both negative and positive. Many of the 408 Squadron crews returned believing the primary was well attacked, but reports indicated otherwise. "Both phases of the bombing suffered from undershooting by some of the Pathfinder backers-up and by many of the Main Force crews. Schweinfurt records refer to 'nominal damage' in the R.A.F. night raid and give a combined figure of 362 people killed by the American raid the previous day," with no breakdown on those German casualties inflicted by the RAF alone. Much easier to quantify was the positive outcome of splitting and stag- gering the timing of the bomber force. Only half as many bombers lost in the second group (eleven, compared to twenty-two down in the first group) demonstrated a significant tactical success.[29]

The next night the boys, including Sgt. Reid as tail gunner, soared into the sky at 2101 as part of the third wave of a raid on Augsburg. A total of 594 aircraft took part, but 408 Squadron could provide only eleven Lancasters. Two of the bombers diverted to other bases after the Schweinfurt raid did not return in time for briefing and had to be scrubbed from the operation.[30]

As in the previous night's raid, the bomber stream was split into two groups, and diversions were varied in an attempt to reduce the number of casualties. And in this case, they were attacking a city that was unaccustomed to being a target. Unlike heavily fortified Berlin, Augsburg had only weak flak defences.[31]

Even from an altitude of 4,800–7,600 metres,[32] some of the squad- ron could see the fires at the target from as far away as 128 kilometres on their approach—and as far away as 241 kilometres on their return journey.[33] Despite the smoke over the target, visibility was very good for the crew of EQ-P. They could see the red target indicator flares dropped by the Pathfinders as they released their 4,000-pound cookie and the accompanying incendiaries at 0117 hours.[34] They could also see that "the town was a mass of flames, and the fires were visible for a great distance after leaving the target."[35] All told, on this night the Canadians dropped 184,000 pounds of incendiaries and 76,000 pounds of explosives.[36]

For the bombers, the tactical advantage of splitting the force con- tinued to work to the crews' advantage, and the Augsburg raid proved incredibly successful. Clear weather and ground-marking, rather than sky-marking, by the Pathfinders resulted in extremely accurate bomb- ing, causing damage to an "important aircraft component factory and to some former paper and cotton mills which had been taken over by the M.A.N. Engineering company." The bombing obliterated the old city centre, with the damage sustained by freezing temperatures, which hampered the use of water hoses to put out the resulting fires. "The Germans publicized it as an extreme example of 'terror bombing.'"[37]

Lumgair's crew landed at Linton-on-Ouse at 0503, safe and sound. Two of 408 Squadron's planes had to land at other aerodromes because of fuel shortages, compounded in one case by failure of one engine. They were the lucky ones.[38] Twenty-five aircraft in all, four of them from diversion and support operations, failed to return.[39] 408 Squadron lost two Lancaster crews:[40] one sprog crew with only one operation to its credit; the other a seasoned crew with more than twenty operations in its log.[41] Experience was not an indicator of survival. Chance and luck remained the main players in determining an aircrew's fate. Casualties "were often depressingly random, and various system malfunctions often claimed many crews who were at the peak of their experience, confidence and productivity. Also, it was frequently just a matter of luck if a particular aircraft was singled out for attack by an enemy fighter, or if a shell from an anti-aircraft barrage exploded lethally close."[42]

In fact, February 1944 proved the deadliest month of the war for 408 Squadron, with eight crews going "down in the most horrible flying weather imaginable. The month was a nightmare. Three times as many trips were scrubbed as flown, and day after day it was a constant round of briefing, standby, scrubbed; briefing, standby, scrubbed. You could cut the tension that gripped the squadron with a very dull knife."[43]

Clearly, it was time for a break.

17

March Holidays and Late-Winter Stand-Downs

ith the end of the Augsburg operation, the boys, including Bud, who had just been released from hospital, were sent on leave. After the tension the crew had experienced over the previous month, it was time to relax, enjoy some freedom, and recoup before returning to the stress of Bomber Command's daily routines.

The boys travelled by train, so they would have been at the York station, with its large iron-framed roof arching above them, listening to the sounds of trains coming and going in the still of the icy-cold late February day, as they watched for their respective coaches to arrive and take them to their individual destinations.

Bob had only a short distance to go to Sileby, Leicestershire, as did Jock, who came from Harrogate, Yorkshire. Being British had its advantages. They could visit with their families and sleep in their own beds, in a home well known to them, with familiar people and surroundings to give them comfort. Bob's sister Pat recalls having a wonderful holiday with Bob in early March 1944. She and Bob went to church on Sunday morning, and, as per the norm that cold winter of 1943–44, it had snowed during the night, leaving a pristine downy blanket of white over the ground. On the way home, Pat and Bob enjoyed the typical sibling pastime of a snowball fight—a fond memory that had to last a lifetime, as it was

Pat's last memory of her brother before he returned to duty with the squadron.

The Canadian crew members, in contrast, had three choices: spend the time alone or with other crew members in the same situation, visit relatives they likely had never met before coming to England, or keep company with a home-stay family who, as Bob's mother would soon come to do, took in airmen during their leave. Some of the Canadians likely ended up on a train together as they headed for destinations farther afield. Bill and Bud spent some time in London during their nine days' leave. Back then it was a trip of five or more hours due to the reduced speed of the trains, not the relatively short two-hour journey it is today. Bill called on relatives, including some cousins, and spent a few days with his uncle Wills. He also visited his aunt's sister, who told him a humorous story about kicking a hole in his father's hat when they knew each other in their younger years. In all, Bill found it to be a "nice change from station life."[1]

George may have returned to his uncle's home at Abbey Farm in Newhall, Darby. Larry possibly travelled to visit relatives in Ireland or Scotland, or perhaps he went to the rectory in Greystoke, where he was known by Mrs. B.S. Watkins, who may have been a relative, a family friend, or another of the home-stay families for overseas servicemen. It was likely during this time that Larry sold his bicycle and bought himself a motorcycle, as he acquired one at some point after February 22.

Norm may have gone to Scotland to see his uncle, who had come out of retirement and returned to policing so younger men could go to war. Or he may have spent time with his older brother Robert, also serving overseas. Norm and Robert both had time off during this period, and they spent at least one leave in Scotland together at their uncle's home.[2] Whatever the boys' destinations, it no doubt proved a welcome break from the month's events.

After a busy holiday in London and southern England, Bud collected a couple of postcards to send to family. He chose one depicting Buckingham Palace as seen from St. James's Park for his mother but did not write her until he had returned to York. In his haste he wrote, "No time for a letter so here's a card. Having fun under the circumstances. Glad your [sic] not here, wish I were there. Say hello to the kids for me. So long. As ever Bud. P.S. Just grunt at the old boy for me eh?"[3] He sent another postcard to his sister, calling her a "twerp" and asking her to "drop a few pages when you can. So long. As Ever. Your Loving brother??? Bud."[4]

Larry, Jock, Bob, and Bud returned to squadron duties on schedule on March 5 to find the base stood down from operations, likely owing to the moon period. Bill and George had been given an extra forty-eight hours' leave, while Norm had returned to base a day earlier than expected and been admitted to hospital with acute pharyngitis.

While waiting for flights to resume, Bud wrote to his grandmother about his time on holiday. "I spent most of it in London except two days when I was down to see Ken [Bud's cousin]. He arrived over here just recently. I sure hope the climate agrees with him better than it does me. I've been in the hospital twice. I had phneumonia [sic] and tonsilitis [sic] the first time and a heavy cold. The second time was just about the same. . . . I was a mid-upper gunner but I'm a tail gunner now."[5]

On March 7 the squadron prepared for operations, but with Norm still in hospital the crew was without a pilot. They took part in daily inspections and ground training during the day,[6] while ten crews from 408 Squadron participated in an operation to Le Mans, France, "despite unfavourable weather conditions over the target." This city was a rail centre, "a convenient funnel for routing big rail shipments between the northern and western and southwestern French coasts."[7]

The crew of EQ-P may have had a reprieve on this night, but their plane did not. W. Off. Second Class W.W. Kasper and his crew flew EQ-P as part of the second phase in the second wave, the last to leave 408 Squadron at 1930 hours.[8] Although all ten of 408 Squadron's Lancasters reached the target, only six bombed it; the crews in four, including EQ-P, couldn't see the target marker flares.[9] Despite descending to 1,500 metres, they were unable to identify the target and thus jettisoned its bomb load. The crew returned safely, landing at Tholthorpe at 0045 hours.[10]

Discharged from hospital on March 8, Norm found the squadron stood down two days in a row.[11] This gave him a little extra recuperation time before he returned to practise flying duties. Finally, for the first time since February 12, the original crew was back together, with both

Bud and Norm returned to health. The boys took part in an hour-long fighter affiliation practice, practising their evasion techniques such as the corkscrew, in EQ-S (normally flown by J. Douglas Harvey),[12] while under attack by a friendly fighter, before a night-flying exercise was cancelled in the afternoon.[13]

On March 10, Bomber Command requested eleven aircraft for bombing operations. However, less than three hours later, the operation was cancelled.[14]

Over the next three days the crew saw no reprieve from the monotony of waiting, with the squadron stood down and more training as the call of the day. The boys remained on the ground. Bill received a "welcome letter" from his sister Irene on Monday but did not get a chance to write her with all the day's goings-on.

At this point, after countless days of stand-downs and cancelled operations in the damp cold York environment, many of the young men were likely edgy, anxious to get up in the skies for a real bombing run. Daily training was tedious and only added to the tension. Those close to completion of their thirty trips just wanted to get it over with, haunted by the ever-present question, "Will I make it back?" As Harold Davis, a pilot of 101 Squadron, noted, each trip became "a strain towards the end." Those halfway through probably dreaded the unknown threats of each day but, according to Davis, they took it "just as another job of work. The old fears are still there but you are settled well in the groove."[15] Crews that still had a long way to go to reach their thirty missions, like the boys of EQ-P, remained scared and unsure, not yet settled in that groove. And Bud would have felt a good deal of anxiety as well as pressure to prove himself as he waited day after day for his first operation. The stories his crew mates told him of their experiences over Leipzig, Stuttgart, Schweinfurt, and Augsburg may have been frightening, but they also gained a sense of confidence in their pilot. This trust may have played on Norm's fears, adding to the pressure on him, even as he remained outwardly cool and level-headed.

Tuesday, March 14, dawned with no operations requested by Bomber Command, but it was a day of action for the squadron and the crew. In the morning, navigators took part in ninety minutes of Link training, while others had ground training in "Astro" (astronomy) and GEE, as well as a lecture on night vision. Later, one crew took part in an air test, checking to make sure their bomber was fit to fly after either being damaged in the previous raid or suffering from some general technical failure. That evening there was flight training in bombing and fighter affiliation.[16] Bill received a letter, dated January 3, from his sister Edna, and somehow found time to write and post a letter to his sister Irene, describing his recent nine days' leave and remarking on his visits to see relatives.[17] To finish the day, he and the crew left the ground at 2028 hours as one of ten crews carrying out a command bullseye exercise.[18] Command bullseyes were similar to any other mock bombing run but included other squadrons in the task to make it even more realistic. A wireless operator from 408 Squadron took sick during the practice, causing one crew to return early, but the nine remaining crews reported completing a successful exercise that took four hours and forty-five minutes.[19]

Most likely tired and cold, the boys headed home to Beningbrough Hall either in the back of a truck or by bicycle or motorbike so they could crawl into their waiting cots for much-needed sleep. It was late and a weeknight; there would be no time for a drink at the Alice Hawthorn or for socializing in York on this occasion.

PART 4

GET YOUR GEESE IN FORMATION

18

Walking in Their Footsteps

H aving spent well over twenty-four hours travelling via one taxi, two aircraft, the London Underground, and a train, we arrived in York in time to see the grand spectacle of horse race fever. Suits, fancy dresses, and hats of many colours, shapes, and sizes swirled by as we gained our bearings. I felt underdressed and a tad wrinkled in my comfy travel wear, not to mention disoriented as I tried to see through the fog in my brain. I wondered if the train station had felt so daunting to the boys, and I tried to picture the crowds of people stepping off the trains in Second World War-era clothing—a large proportion of them in uniform, holding duffle bags, chatting, smoking cigarettes—before carrying on to their base or heading out on leave. The boys had stood on these very platforms, stared at the grand arched roof, and walked out these doors on their way to the squadron, just as we were doing now.

After several minutes we found a taxi and set off for our bed and breakfast. I had initially planned to walk the distance, but I was glad to avoid the throngs, letting the driver find an alternative way along the congested streets.

Once we were checked in, a nap was the only plan of action my clouded brain could muster, even after a much-needed shower. Two o'clock in the afternoon or not, I snuggled down into the comfort of clean white sheets, giving into sheer exhaustion, and slept soundly for the first time in days. When the alarm went off sometime around five in the evening, I groaned my dissatisfaction and stuck my face into the pillow beside Michael's shoulder.

"A little longer?" he mumbled, more awake than me but not ready to get up either.

"Um, no, I should get up." But I didn't.

The next time I opened my eyes, darkness had dimmed the mellow painted walls to shades of grey. "Oh god, what time is it?" I asked, jumping half off the mattress, realizing we had both fallen back asleep and had not reset the alarm. I scrambled the rest of the way off the bed in a hurry.

Was I insane? No matter how many times I flew between England and Australia, I never accepted the fact that jet lag always won out. How did I figure I could manage an engagement right after a marathon flight? Luckily I had pulled out a fresh set of clothes before crawling into bed, so getting ready proved less harried than expected. Still, we were about fifteen minutes behind schedule when we headed out the door to find Bob Hudson's sister Pat and her daughter Barbara.

Downstairs, everything was dark. It seemed the family running the B&B had retired to their own private quarters. With no way of knowing if Pat and Barbara had arrived, I wondered what to do. This was not how I had pictured our first meeting. We made our way back up the stairs, and, standing on the landing, I contemplated knocking on doors until I found my contacts. Then I heard the muffled voices of two women coming from the room next to ours. I tapped on the door.

"Barbara?" I asked hesitantly when a woman answered the door.

"Yes," came the reply, and Barbara Bignell, Bob's niece, invited us in. We made nervous small talk and then arranged to meet again in a few minutes, when Pat and Barbara were ready, to go out for dinner.

In the meantime, I mused about how the boys might have felt, coming together as a crew. Had they hesitated when they first met each other or did they just barrel in, head first, without any nervousness? Crews were made up of men from all over the Commonwealth—Canada, Australia, New Zealand, and Britain—but also from Allied countries, some of which had been invaded. These crewmen had escaped their country to fight another day. The boys of EQ-P came from all walks of life, and although all were young, their ages varied by as much as a decade. Some were married, some had children, but most were single. What were their impressions of one another?

My jitters did not last long. The four of us found a local pub, and before long we were chatting away, sharing personal stories, as if we had known each other for years. Despite the separation of time and space, we shared a special bond that remained constant. We were connected by past tragedy, but the present promised something brighter.

The next morning, as we walked down the street toward York Minster, Pat, Barbara, Michael, and I enjoyed the sunny morning light and the newness of our relationship. Our boys represented the youngest members of the crew, both nineteen, Bob a little younger than Bud. We took pictures along the way and marvelled at the old buildings and cobblestone streets. The boys had passed along these same streets, and here we were, decades later, walking on them together.

At the cathedral, Pat pulled out an invitation to the "Unveiling of the Thanksgiving Memorial by His Royal Highness The Duke of Edinburgh in York Minster on Tuesday, 1st November, 1955," which had been sent to her mother. She joked to the staff that she had come for the dedication, although a tad late. After we explained our situation, they directed us to the memorial, an astronomical clock, that stood at the far end of one of the aisles. In a case below the clock was the illuminated *Book of Remembrance* listing the Allied aircrew casualties in Yorkshire and the northeast of England. On the wooden base of the clock, above the glass-encased book, was a plaque bearing the statement "They went through the air and space without fear and the shining stars marked their shining deeds."

I doubted any of them went without fear. However, I was immediately struck by the mention of stars, which reminded me of a poem written by Bill's sister Isabel, shortly after he went missing.

TO AN AIRMAN
Last night a star fell from the sky,
It seemed so sad its light had gone,
Till I looked overhead and saw
A million others shone.

Last night a plane fell from the sky,
A brave young airman met his doom,
Yet through the tears I also saw,
That others took his room.

This brave young airman feared not death,
He saw countries torn with strife,
Poor people wronged and starved and killed,
And so he gave his life

That you and I might live our life
In constant faith and joy and peace.
Our heritage for years—from one
Whose light will never cease.[1]

A staff member opened the case, giving us access to the book. We searched the pages and found each boy's name. I knew they were all there, but I had to check each one. The poor man waiting for us to finish so he could close the case must have wondered how many family members we had in the air force, but he was patient while we found the appropriate pages. It seemed fitting to start our journey in York by remembering the boys in a holy place.

After leaving York Minster, we walked along the streets in search of Betty's. A favourite pub during the war, it had not diminished in popularity over the years. When we located it, only a short distance from the cathedral on a jam-packed York street, the place was full and there was a line of customers at the door, waiting for seats. We eventually got a table in the main dining area. After our hearty B&B breakfast, none of us felt that hungry, so at first we just ordered drinks. When we saw the desserts roll by on an old-style tiered serving trolley, however, we changed our minds and opted for some delectable cakes and pastries as well.

Looking at the interior of the building and its grand style, with the old features still evident, I wondered how Betty's looked back in the 1940s. The room seemed massive, an impression enhanced by the full-length windows. I could not help but enjoy the old-world charm.

After finishing our sweets we headed downstairs to the wood-panelled dining area with its famous mirror. Numerous fly boys from all over the world had scratched their names on the mirror during the war years. Legend had it that they used the diamond engagement ring of the barmaid. My boys had not written their names on the mirror, but Norm, according to his brother Robert, had carved his name into one of the beams or supports in the downstairs bar area. Sadly, that lower room had been refurbished years earlier, and the beam had disappeared, along with many other old bits. No matter. I knew he, and most likely the rest of the boys, had been here, gone down the very same steps, and seen himself reflected in the mirror, just as I was doing now. I scanned the downstairs area before examining the scrawls on the mirror. If only I could step through the glass and into the past and share the experience of being here, for just a moment, with them.

Fed and watered, we stepped back out into the sunny afternoon. On our way along the cobbled streets to the B&B, we stopped at a teddy bear store and, after searching for nearly two years for my wedding gift, I found the Steiff I wanted there at the back corner of the store. He caught my eye, standing at attention between a selection of others, covered in a light grey-brown mohair or "caramel" according to his Steiff identification. A skeleton key hung over his heart, held at his neck by a strip of leather. He was a "keepsake" teddy bear, full of old-world charm. I could have stuck a miniature flight cap on him and he would have looked the part of a bomber crewman. We bought the bear, and I also got a teddy bear passport for the little bear that had accompanied me on all my travels since I had purchased it years earlier. Gap, as he is known because of his "Mind the Gap" London Underground T-shirt, had originally come from Britain, and had been to Canada, Germany, Austria, and Australia; had passed through various airport terminals, including Singapore and Thailand; and in just a few days would accompany me in the tail end of a Lancaster bomber. I figured it would be good for him to start entering countries legally for a change, considering most of the time he sat in my hand luggage or came out to look at the sky through the window of the aircraft.

Pat asked what I was going to name the new bear, and we tossed around a few names, like York, but nothing seemed to fit. I wanted it to have some significance for our trip. In the meantime, he remained nameless and tucked away in his box, ready for travel.

We spent the late afternoon at the Yorkshire Air Museum, which has a room "dedicated to the memory of the 20,000 Air Gunners who lost their lives in WWII," which is "believed to be the only one of its type in the world."[2] Pat and I represented the gunner families, so we were particularly interested in seeing this display. It would give us a good idea about the turrets, clothing, and all things gunner.

Looking for the uniform display, and not paying much attention to where we were going as we chatted away, we walked straight through the doorway of the gunner room. We looked up and were unexpectedly confronted by several mid-upper and tail turrets, resting like caskets in the quiet of a funeral home. Pat gasped as she clasped her hand over her mouth, could go no farther, and had to leave. I swallowed hard and resisted the urge to follow. The passage of sixty-six years did little to soften the pain inflicted by the simple presence of a row of metal turrets, still clearly associated with losing her brother.

Michael and I remained behind to gain a better understanding. We spent a good deal of time looking over the numerous displays that dotted the room. Gunners wore layers of clothes along with a heated suit to keep them warm in the cold of the turret. These suits did not always work properly, however, leaving some freezing and frostbitten while others received burns from the malfunctioning gear. They could count on their gloves and boots, thick and insulated, for warmth in the cramped confines of the turret, while face masks provided both their lifeline of vital oxygen and their only communication link to the rest of the crew. The gunners sat silently for hours, searching the skies as they moved their turrets through quadrants of darkness, hoping there would be no reason to yell for the pilot to dive in a corkscrew to save their lives. In EQ-P, this was the job of two smiley young boys just nineteen years old.

My husband, kinesthetic learner and avid gun lover that he is, noticed an interactive gunner display in one corner. It detailed how gunners adjusted their shooting in order to hit a moving target in air combat. He waited, somewhat impatiently, for the young boy playing on the simplified simulator to move on before taking up the challenge himself. It seemed gunnery still had a following and could attract boys of all ages.

Leaving the room with a better understanding of the gunner's role, we rejoined Barbara and Pat, who were sitting at a picnic table, talking to a friendly elderly volunteer. Fully refreshed and cheered up by the man, they came with us to the Canadian Memorial T2 Hangar, where numerous display boards held information on Yorkshire-based squadrons. Before long, evening heralded the close of the museum, so we returned to our lodgings to rest up for another big day.

19

Beningbrough Hall

We got up late in the morning on Sunday, and joined Barbara and Pat for breakfast in the dining room at the B&B. There was no need to rush; Beningbrough Hall, where the boys stayed after they were assigned to 408 Squadron, would not be open until eleven.

As we chatted over breakfast, we came up with the perfect name for my new teddy: Beni, a short form for Beningbrough. This proved to be an ideal choice, as he is a constant reminder of my visit to the hall.

We also spent a lot of time glancing anxiously out the window. The sky looked undecided and as fickle as ever. Some things never change. This was the kind of weather described by many veterans who served in the north of England. However, when we headed out to Barbara's car, equipped with camera, voice recorder, jackets, and umbrellas, we were met by blue skies and white puffy clouds. I hoped it was a sign of the day to come.

The drive was short and full of the typical little villages and narrow roads that seem more appropriate for bicycles and walking than motor cars. Following the National Trust signs, we finally entered the grounds of Beningbrough Hall. I leaned forward in the back seat, anxious to catch a glimpse of the building among the trees. Minutes passed. Still no sign of the hall. We turned along the lane, and there it finally was, filling my visual field with its imposing presence.

Michael leaned toward me and asked, "Are you excited yet?"

"Now I am excited," I replied with an ear-to-ear grin frozen on my face. My mind raced. What were the boys' thoughts when they set eyes on Beningbrough Hall for the first time? It must have been an impressive sight for the five from Canada especially. In my mind was the thought that the boys had been here in this hall, and I was about to walk in their footsteps. I felt like I had come home to be with loved ones after a long time away, something the boys would never do.

We were early; the grounds were not yet open, but after a short wait with some other eager visitors the doors opened at last. I had to make a huge effort to keep myself from running down the lane toward the hall. I was already ten steps ahead of the others, eager to dash forward and yell to the boys, "I'm here," as though they would somehow be there, standing at the front door to greet me.

When we entered the hall, once again I thought about how they must have marvelled at the sheer size of the building and the space in each room, considering what they were used to back home. Moments later we turned a corner and confronted a staircase the squadron boys had raced down on their bicycles. How dangerous it appeared. But compared to being on operations, it must have seemed trivial and fun.

I wondered what Beningbrough looked like in those days. Lady Chesterfield had transferred most of her furniture and belongings to other buildings, and what could not be moved was covered over to protect it from damage. Despite the hall's present beauty, with numerous portraits and old furnishings in each room, I could imagine crowds of young men gallivanting around in what might have looked like the wild abandon of naughty children. My mouth twitched. Bud, Bob, and Norm popped into my mind as the type to get up to mischief.

We proceeded to the next floor, which was used for sleeping quarters. The vision of rows of uncomfortable cots spread out over the large open area before me. And just as Bud had written to his sister, there was a fireplace in each room.

At this point I found myself swaying as an uncontrollable anxiety pushed me to move on, while my brain fought to slow me down so the rest of our little group could keep up. Michael asked if I was okay, putting his arm around my waist to steady me.

"I'm fine," I responded, pausing before declaring in a strained, almost hoarse voice, "I want to find the bathtub."

It was the best explanation I could provide in words for the emotional turmoil I was feeling. It was akin to religious fervour, a desire to reach the altar at the front of a church to quench my thirst for God. I needed to move on to the next room, to wherever the tub full of neck-high water sat. We moved on through another chamber and another before finding the room in question.

There was no doubt that all of the boys had been in this tub at one point or another—it was the only one in the house. I had the urge to stroke the rim of the sunken tub like a pilgrim touching a holy relic. I was walking along the same halls, through the same rooms, and here I was crouched in front of and touching the same bathtub they had used. How much closer could I possibly get?

Later we walked around the gardens and out onto the back lawn of the hall. It was a fitting tribute to the boys to see children happily playing, running about in pure delight without a worry. Wasn't that the point of this after all, preserving the freedom to just be? I smiled to myself, remembering the wild nature of the squadron boys, most not much more than children themselves. I could not blame them, considering the end many would eventually face. These children would probably not have such cares, and I wondered if they would ever understand what sacrifices my boys and so many others had made for all of us.

After our break outside we went to the top floor. Despite the interesting displays and educational information, I could not focus on the hall's present purpose as a portrait gallery. My heart was in the past and refused to be pulled forward.

Before we left, I revisited the sleeping quarters and returned to the bathtub for the last time. I needed to say my goodbyes. A great aching sadness settled in my heart. I tried to etch the rooms into my memory as I walked slowly to the ground floor. The ghosts of the past stood silent and still. They could not follow me. I mentally kicked and screamed, refusing to surrender them to the past, but the walk down the stairs shoved me forward into the present.

After leaving the hall we headed for the Alice Hawthorn pub. The boys had got there by boat, but for us it meant a lengthy drive to find a crossing over the River Ouse. Once we entered the village, we passed the pub with the hope of seeing the river crossing, but the road led to what looked like a private property. Unsure of exactly where the boat crossed, we abandoned the search and went back to the pub.

I knew the pub had been renovated since the war, so although I expected a lovely old pub, I did not anticipate feeling the old heart of the place within the new. The low roof of the original barroom spread out before me with a fireplace at the far end. I squinted and imagined the bomber boys gathered around the tables, some making a boisterous ruckus as they chattered on about their experiences or their newest girlfriend, while others sat more quietly, sipping their beer and thinking of home. I thought back to the stories I had read about the sense of home felt by the airmen who frequented this pub and wondered if the boys experienced that warmth. One local writer described how, "to the kind-hearted innkeeper and his wife, these boys from across the Atlantic have become adopted 'sons.' The young men often cook their meals at the pub, sometimes sleep in the attic and even borrow money from the landlord and landlady. When the boys yearned for corn-on-the-cob, a favourite back home, the landlady, despite knowing very little about the dish, bought some seeds and planted them in the garden. In due course, corn-on-the-cob was served to the delighted airmen."[1] Considering the bland and monotonous station meals, no one could have had anything but affection for a woman willing to give them a taste of their beloved home.

Bud's brother Ken, fully informed of my travels, had instructed us to have a drink for the boys at this pub. Those of us not driving happily obliged. However, there was a problem. I didn't like beer and couldn't imagine swallowing an entire pint and then eating a meal. I opted for my usual, a Jack Daniel's and coke, while Michael drank the beer in my stead. When I emailed Ken later, apologizing for not drinking a beer and telling him my preference for whiskey, he was his usual supportive self, telling me, "You're my kind of gal." I smiled, remembering Bud had often gone for wine. I wondered if any of the boys had been whiskey drinkers. The four of us drank to the boys and then to Michael's and my second wedding anniversary—a day I would never forget.

When the food arrived, we tucked in to our roast dinners with all the trimmings. I doubted the boys managed to eat quite so well, given wartime rationing, but we ate heartily and chatted about our adventures, and I imagined they did just the same.

It had been a long and emotional day, and tonight Pat and Barb would head for home. We would see them again in just a few days, and I looked forward to having them along to see us on our Lancaster ride. Our shared journey not only revived a bygone time but also wove us together into a greater whole, entwining past and present, as bits of the boys' spirit flowed within us. My eye colour, Pat's wide smile, and a number of other little traits, easily overlooked, conjured up the ghosts of fly boys departed as we sat in the present, bidding cheers to the past.

20

Present Meets Past

O n Monday morning, Michael and I hopped into a taxi and headed to RAF Linton-on-Ouse. As it is still a working base, we pulled up outside the gates and walked to the guard room to wait for our guide. Wg. Cdr. (retired) Alan Mawby, curator of the Memorial Room on the base, greeted us and, after we acquired the appropriate passes, took us on a tour of the station.

While we walked along the quiet roads, he gave us a brief history of the base and pointed out buildings and features dating from the time the boys had been there. A total of 2,009 airmen from this base and its satellite fields lost their lives flying on operations during the Second World War.[1] With 933 coming from 408 Squadron, the boys and their squadron mates made up nearly half the casualties.

Partway through our tour, Alan took us to a building and told me to have a look in the window. I could see a parachute hanging up inside, and Alan told me that Bud would have "gone in through that door, he would have signed for his parachute . . . he would have definitely gone in that building, without a shadow of a doubt and picked up his parachute . . . and that was probably the last building on the station that he went into, because he would have then gone out and walked over to the wagon to take him to the aircraft and then flown off on his mission."

I had trouble absorbing this. The building was still there, used for the same purpose. But sixty-six years earlier, Bud and the rest of the boys had stood in that exact spot and taken their parachutes.

Oddly, the parachute building and the others seemed too new to have been built in the 1930s and '40s. They also did not match the black-and-white image I had absorbed from photos of the base. The buildings at Linton had been sandblasted in an attempt to remove the camouflage paint enshrouding them, and the result was modern and stark brickwork unidentified with a bygone war. In contrast, the Yorkshire air museum, and the Lincolnshire museum that we visited later, which were no longer working stations, retained a sombre, monotone appearance, more in keeping with our modern vision of the war era.

We went up into the air control tower and looked out over the runway. I tried to picture the Lancasters dotted around the field and the bomb dump, but the silent expanse was devoid of Lancasters and crews now: no ground crews working on the damaged aircraft, no preparations for bombing up for an operation ahead, no aircrew doing checks or walking to and from briefings. Young men still trained here, but in place of the large four-engined Lancasters, single-engined Tucanos rolled down the runway and up into the sky or came around for a landing as we stood and talked.

Later, at the officers' barracks, faint hints of tri-coloured camouflage paint embedded in the brick walls hearkened back to the past, refusing to let the building's heritage fade away. Alan noted that the boys would have had breakfast in the large dining rooms and then continued the day with a parade in army style before going off to do their required work at the aircraft.

After the tour we headed to the Memorial Room, where Alan described the events that led to the beginnings of the memorial. Initially, the 408 Squadron Association planned to present a stuffed goose to the base in 1975, but somehow the goose disappeared in London's Victoria Station. How one loses a stuffed Canada goose we could not imagine—it's not exactly a small item, and it would not have the sentience to waddle away. I had to wonder if, like the doorknobs of Beningbrough Hall, it was sitting in someone's attic or living room, or perhaps it still waited in Victoria Station's lost and found. Undeterred, the 408 Squadron Association presented a second goose two years later.

Still, this was not much of a tribute for so many brave men. When Canadians asked Sgt. Bill Steel where the memorial was for the crews who had flown at Linton, he decided something more substantial was needed and set about creating a memorial to all the Linton-based squadrons from the war years.[2] Today the memorial is a mass of information and photographs gathered from the RAF's holdings and donated by veterans, their families, and other interested parties.

Feeling satisfied that I now knew a little more about the boys' surroundings and their daily routine, I searched the Memorial Room for evidence of their existence. I did not find any photographs of Bud, Norm, Bill, Bob, Larry, George, or Jock, but there was something equally intriguing. As I looked over the photographs of men from 408 Squadron, I identified two without even looking for their names. There, at his tail turret, stood Wally Richmond, the original tail gunner before Norm's crew arrived at 408 Squadron. In another photo was George McKillop, an aircraft mechanic, my mentor from the beginnings of my research on the boys. They stood like shining lights, telling me to "keep going," pushing me forward on my mission.

Like the newly qualified pilot Flying Officer John Gwinnett, I found the Memorial Room a "humbling place." In his words, "this room paints a picture and the stories here are extraordinary. It would be a travesty if they were allowed to fade into the background."[3] Seeing the personal history of the crews from Linton as I looked around, I knew I couldn't let the boys fade. They deserved their place as much as any other.

21

Just Jane

O ur time in York done, we spent the next day travelling by train to Lincolnshire for our mutual anniversary present at the Lincolnshire Aviation Heritage Centre. We arrived there early, around 8:45 AM. As we waited for the museum to open, we watched from the fence as the hangar doors trundled back and the reason for our trip slowly rolled out onto the tarmac.

Upon entering the centre, I let my husband take the camera and snap away at *Just Jane*. She posed like a 1940s pin-up girl, smooth and rounded with feminine poise. I stood and stared, then moved a little, stopped, and stared again, in complete awe, my heart bursting with happiness. *Jane* was a beauty.

Near the front of the plane stood two elderly, well-dressed gentlemen, obviously emotional yet pleased to be there having their picture taken. I wanted to talk to them but I did not approach, and instead just watched as the photographer took photos of the pair.

When I saw them and the plane, the full impact of what was about to happen finally hit me. Soon I would be inside this bird of war—not just any bird, but the greatest bomber of the war—going for a ride. This was an aircraft meant for men, a plane very similar to the one my boys had been in the night of their deaths. A niggling pain crept up my throat, and tears stung the back of my eyes. I continued to follow Michael around the aircraft like a lost dog, my eyes filling to glassy pools that I tried not to let spill over. This was it. This was the closest I would ever get to EQ-P in its full three-dimensional glory.

I swallowed hard, pushing the welling emotions down. Bud had only had one operational flight. It was his first and last, yet in his records the squadron listed his operational hours as "NIL." The flight was never finished, so it was impossible to determine the hours served. But, irrationally, I resented the "NIL" hours record, for if Bud had had no operational hours, surely he should still be alive. I doubted if he or any tail gunner would consider those last hours to be "NIL." Bud would have spent the time making sure his guns were free of ice and working, emptying his mask of condensation, freezing in an open-ended turret, alone, turning through quadrants of the dark night sky looking for night fighters. What had he seen that night?

I wandered around the back and looked at the tail turret. A skull and crossbones painted below the Perspex marked the deadliest position of the plane. Luftwaffe night fighters "preferred to attack from the rear and under the belly of the bomber, so he was often first in line for elimination."[1] If that was not bad enough, the tail gunner, as well as the rest of the crew, was at risk from their fellow bombers. When one plane was shot down or blown up, it could smash or break off the turrets or other parts of airplanes below it as it fell from the sky. And in some cases, cookie bombs and incendiaries, dropped from the aircraft above, landed on bombers in the same or other Allied squadrons.

The lifespan of a tail gunner varied from two to five weeks, or approximately five operations. If an operational flight averaged around seven hours, then a tail gunner survived approximately thirty-five hours of operational air service before he died. That would have been about the length of Bud's operational service if he had not been sick the month before the Stuttgart operation.

These were some of the thoughts rampaging through my mind as I studied *Just Jane*. Later, while we waited to enter the plane, I was distracted by another observation: I was the only female inside the roped-off area for passengers. Where were the women? Didn't any other females have an interest in stepping inside the greatest bomber of the war or knowing what it was like for their relatives? Some must, but perhaps they were intimidated. I felt it myself as I stood on the edge of the group, facing a wall of burly male backs. They chomped at the bit to hop into the plane.

As we prepared to board, the organizer asked who wanted which spot in the aircraft. I had requested the tail gunner position when paying for the ride months earlier, and now I held my breath as the organizer said first dibs went to Second World War vets and their families. The elderly veterans who'd had their pictures taken earlier in the day happily requested the cockpit. My panic subsided.

When it came to family members of veterans, a number of hands went up directly in front of me. I doubted my hand could be seen behind them, and I stopped breathing again. Would I lose the only place I wanted, the reason I had come halfway around the world?

At this point the organizer said there had been a request for the tail gunner position, and she called my name. The men all looked to their left and right and, not seeing a woman, turned around. One fellow ahead of me and slightly to the right quietly said to his friend, "Didn't you have a relative who flew as a tail gunner?" and I realized my dreams of taxiing in the tail turret might still be contested. For a Second World War vet I was willing to step aside or perhaps share the turret by sitting behind, just outside on the spar, but the thought of having to give it up to another family member, and one who had not previously requested the turret, did not sit well. My heart pounded, and I strained to draw in enough air with each breath to maintain my calm. The man's friend answered in the affirmative but waved at him to be quiet and let the position slide in my favour without any remarks. The two of them took the mid-upper turret, a place that I would not have been able to see out of, given my height. I waited gratefully at the back of the line as the others took up their favoured positions.

Once inside, my husband went up to the cockpit while I remained in the back with the men who had been in front of me. Each person had a chance to check out the tail turret, and I watched them sit on the spar, turn, and slide down to the small open doors before entering the turret. I thought of Bud doing this with bulky clothing on. Then each took his turn sitting in the space that was Bud's, and I smiled as they, unburdened in polo shirts and jeans, sat in the turret seat and inevitably bumped their heads on the back of the turret opening as they tried to get out of the tiny space and push themselves back up the spar to make room for the next person.

When they all finally headed for their positions in the mid-upper turret or farther forward, to the navigator or wireless operator post, I hopped up and, at the dizzying height of five feet and three-quarter inches, had no problems sliding down the spar and entering the turret. I settled into position, alone with my thoughts. As the lone female I had the distinct impression I did not belong—but I pushed the thought aside. I was on a mission and no one was going to take that away now.

I sat in the seat and looked at the controls and the space. The turret offered little room, even for a shorty like me. Leaning back to look around, I too scraped my head on the top of the door opening. I scanned the turret, absorbing everything, and tried to imagine what it would have been like to sit here in the cold for hours, in bulky clothing, freezing, in the dark. I was pretty happy by this point, waiting for the pilot to sort everything out for the ride and enjoying the freedom of being on my own in the turret. Well, on my own but with my little teddy Gap, riding shotgun, clipped to my belt loop. My own little talisman. It seemed appropriate for this ride.

As I sat, trying to take everything in, I turned to my right and caught sight of an axe wired into a crevice within reach of my hand. I felt the blood rush to my brain and my gut, a sickening feeling as if I were being swallowed whole by a thick, rising liquid. I jolted upright in my seat, drawing my knees in to my stomach and then shoving them, full force, straight out on a diagonal, with an audible *humph* escaping my mouth. Thank goodness my legs were so short or I would have broken my ankles on the foot controls.

"SHIT, shit, shit!" I half yelled the words silently in my head, half whispered them out loud through gritted teeth. I looked up at the top of the turret, sucking in air and fighting to stem the tears and ease the pain in my chest as I sat in Bud's coffin.

Moments later, Barbara Bignell came toward the turret, camera in hand, ready to take some pictures. How could I smile, knowing what I knew? But I did. I smiled for Ken and for Bud. The photo would be sent to Ken when I got back to Australia, and I'd be damned if I was going to be crying in it. I pulled myself together, and when I heard the sound of one of the four engines chugging, I smiled all the harder.

The engines came to life one by one, and before long we were moving out into the open field. Riding over the grass, the engines roaring, though not even near the full sound that Bud would have experienced, I smiled without force. I knew the thrill of Bud's heart. The movement and the power of the plane, the noise of the engines buzzing in my ears—I loved every precious minute. I could see why so many volunteered to join the air force despite the deadly statistics. There could be nothing like flying free at the tail end of a plane.

The grass lay flat under the generated wind, and I swung and bumped around in the turret. Looking up to the sky, I focused my view through the gun sights. I wished I could turn the turret and shoot the guns, feel the tail rise up and go barrelling down the runway backward with the ground dropping away beneath me. What would it be like to see the squadron planes rising up into the dark in front of me and to look at the ground below?

Later, I had the luck to meet 514 Squadron tail gunner Robert Chester-Master, who recalled, "One could always see your mates taking off in the line before and I used to say a little prayer for us all. God speed [sic] and safe return." As for his view of the ground below, he told me, "On one wonderful occasion as our dispersal area was close to the road, a young English girl got off her bike and knelt and prayed. . . .I felt very humbled, knowing the problems that they and their family and friends were being blasted with bombing on a regular basis and that she still had thoughts for others, such as us."[2]

All too soon the ride ended. As we returned to the tarmac, and I sat there for the last moments in the rear turret, I noticed a man taking photos of the plane. Pat and Barbara stood beside him, and I waved at them, not sure what to convey about the experience. The photographer continued snapping shots and seemed to be focused on the rear turret. I wondered if I should move so he could get a photo without me in it, but as he came closer, I realized I was his focus.

When we finally left the plane, Pat and Barbara introduced me to the photographer, Terry Mason, who told me that his father had "worked for AVRO and carried out the final aircraft inspection and pre fly out checks before the aircraft was flown out from England to Agadir in Morocco having been purchased for maritime reconnaissance use by the French Navy. He was then sent out to Morocco by AVRO to carry out servicing and repairs to this Lancaster along with several others purchased under the same contract."[3] That plane had gone through a long restoration to become *Just Jane*.

The day was an incredible journey, and Terry, the cameraman, captured the most poignant picture as I waved at Pat and Barbara, one gunner family to another, caught between two worlds and two states of being. I glimpsed the life of a tail gunner and found Bud on that first and final night. I had done it for Ken and Bud, and for Bob and his family as well, and no one could ever take that away. I was a girl in a turret thousands of kilometres from home. I had become one of the boys.

above—Outside Betty's, York, 2010. LISA JEAN/MICHAEL RUSS

below—Mid and tail turrets at Yorkshire Air Museum, 2010. LISA JEAN/MICHAEL RUSS

top—Beningbrough Hall, 2010. LISA JEAN RUSS

middle—Pat Johnson and Lisa Jean Russ visiting Beningbrough Hall, 2010. MICHAEL RUSS

bottom— The Alice Hawthorn pub, 2010. LISA JEAN/MICHAEL RUSS

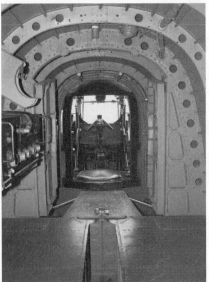

top—The Lancaster *Just Jane*, 2010.
COURTESY OF HUDSON FAMILY

middle—View from tail spar into tail turret in *Just Jane*, 2010.
LISA JEAN/MICHAEL RUSS

bottom—Lisa Jean Russ in tail turret of *Just Jane*, 2010.
COURTESY OF HUDSON FAMILY

top—The Lancaster *Just Jane* heading out to the airfield, 2010. LISA JEAN/MICHAEL RUSS

middle—Lisa Jean Russ, Monique and Claude Bouleaux, Jean-Paul Steydli, and Patrick Baumann, 2010. MICHAEL RUSS

bottom—Lisa Jean Russ sharing photographs of the boys with Rene Steydli, 2010.
MICHAEL RUSS

top—Sharing stories around the table with the Steydli family, 2010. MICHAEL RUSS

middle—Lisa Jean Russ with the Steydli family; seated are Rene and Marie-Thérèse Steydli, 2010. MICHAEL RUSS

bottom—The graves of Lancaster crew BQ-J, Artolsheim Communal Cemetery, France, 2010. LISA JEAN/MICHAEL RUSS

top—Hilsenheim Cemetery, France, with the graves of EQ-P at the far end, 2010.
LISA JEAN/MICHAEL RUSS

middle—Reaching the graves at Hilsenheim Cemetery, 2010. LISA JEAN/MICHAEL RUSS

bottom—The graves of the boys of EQ-P in Hilsenheim Cemetery, 2010.
LISA JEAN/MICHAEL RUSS

top—Parts of LL637 EQ-P dug from the Steydlis' field during the war, between Hilsenheim and Wittisheim, 2010.
LISA JEAN/MICHAEL RUSS

middle—Pitch motor, 2010. The Steydlis hid the plane fragments in their barn.
LISA JEAN/MICHAEL RUSS

bottom—Remnants of LL637 EQ-P's wooden propeller, 2010. LISA JEAN/MICHAEL RUSS

Looking for pieces of EQ-P in a farmer's field, 2010. MICHAEL RUSS

above—Matthieu Steydli and Lisa Jean Russ at the main crash site near Hilsenheim, 2010. MICHAEL RUSS

below—Pieces of EQ-P found in 2010. LISA JEAN RUSS

Bud Burt's grave,
Hilsenheim, 2010.
LISA JEAN RUSS

Steydli memorial
to the boys of
EQ-P, once the
propellor engine
casing, 2010.
LISA JEAN RUSS

PART 5

I REMEMBER YOU

22

To France

felt more than a little nervous as we rode in a London cab through the early morning dark toward the Eurostar station. I was racking my brain to remember French words that might be useful. Despite my Canadian roots, my French language skills were poor at best, and my ability to follow a French conversation even worse. I had tried hard to learn during my school years, but languages were not my strength.

When we stepped onto the train, trepidation followed me as dark as the clouds forming overhead. At first I spent time looking out the window at the dark green landscape and gloomy grey skies, wondering if I would notice a distinct difference between the English and French countrysides. As we entered the Chunnel, I put the question out of my mind and pulled out my newest purchase, a copy of Leo McKinstry's *Lancaster: The Second World War's Greatest Bomber.*

For a while, reading helped me relax and focus on my research. What else could I do? The window only gave me a reflection of myself. When we emerged into the light of day, I looked up and wondered if I had indeed been beneath the murky water of the English Channel. The announcement that we would soon be stopping in Calais answered my unspoken question.

As the train sped on and my husband slept beside me, an indescribable feeling swept through me and lay heavily on my chest. My destination neared. I was going to see the boys. Michael's constant question, "Are you excited yet?" nagged me. Excitement did not describe the feeling. Emotional, yes, but . . . words escaped me.

I stared into the back of the seat ahead and the graves appeared before me. All seven of them. I could see them waiting for me. Yes, that was it, they waited for me. The boys beckoned to me as though they knew I had arrived in France. I sped toward them. They were not far away now.

At Paris Nord station we rendezvoused with Damien Bouleaux, one of the Steydli grandchildren, who rushed us along the platform under puffy white clouds in a sunny blue sky. We had planned to take a later train, but with Damien's help we hoped to board an earlier Paris Est TGV train, which Jean-Paul, Damien's uncle and my main contact with the Steydli family, would be driving.

Indeed, with five minutes to spare, we were walking along the TGV platform an hour earlier than expected. I figured Damien would see us safely on the train and be off, but as we walked nearly the length of the train, I looked up to see Jean-Paul approaching from the opposite direction. This man, whom I'd never met in person, was coming to greet us with a smile that welcomed us as though we were long-lost relatives. That smile overcame any language barrier.

We said our goodbyes to Damien, boarded the train, and settled ourselves in the coach as Jean-Paul got on with the task of driving. My earlier question was now answered. It was evident we were no longer in England. The houses looked different, roofs were steeper in pitch, and the farmland stretched out before us from the time we left Paris all the way to Strasbourg. These places had seen war, endured occupation, and now lived free. Soon we would be in territory that had been annexed by the Germans during the Second World War, just as it had been from 1871 to 1919, after the Treaty of Frankfurt. Tossed back and forth over the centuries between the French and Germans, the Alsatians developed their own language variations and unique identity.

When we stepped off the train in Strasbourg, we rejoined Jean-Paul and headed out of the station to meet his sister Monique and her husband, Claude Bouleaux, Damien's parents. My heart leapt excitedly at our introduction. I had only seen one picture of them and sent the odd email, but it meant there was something more familiar than what lay at the surface.

The five of us spoke in broken phrases, mixing English and Alsatian French with gestures to aid communication as our hosts gave us a brief tour of the city. We stopped for our first drink in an Alsace pub, and I pulled out photographs of some of the boys, which I carried with me. Jean-Paul, Monique, and Claude had never seen most of the boys, so these photos provided a visual reference for the names on the gravestones, making the boys more three-dimensional and helping to develop their personalities.

Later, after Jean-Paul left for Hilsenheim to have supper with his family, we stayed in Strasbourg for a while longer and had dinner with Monique and Claude, sampling some of the Alsatian cuisine, before heading home with them to Hilsenheim for the night.

23

Expectations and Realities

T he next morning, at breakfast with Monique, Claude, and Jean-Paul, our hosts urged me to eat a huge assortment of Alsatian food—fresh breads, cheese, cold meats, giant croissants, glass pots of yogurt, and various other treats—along with coffee and fresh apple juice made with apples from Jean-Paul's own trees, all of which threatened to replace the weight I had lost while Michael was overseas. They had invited Patrick Baumann, an amateur historian with a keen interest in the planes that had crashed in France, particularly Alsace, during the Second World War, to join us, and as we ate, we talked.

I had a few ideas about which night fighters might have been in the area on the night of March 15–16, but I had made no real effort to delve into the German side of things. When I asked Patrick if he knew who had shot down EQ-P, he calmly named a night fighter whom his research suggested had been in the area: Reschke.

My heart skipped a beat.

Who? What? Did I hear him right?

My brain reeled. I had not expected it to be like this. I was unprepared. Despite knowing that Reschke might not be the one—there were many night fighters in the air that night—hearing a name somehow changed things.

How do you feel when you learn who may have instigated a loved one's death, even a loved one you have never known? How do you explain that, despite the unrecognizable feeling you cannot name, you don't hate the person? Hate had no place. He was only doing what the boys were doing, defending what each thought was right, following orders and doing their best for their respective sides. Still, this knowledge didn't make me feel any better.

It was as if I had been hit hard in the gut and lost my wind. I found it hard to breathe and to swallow, but there was no pain from the attack, just the lack of oxygen. Somehow my brain was forgetting to tell my lungs to work. Nor could I find my voice. I gestured to Michael and pushed out a few monosyllables: "You . . . do . . . it."

I listened, and slowly air began to return to my lungs, but my mind had gone off in a fog. I was dressed respectfully in black and grey, prepared to visit the graves after breakfast. I doubt any colour could have brightened my thoughts. They were already subdued beyond my clothes.

24

Honking of Geese from Above

O n the night of March 15–16, 1944, Alsatians went about their business as usual. Families had their evening meal together, taking care to black out their windows. "It was forbidden to turn on a light, which could be seen from outside," Jean-Paul's parents told me. Bombers were flying over the area more frequently, so the Germans ordered the Alsatians to turn off or black out their lights to conceal the whereabouts of towns and villages. The families, in turn, hoped no bombs would fall and no planes would crash into their homes.[1] On "la terrible nuit du 15 mars 1944," their fears would be realized.[2]

Around 2230 hours on that clear winter evening, the bomber stream spread over Alsace, headed for Stuttgart and a zero hour of 2310. As 863 planes thundered above the narrow valley, they rattled the windows of the houses in the villages below. Among them flew a number of aircraft tasked to perform Airborne Cigar (ABC) duties.[3] Lancaster Mk I ME558 SR-Q of 101 Squadron, from RAF Ludford Magna, Lincolnshire, was one of them. ABC required a special radio operator, so SR-Q had an eight-man crew instead of the usual seven. The extra man, in this instance J.B. Bull, was usually able to speak German. He scanned for the "relevant frequency of the Luftwaffe night fighters. He could then use his powerful transmitter to either jam the ground-control instructions or, in a suitably convincing German voice, issue his own false instructions."[4]

At this point in the war, ABC-equipped Lancasters accompanied "all major main force raids." To accommodate the additional weight of an extra person and extra equipment, these bombers carried fewer bombs, and they "were distinguishable by the three large transmission aerials they had installed, two in front of the mid-upper turret, and another in the nose, in addition to a small dorsal reception aerial." Although these Lancasters were not obviously different from the others, especially in the dead of night, the night fighters discovered they could detect them by picking up the ABC signals,[5] and finding these bombers gave the fighters and their controllers two significant advantages. Destroying these planes freed the fighters of irritating communication problems, but merely locating them placed the fighters within the bomber stream the ABC-equipped Lancasters were trying to protect.

In the dark sky, Major Rolf Leuchs of Night Fighter Wing (NJG) 6 spotted a Lancaster, likely BQ-X of 550 Squadron.[6] Whether as a result of Leuchs's attack or a separate mechanical failure, a bomber, probably BQ-X, had one wing on fire. It is believed to have passed over Illhaeusern, headed in the direction of Münster, as a few bombs from an aircraft dropped on a barn. Villagers in the valley of Münster also saw a bomber, again likely BQ-X, circling at low altitude before crashing near another farm in the village of Sondernach.[7] Only two men, Sgt. Kenneth Rowland Sumner and Sgt. Harry C. Petty, managed to bail out of the aircraft. Both landed close to the crash site. Petty had received injuries to his legs but was able to move and went in search of his crew mate. Sumner had landed in the trees and was severely injured, but Petty found him and remained with him until Sumner died. After covering Sumner in a parachute and leaving a note stating Sumner's name, Petty headed for Sondernach around three in the morning. Petty received treatment for his wounds, and in the morning the police turned him over to the Germans.[8] He spent the rest of the war as Prisoner 3651 in Camp L1.[9] When he returned to England after the war, Petty spoke little about what happened the night of March 15–16, so his story of the events died with him.[10] Those who perished in the incident were originally buried at Maettle, but were reburied at Choloy War Cemetery after the war.[11]

On the night of March 15–16, the noise of the bombers drew the attention of people in various villages farther north. In Sélestat, Alphonse Spiller, a sixteen-year-old apprentice baker, peered out his third-storey window, while fifteen-year-old Louis Rudloff sat with his family in the kitchen of their home in Artolsheim. When they heard the loud hum of bombers overhead, so penetrating that the windows of the house vibrated in their frames, the family went outside to determine what was going on, concerned that they might be bombed.[12]

Rene Steydli, then twenty-one years old, and Marie-Thérèse Hipp, then seventeen (who married Rene many years after the war), both lived in Hilsenheim, about half a kilometre apart. They also heard the "amazing noise of all the planes." Marie-Thérèse had gone to bed but got up when she heard the planes arrive over the village. Rene was still up at the time. They "both looked out of the window, but couldn't see anything."[13]

Alphonse, in Sélestat, watched as a night fighter attacked a bomber. In an attempt to escape, the bomber collided with another bomber, which in turn hit a third. The first bomber, assumed to be EQ-P,[14] broke in two from the force of the collision.[15]

As the pilot of the first aircraft, Norm likely ordered the crew to bail out when EQ-P was attacked, but Bud did not leave from the turret or attempt an escape through the side door of the plane's flaming fuselage.[16] He may have found himself in a situation similar to that of tail gunner Pat Brophy, who was trapped when damaged hydraulics, a broken turn crank, and damaged turret doors made the turret inescapable. (Brophy was able to shift the doors between his turret and the Lancaster interior enough to attach his parachute, but was unable to free himself from the turret in either direction.[17] Unlike most in such a situation, Brophy survived to tell his amazing tale.) Bud grabbed the axe beside him in the turret and began to chop at the turret mountings. According to tail gunner Steve Fortescue, gunners received no instruction in using an axe, but "[we] felt comfortable knowing there was some means of smashing our way out in an emergency if necessary. If the engine supplying hydraulics to the plane failed, there was a little crank handle to wind like mad to rotate the turret."[18]

When EQ-P split in two, Bud was at the mercy of the wind and gravity, tumbling wildly to the ground, trapped in his turret and clinging to his axe, with his crew mates still in what remained of the front fuselage. The tail gunner in an American bomber had just such an experience when his plane "could not take the strain and . . . broke in two at the radio room . . . The tail section was whipped round like an autumn leaf from a tall oak tree in a high wind. By this time, although I was scared as hell, I did not know what had happened, but there was no noise of any kind. I released my flak jacket and finding my chest chute snapped it onto my harness. I then pulled the release on my escape hatch—nothing happened; then struggling to escape, I banged the door with my shoulder and it finally blew out with Yours Truly following."[19]

Rene Steydli heard what sounded like an aircraft with engine trouble descending before crashing in the middle of his family's farm, about three hundred metres from the nearest house in Hilsenheim. Soon after the crash, explosions sounded from the wreckage of the plane and fire illuminated the night sky.[20]

In Artolsheim, Louis Rudloff and his family heard a burst of machine gun fire from above. Immediately after, an aircraft, with its interior ablaze, swept over the roofs of the houses in the village.[21] This plane, BQ-J, likely one of the other two planes in Alphonse Spiller's account, was from 550 Squadron.[22] It appeared to have a damaged engine. The Lancaster missed the homes of Artolsheim and struck the ground five hundred metres away, on residential property, close to what is now the village's soccer field. Some of the young people in the village wanted to go out to the plane, but abruptly an inferno began, followed by the explosion of bombs and the ejection of incendiaries, which set multiple fires in the community. The local firemen struggled to control the situation as BQ-J and many barns and houses in the village continued to burn through the night. In all, the fire incinerated nine barns, killing a horse belonging to one resident and cattle belonging to another. None of the inhabitants of the area died, but the blaze destroyed one villager's home.[23]

All of the crew perished in the crash. They were initially buried on the morning of March 16 in a collective grave without coffins, but ten days later the International Red Cross exhumed the bodies, placing the burned remains in wooden coffins before reburying them in Artolsheim Communal Cemetery. In 1974, the propeller and hub of the aircraft were found buried in the ground.[24] Today they stand in front of the graves as a memorial to the men, shining brightly in the sun, as bent and broken as the crew.[25]

Sgt. Ennis, the flight engineer from the ABC-equipped Lancaster, SR-Q, likely the other plane in Alphonse Spiller's story, parachuted from the plane, which was seen "ablaze" in the sky "and partly burnt out before crashing" at Breitenheim near Mussig.[26] Ennis was later found dead, floating on Lake Baggerloch on the edge of Wittisheim,[27] not far from the tail end of EQ-P. His last moments remain a mystery. Those who found the body first assumed he had drowned or died of some injury incurred while parachuting from the plane, but a bullet hole in the nape of his neck suggested another cause.[28]

The rest of the crew on SR-Q plummeted to the ground in their metal bird. The "charred and burnt parts of human remains," which were recovered from the wreckage, were "buried without coffins" in Mussig Communal Cemetery.[29] Ennis, found some distance from the plane on the edge of Wittisheim and originally believed by the Germans to be linked to EQ-P, was buried on March 19 in Wittisheim Communal Cemetery. In 1953 he was exhumed and reburied in Choloy Cemetery along with others who had been buried in places throughout northeastern France that were not easily tended.[30]

25

The Cold Dawn

On the morning of March 16, 1944, Marie-Thérèse Hipp's brother, cycling along the road between Hilsenheim and Wittisheim on his way to school, saw the front of EQ-P, still in flames, in the Steydlis' farm field, after seven o'clock.[1] Marie-Thérèse learned of the crash when she went out to do some shopping and met a neighbour who told her what had happened the night before.[2] She arrived at the crash site after 8 AM. The German police reached the site about the same time, but some other locals and possibly some people from Wittisheim were already there. By this point the fire was out, but the aircraft was "nearly completely destroyed."[3]

Marie-Thérèse noticed two or maybe three bodies lying near the plane outside the fuselage. Their clothing showed "no sign of burning" despite the charred wreckage beside them. She saw one of the Germans opening the coveralls on one body, extracting a wallet of personal documents and revealing to her "a wonderful white sweater with a turtleneck."[4]

The bodies Marie-Thérèse glimpsed were likely those of Bill and Bob, who may have been thrown from the broken aircraft when it crashed or exploded, as happened in the case of a Liberator where the "explosion threw the crew out in mid-air. Their shattered bodies [lay] beside the smoking remains of the aircraft."[5] With the tail end of Lancaster EQ-P open, the intense force of the crash and explosions could easily have ejected the men from the aircraft, whether they had been moving within the plane in an attempt to escape or trying to put out the fire in the fuselage.

Norm, Larry, Jock, and George had died in the front fuselage during the crash, and were all badly burned in the wreckage.[6]

Bud had crashed by the forest at the edge of the nearby village of Wittisheim. The villagers found him entombed in his turret, axe still in hand.[7]

All the townspeople had to leave the crash site after the Germans arrived, and the bodies were later removed.[8] The following day, March 17, a local living beside the cemetery saw the naked bodies of the crew at the entrance to Hilsenheim Communal Cemetery.[9] Nothing had been left on the bodies, not even the ring on Bud's finger, the only effect (other than identity discs belonging to Bill, Bob, Jock, and Bud) known to be found in the wreckage of EQ-P. The German authorities had removed the ring and retained it with the information surrounding the crash.[10]

The Germans buried the boys themselves. Bill, Bud, and Bob, each identifiable, occupied individual graves. Norm, Larry, Jock, and George, unable to be separately identified, rested collectively beside them.[11] "No ceremony of any kind was permitted by the Germans," but, undeterred by German commands, the villagers of Hilsenheim "went secretly the following night and placed flowers on the graves, much to the anger of the local German Commandant, who threatened to shoot the villagers. Fortunately, however, he did not carry out his threat."[12]

It took approximately "three days to load everything with a crane on trucks and to take it away. During this time, the crash place was guarded by the military. They took away every little thing they could find," and then they left the field.[13]

Unbeknownst to the Germans, a piece of the plane had landed about two hundred metres from the main crash site, in a field belonging to the Steydlis. Rene's father wanted to prepare the field for sowing, so Rene, his father, and his younger brother, knowing they could get into trouble for not reporting the find, took a horse into the field late one evening and "dug around the place where a cable was visible from the surface." By the time they had unearthed the part, loaded it onto the wagon, covered it with a tarpaulin, and headed home, it was nearly dark.[14]

What they had found turned out to be a propeller hub, cowling, and pitch control motor. They placed the wreckage in their barn and concealed it under hay in hopes that the Germans would not come looking for it.[15] "Except for the family, nobody knew about the aircraft parts until after the war."[16]

Despite the sad outcome, the boys were not neglected or forgotten over the years. After the war, family members and villagers alike continued to place flowers on the graves of the crew. Their full story may have been fractured by time and place, with some knowing their beginnings while others knew their end, but the respect and love for these men never wavered.

26

A Long Walk to Be with Them

L ater that morning, we left the house with Jean-Paul, Monique, and Claude, and walked the short distance down the road to say a quick hello to Jean-Paul and Monique's parents before proceeding to the florist and the graves. Rene and Marie-Thérèse Steydli welcomed us into their home as though they had been waiting a long time to see us. In fact, they had been waiting for over sixty-six years. They had been among the last people to see EQ-P, and Marie-Thérèse had witnessed the devastation of the burned and mangled wreckage, but they had not met any of Bud's relatives in person until this day.[1]

Rene Steydli stared up at me from his wheelchair, searching my eyes. There was so much that could not be expressed in words, even if we had spoken the same language. Did he try to picture Bud in me? Did he look at me and see the past? Sadness and happiness mixed, along with a feeling of helplessness. I knew he and his family had done what they could for the boys and for their families at great danger to themselves, and for that I would forever be grateful.

We would return to talk later, but for now we were off again, heading down the street to the local florist to buy flowers for the graves. I had thought about the flowers a long while before coming to Europe. I wanted to make a special statement. Bud's brother Ken had sent me money, wanting to contribute. It was not necessary, but I understood his wishes and I happily obliged.

While selecting the flowers for the graves I did not explain my reasoning to anyone. Too much emotion flowed through my veins, and words, whether French or English, escaped me. I spoke like a child, using single terms, as if I were learning to speak for the first time—*sept, rouge, jaune, vert, oui, merci*—with Jean-Paul gracefully reiterating and elaborating on them for the florist. I chose each flower and colour with a sense of symbolism that came to me as I contemplated the selection of blooms offered in the little shop. The most serene golden retriever came over and leaned heavily against my thigh, looking up at me with adoring brown eyes as though he knew why I was there. I stroked his soft golden head and neck and made my choices.

I selected seven red roses to symbolize the love the crew families shared for the boys. I chose seven yellow roses to represent the friendship and unity sought by the crew families. Over the years it seemed we had all tried to connect in one way or another, but for some reason were unable to arrange for all of us to meet. The shop had no white flowers available, so I chose light green carnations as a symbol of peace. The boys at least rested in peace, together. I asked Jean-Paul if there was a flower unique to the Alsace. He could think of none, and the florist suggested wheat-like plants, which I agreed were perfect. The plane had crashed in the Steydlis' farm field, and the seven wheat-like plants represented the loving bond between the Steydli family and the boys of EQ-P, which forever entwined the Steydlis and all of the boys' families. The florist added greenery, and the bouquet was complete. It seemed too small, not grand enough for the occasion, but I had taken almost all of the roses and carnations on display, so I consoled myself with the knowledge that the sincerity of my gesture was more important than the size.

We left the florist and headed the remaining distance to the graveyard with vase, flowers, and mixed expressions. From the entrance I could see where the boys rested, at the far end of the graveyard. Theirs were the only military graves in the cemetery, and they stood out as a neat, stark row of seven curved white stones in front of a cedar hedge. Between the gate and the boys were numerous family graves of Hilsenheim residents. I have never seen such beautifully preserved graves. Bright flowers sprawled gloriously over the dark headstones, emphasizing the seven white stones in the distance.

My heart thumped hard in my chest as my anticipation and anxiety grew, seeing them there, waiting. I could feel the pull of the graves, but my feet were reluctant to move quickly as we began to walk, the Steydlis hanging back slightly to give us space. I began to shake with little sobs.

I remembered a letter I had read that Bud's brother Ken had written to Jean-Paul Steydli in 1981, when Ken had visited the cemetery, and his words could as easily have described my experience. "Our entry into Hilsenheim was an indescribable event; it was like a revelation of arriving at the finish line of a long sought after goal. The entry into your town cemetery and through to the far wall, where the boys' graves were so beautifully cared for, was an intense emotional experience that I will never forget."[2]

Michael put his arm around me as we walked and asked if I wanted to stop, but I shook my head. We continued down the path, with me alternating between a forced silent reserve that pained the back of my throat and falling back into jittery sobs.

I had not prepared myself for this moment. I had spent more than a year learning all I could about the seven crewmen of EQ-P, and they had somehow become "my boys." I had flown halfway around the world to be where they had been—Beningbrough Hall, Betty's, the Alice Hawthorn, and Linton-on-Ouse—and shared some of their experiences, even riding in a Lancaster bomber. Now I stood before their graves as the only person who knew all the boys as a collective whole. I grieved, not for the loss of one life but for the great loss of all seven. I was not there for one but for all. It came with a pain I had not expected.

My husband gave me his hanky, and I wiped my wet eyes, trying to keep from tearing up again. I had always thought hankies an old gent's thing, something from another time and generation, and frequently kidded him about carrying such an item. In protest he usually replied, "A gentleman always carries a hanky," and pointed out how one never knew when it might come in handy. Well, it was coming in handy now! Dabbing away, I tried to remember how many of the boys had hankies listed in their personal effects. Almost all had at least one. Larry had thirteen returned to his family. I imagine the fourteenth was with him the night of his death.

The Steydlis busied themselves sorting the flowers. Having filled the vase with water, they added in pebbles from the graves so the vase would remain upright in a blustery wind. They set the bouquet near Bud's grave and pushed more pebbles around the base of the vase to hold it in place.

It joined a very sturdy urn full of fresh-cut flowers that sat front and centre before the seven graves. Puzzled, I asked Jean-Paul where the flowers had come from. He told me that his mother had wanted to make sure the graves looked welcoming when we arrived, so she had come down the day before with flowers from her garden and placed them there. Even now, after so many years, she made sure the boys and their families were taken care of.

I was speechless. The boys were not her flesh and blood. They belonged to families in distant countries, and her only contact with them had been the brief sight of some of them in death, lying near the plane, yet she came many times each year to remember them, showing her respect for men she had never met in life. She understood a mother's love and gave it sevenfold in the place of the mothers and wives who could not visit them. I knew they had been truly cared for and dearly loved for all these years. They were not forgotten in this far-off land.

27

Picking Up the Pieces

After visiting the graves we went back to the Steydli residence. In the driveway, Jean-Paul and Claude arranged the Lancaster parts that had been dug out of the field by Rene, his father, and his brother. They looked pristine. It was hard to imagine them driven so deeply into the ground by the force of the crash or explosions. Nothing seemed bent or damaged. Lovingly preserved, the parts spread out before us told a story all their own.

Rene Steydli, a curious man by nature and, at the time, a young man himself, had taken the large piece apart out of interest in its mechanical workings. Now, as Rene sat inside, housebound in his wheelchair, his son and son-in-law laid the pieces out in the order they would have gone together, outside in the driveway, and we looked at each part in turn. What wonderful craftsmanship.

A never-ending lineup of surprises proved the norm on this trip. We could see evidence of some of the differences between the Lancaster Mk II and the other models. Remnants of wooden propellers, not metal, remained at the hub. Perhaps it wasn't only the Merlin engines that were in short supply, but metal as well. Serial numbers were clearly visible on another piece. To top it off, Jean-Paul attached the motor that adjusted pitch in one of the Hercules' propellers to a battery to show us that, even after all this time and after all it had been through, it still worked. Hercules seemed an apt name for this small piece of the whole.

Alan Mawby, curator of the Memorial Room at Linton-on-Ouse, had talked about "bent metal" and the importance of people keeping the story with the pieces so neither would be lost. Here in Hilsenheim, provenance abounded. The parts were a small gold mine for an aircraft enthusiast, historian, or archaeologist. No Lancaster Mk II bombers exist today, and these pieces likely represented one of the last vestiges of an Mk II left in the world. What made them so special was the fact that they came with a rich story that was not only still remembered but that continued to be shared—and added to—by each generation of the crew families who came to visit the Steydlis. Theirs was a living history.

Early that evening, when we returned from visiting a local museum and the graves of crewmen from SR-Q and BQ-J, Jean-Paul, Claude, and Matthew, Jean-Paul's young son, took us out to the EQ-P crash sites. We stopped on the edge of the village of Wittisheim. At the time of the crash there had been a railway line and a bridge over the tracks here. They had since been removed, replaced by a small heritage marker. Nearby was a small section of rail track with a replica locomotive resting upon it. Jean-Paul pointed to the other side of the road, where he believed the rear turret had landed. I found it hard to believe the turret could have landed so far from the front of the plane, and I could not imagine how the people of Wittisheim must have felt, coming across the turret on its own, a dismembered entity of the burned-out Lancaster in the adjoining village, with the body of the tail gunner, my Bud, still inside holding the axe.

Later, after changing our clothes to suit the conditions of the field, we headed out to the main crash site. Jean-Paul was worried that the field would still be full of the year's crop and there would be nothing for us to see. However, when the vehicle stopped at the parcel of land and we got out, the Red Sea parted. I don't know if Jean-Paul had mentioned our visit to the farmer now using the land, but he or someone had cut a swath that cleared the section where the front of the plane had crashed.

We walked over the clipped plants, looking for signs of the crash as the sun hung low in the sky. Jean-Paul wondered if we would be able to find remnants of the plane without the ground being tilled. He told us that for a good twenty years after the war, the soil had stayed a lighter colour and nothing grew in the spot where the plane had dug into the fertile earth. With the passing of much time, the earth had healed itself and once again produced sustenance for the living.

We kicked around, looking for items that might be parts of the plane. I had no luck. Matthew, however, eager to help and with sharp young eyes, dug up various bits and pieces. The earth continued to expel her story, and in doing so sealed the wounds that had once left her barren.

In the end I carried away a number of pieces, small but indicative of a Lancaster, the remnants of EQ-P. There were pieces of Perspex, bubbled from heat and melted; twisted bits of aluminum metal; and an unheated piece that looked as though it might be a joiner plate with rivets. I was amazed to find these small pieces so long after the crash, as if the boys refused to stop sending messages to those willing to seek: *We are here, we existed, do not forget us.*

Standing there with the sun setting over the field and the village of Hilsenheim, I realized the boys could not have crashed in a better place. They died between the Black Forest and the Vosges mountains, in beautiful farmland with a church in the distance. The crash site clearly remained important in the memory of the Hilsenheim villagers, and especially so for the Steydli family, generation after generation, down to the youngest of their children. What more could a relative ask for when it came to providing a final resting place for their loved one? Here, beauty, respect, love, and remembrance surrounded them. They lived on.

28

A Celebration

We spent our last day in France travelling around Alsace, enjoying the sights with the Steydli family. They took us to Château du Haut-Kœnigsbourg in the Vosges range, where Sélestat, Hilsenheim, and Wittisheim spread out below us. We ate more of the delectable delights of Alsace and visited another museum. It was the evening, however, that will remain deeply embedded in my soul.

When we returned to Hilsenheim, the Steydlis made sure we had time to revisit the graves. I managed to keep myself together, but the pain of knowing this would be the last visit with the boys made me incredibly sad. I yearned to be able to walk to the graves whenever I wanted, to tend them and fill them with flowers as the Steydli family did. But I would have to content myself with saying goodbye and leaving the boys in their hands. After saying my final farewell, we walked back to the car and rode the short distance to Mr. and Mrs. Steydli's home.

The simple pleasures of family, food, and laughter filled the evening. Most of the family was there to share in the festivities, and hanging over all of us was a painting of EQ-P taking off on the night of March 15, 1944, which had been commissioned by Bob Hudson's family for the Steydlis in gratitude for all they had done for the boys and their families. There were several courses of food, each with a special drink to accompany it. There was a feast of culture as well. Mr. Steydli, in his wheelchair and with only one hand (he had lost the other in an accident), shared his love for music by playing a few tunes on his electric piano. The sense of vibrant lives lived in a caring and simple manner, void of pretence or pessimism, filled the house. Again I was reminded of a letter from Ken to Jean-Paul, quoting Tomi Ungerer's book *Alsace, The Open Heart of Europe*: "'Allergic to arrogance and adaptable, we take pride in being reliable. We like to share food and wine as well as opinions and ideas. We are salted and seasoned, knowing that one man's enjoyment is another man's pleasure' is a neat summation of the people of the Alsace."[1] And so it was.

We shared in a family celebration that included popping open a bottle of bubbly, with a whooping cheer from Mr. Steydli. He reiterated several times that night how words within various languages were not so different, using wine, with *vin* (French for wine) and *vino* (Italian), as his example as we drank. Thinking back, I believe he was trying to convey an important message with that simple example, communicating it the only way he knew how, given the language differences: we are not so different; we are, in fact, very much the same. We share a common background, a common goal, and, as such, are one family. His sheer pleasure made me realize what it meant to the Steydlis to have us there. His act of saving the Lancaster parts bore fruit each time he and his family celebrated meeting another family member—"the more the better," as Jean-Paul interpreted for his father.[2] I represented another link to the boys of EQ-P that until now had remained distant and uncelebrated. I also embodied another generation that would remember the story. Mr. Steydli's faith in keeping the salvaged parts of EQ-P was being rewarded, although he "never thought it would take so long."[3] It took nearly half a century before he began meeting the boys' relatives and sharing the pieces of the plane, but he gained deeper satisfaction with each family member who showed up searching for the past.

Brought together, our families celebrated, as one, the simplest yet deepest pleasures of life. We were free to speak, free to share, and free to enjoy those freedoms and continue our lives as we wished, thanks to the boys and all those who died to protect that right. We owed it to them to give our best in life. We had everything to celebrate.

=== 29 ===

"Why Now, Why So Late?"

————— ⚬ —————

We stood in Sélestat in the chill of the late-August dawn, waiting for the train that would take us to our Strasbourg connection for Paris and then back to London. I wished I had more time. The entire trip had flown by so quickly, and my brain desperately tried to absorb and process all the information I had collected over the days. We said our teary goodbyes to Monique and Claude before boarding the passenger coach with Jean-Paul and his family. The train began to move and we were off again.

During the short trip I struggled to express my feelings to Jean-Paul for what his family had done for us. With no clear way to say it in my own language, I knew there was no point in even attempting to articulate it in a language I hardly knew. I felt inept as I took the wad of cash from my pocket and handed it across the aisle to Jean-Paul, asking him to spend it on flowers for the graves on Remembrance Day. Jean-Paul protested that it was too much, but I explained as best I could that Ken had given me money for flowers, and I had added to his total, and that was its purpose. The amount did not matter.

The train stopped, and we hopped off and walked across the platform to where the TGV train would shortly arrive to take us to Paris. Jean-Paul and his family waited with us, all of us looking a little forlorn at the prospect of going our separate ways. Jean-Paul's eyes were as glassy as mine as we spent our last minutes in chat. This trip had affected him as much as it had me. Neither of us had existed the night of the crash. We had not been there to witness the devastation first-hand, yet we both carried the story of our families' intertwined pasts, and we both felt compelled to speak for the boys and share their story to make them a permanent part of history. I realized I would be leaving behind not only the boys, but also a kindred soul and a new part of my ever-growing family.

Too soon the train rolled into the station. I squeezed Jean-Paul's forearms and said goodbye and thank you, more with my eyes than with words. Michael and I got on the train and settled into our seats. Jean-Paul and his family stood near our window. As the train pulled out, we waved farewell, and that was that. We were on our way back to London and, the next day, to Australia.

"Why now, why so late? Why didn't people come ten years after the war? There would have been witnesses still around," Jean-Paul had stated in dismay as we stood on the platform at Strasbourg. I took these questions away with me to consider in more depth as we sped along the TGV line toward Paris.

I knew there were many answers. The First World War, the Great Depression, and then the Second World War had taken an emotional and financial toll on the people of North America. Many struggled desperately just to get by. Overseas travel was something for the rich or, for those travelling from Europe to the West, a means of finding a better prospect in life, as many of the boys' parents had done before the boys themselves were born. The five Canadian boys had never been off the continent before enlisting. For some, that was part of the enticement of joining the RCAF: it was a chance to be something better, to see new places, and to do what most others before them had not done—fly. They envisioned adventure.

When the war was over, with many a family having lost at least one member, they may have wished to ease their pain by allowing time to pass before looking for the missing. In the first five years after the war, the simple answer would have been that families did not know where exactly their loved ones died, let alone where they were buried, and were waiting for confirmation from the Casualties Office or the Missing Research and Enquiry Service.

Perhaps, when they learned where the boys rested, they feared what they might see if they visited war-ravaged Europe or how they might be treated as the family of a bomber crewman or that, knowing no language other than English, they would be unable to make their way in an environment so totally alien to that in which they lived.

As a child growing up in a later generation, removed from war, I wished, like Jean-Paul, that someone had come sooner and written it all down. The story would have been clearer and easier to put together. Even so, it would not have been easier for the families to bear. After all they had been through, even old wounds that appeared to have healed were forever evident. Each new laceration meant a more difficult and lengthy mending process. Some things, perhaps even now, are still too close to the heart to be opened up, to let the overwhelming pain seep in again.

Staring out the window as I pondered, I realized I would never know every detail of the boys' lives and deaths. I had, however, come an incredible distance from knowing not much more than their names.

PART 6

HOW COULD I FORGET?

30

Mizpah

H aving come so far, one would think I could put the past to rest, but that is not the case. Hardly a day goes by when I do not think of the boys. My mind continues to mull over what I do not know, those seemingly endless possibilities and questions that remain undefined and unanswered. Is it ever truly over? For me, the answer is no, and I suspect the same can be said for the rest of the families.

Looking through the photographs obtained on my travels, I take a closer look, without distractions, at the small and often overlooked aspects, like the epitaphs written at the bottom of each tombstone.

After the war, the graves of the many dead were officially marked by white headstones. The RCAF gave the families sixty characters at the base of the stone for a personal message. But how do you sum up a young man's life in sixty letters or fewer? What inscription could convey the sacrifice of losing your loved one in war?

We had taken photographs of the stones marking all the graves we visited, for the crews of BQ-J and SR-Q as well as EQ-P. Of all of them, one stone in particular evoked an immediate strong emotional response. On the tombstone of J. Clegg of SR-Q are the words *Beautiful memories silently treasured of a dear husband, son and daddy.* The words *memories silently treasured* and *daddy*—not *father* but *daddy*—burned my throat as I realized that memories are silent often because they are too painful to be spoken and that, sadly, most of those who lost their fathers were so very young.

The epitaphs on Bill's stone, *Thy will be done*, and Norm's stone, *After he in his own generation served the council of God, he fell asleep*, are quotes from the Bible, while Bob's, *At the going down of the sun and in the morning we will remember him*, is adapted from Laurence Binyon's poem "For the Fallen," originally written in 1914 in response to the great loss of life at the beginning of the First World War. It has come to mean so much more.

The inscription on Jock's stone reads *Ever remembered by his father and mother, brother and sisters*, while Larry's states *We loved him in life, let us not forget him in death*—both expressions of personal remembrance.

Bud's stone remains blank. Perhaps no words could come, no epitaph could appropriately express the grief felt by his family. That continues to bother me, but I too do not know what belongs there. It harks back to Clegg's *memories silently treasured*.

One stone alone carries a combined biblical and personal message. George's bears the epitaph:

MIZPAH

EVER REMEMBERED BY

PAT, GAIL, GEORGE, LEVI PARKER,

EDMONTON, ALBERTA

Mizpah means "watchtower" and appears in the Bible in Genesis 31:49—"The Lord watch between me and thee when we are absent one from another." It signifies an emotional bond between two people who have been separated, either physically or by the death of one of the two persons.

The use of the word *mizpah* on jewellery, such as brooches, rings, bracelets, and lockets, and on tombstones goes back to Victorian times, and it has continued to be used, especially in times of war. Such trinkets of love were like a talisman keeping a loved one safe. For those who could not be saved, the word was written on the stone as a final act of undying love, expressing the hope of being together again one day. The bonds of love refused to be broken even by death.

Although a *mizpah* was normally deemed a bond between two people, I believe the crew families and the Steydli family have made this a greater whole, a bond between many. A bond between those alive and those long since passed. The living look after the dead, remembering them through shared stories and by visiting the graves, while the dead unite the living, one generation after another, through those very same acts. There is an ongoing watching over of both those remaining and those gone. Not time, nor space, nor death itself can break that bond. The hope of all that *mizpah* implies remains.

31

In Memory

T oday the crew of EQ-P is remembered in a variety of ways, as a group and individually. Physical memorials as well as personal forms of remembrance of the boys remain. They are noted for their part in protecting our freedom.

The crew is remembered as part of the greater number on monuments such as the Bomber Command memorial in London, England, which opened on June 28, 2012. In Canada there is the Bomber Command Memorial in Nanton, Alberta. The 6 Group Memorial at Trenton, Ontario, and the Escadrille 408 Squadron Memorial in Edmonton, Alberta, also commemorate the dead. At Linton-on-Ouse there are two memorials: one is the Memorial Room at the RAF base; the other, a memorial specific to 408 Goose Squadron and 426 Thunderbird Squadron, is on the village green. The names of those who died in the air force are listed in the *Book of Remembrance* on Parliament Hill in Ottawa, Ontario, and in the Memorial Book in York Minster, York, England.

Individually, there have been three types of memorials to the boys: those in places related to the boys' upbringing, mentions in books, and geographical memorials. For example, Larry Doran is included in a list of volunteers from Kitsilano who served in the Second World War, which hangs in Kitsilano Secondary School in Vancouver, BC, where Larry went to school. Norm Lumgair is listed on the Thornhill Community Memorial at the Legion in his hometown of Thornhill,

Manitoba. Jock Cruickshank is included on the city cenotaph and the memorial in St. Mark's Church in Harrogate, England, where he grew up. There are many more.

Saskatchewan has an impressive memorial in the form of two books: *Their Names Live On: Remembering Saskatchewan's Fallen in World War II* and *Age Shall Not Weary Them: Saskatchewan Remembers its War Dead*. Both of them include information on Bill Taylor beyond just listing his name.

Three of the five Canadian boys have been commemorated in geographical memorials: Taylor Bay in Saskatchewan (Bill), Lumgair Creek in Manitoba (Norm), and Doran Creek near Quesnel in BC (not far from where Larry spent some years in his youth).[1]

On a personal level, the families remember the boys in their own individual ways. Since 1977, most of the families have made the pilgrimage to the graves in Hilsenheim at one time or another. Ken Burt, Bud's brother, flies the Second World War RCAF flag from his flagpole each Remembrance Day, and he has a painting, similar to the one commissioned by the Hudson family for the Steydlis, hanging in his living room. The Hudsons have a print of the commissioned work in their home, as I do in mine, thanks to their generosity. Each family also holds medals, log books, photographs, and letters that continue to nurture remembrance of those who have long since passed.

The Steydli family also proudly holds several memorials to the boys. Hanging on the wall of their most social of rooms, the dining room, is the painting of EQ-P. Below it is information about the boys' operational flight that night and drawings of the plane parts still in the Steydlis' possession. Some of those parts have taken on a new life as picture frames and the like, given to the families of the crew members and now residing in Alsace, Britain, the United States, Canada, and Australia. Smaller pieces that were dug from the crash site with the help of the Steydlis during various crew family pilgrimages have become the most personal relics from the boys' last moments.

The parts retained by the Steydli family can be found inside and outside their home and make up a permanent personal memorial for them. Some are kept as pristine working parts that have been loaned to local museum exhibits recording the history of the area. Others have been made into something new, such as the urn in the yard that began life in the 1940s as a propeller engine casing but today sits full of beautiful flowers. The date 15.3.44 is painted on the metal as a constant reminder of its original use and of the crew that died on the Steydlis' farmland so many years ago.

The aircraft parts themselves have become a symbol of many things as well as a memorial. They signify a bond between two groups of people on the same side but in different situations, people struggling for freedom, working for a common goal—the crew as liberators and those wishing to be liberated. They represent death and life, both physical and spiritual. And, maybe most importantly, the remaining pieces are a symbol of a united love for the men of EQ-P, who have not been forgotten.

Perhaps one day there will be no one to point out the spot where the plane crashed. Certainly one day, and, sadly, all too soon, there will be no family members who can say they knew any of the crew personally. At some point they will all have died, though most after living a long life thanks in part to the crew of EQ-P.

32

Remembering the Dead

T he seven men whose stories are told here, and whose photographs illustrate this book, represent all the average guys who flew in Bomber Command or, for that matter, were part of any armed forces in the Second World War. Because they did not survive to tell their story or were not part of the most memorable battles immortalized by books or movies, these men have been marginalized, lost, reduced to nothing more than a statistic in most books. However, by researching their individual pasts, searching war records, communicating with their families and those who experienced the night of March 15, 1944, walking in their footsteps, and making their story known, I am trying to ensure the crew of EQ-P is not only not forgotten but also remembered as the real individuals they were. They may have been lost, but now they live once more, to be remembered by another generation, lest we forget.

Nowadays we are far removed from the realities of a life under threat and disconnected from the people who fought in the Second World War, making it all too easy to forget these men. We are absorbed in our own lives and see no point in remembering a past before our own time or in trying to tease out the "truth" from sometimes differing accounts and theories. Too many people view history as a threefold monster—a monotony of facts, lessons we should learn, and often confusing and conflicting esoteric arguments about details that do not always give the whole story and that seem to have nothing to do with our present or future.

It is true that the history we know is but a small part of the whole story and only a fraction of the truth. The official record, factual as it may be, is too often written from the point of view of a handful of leaders—political, military, corporate, or otherwise—who speak for the many, but allow the many only a token appearance in their story.

In the case of the Second World War, for whatever reason, decisions have been made about what is or is not important enough to be included. Often what makes the cut are the biggest battles (even though many smaller battles are often required to get to the point of these larger, more prominent battles), official documents, and the hierarchical view, although no matter how many official views from either side one reads, they are still only the leaders' perspectives, far removed from the varied viewpoints of the common or front-line experience. Major battles and official records make great bones and provide a structure on which to hang more information, but they do not, on their own, create a three-dimensional story, and they do not make a complete history of what actually took place over the course of the war.

By ignoring parts of history because they seem to lack importance in the greater scheme of the war, by separating official hierarchical documents and personal experiences of individuals or groups, we lose the accuracy that history so ardently attempts to present. The complete account from all involved, the real human story, the true "his-story," is broken—and, worst of all, the next generation loses interest in the often inaccessible, remote account that results. Have we forgotten that thoughts and emotions drove our history in the first place? The belief that it is only the big battles that matter and that official documents are the only trusted source of information rips the heart out of history. Every battle, document, fact; each varying viewpoint; every individual's character and emotions are crucial for the retelling and should be brought together. Only then can we know the whole truth of the matter —mistakes, faults, victories, and all. Only then can it be our history.

When I watch a documentary that includes the voices of those average guys in the war, what I remember and talk about afterwards is the person on the front line. I am drawn to him because, even with all his flaws, he is the most human. It is he who makes history come alive. It is he who makes history accessible because the emotions and thoughts, *combined* with official records, create the fullest sensation of the human condition. He was there, he saw it, he lived it, and it shows.

The story of the boys of EQ-P would be very short, and would lack this human element, if I only looked at the big picture and did not consider their place within the war, the various records available, and the accounts of others.

However, it is easier to accept the history of leaders and official records than to seek out the individual human story. It is easier to accept or repeat what has been written than to make the effort to dig through the larger truth that sits silent and unspoken in the countless boxes in our own attics, in archives, and in the living who experienced the war. There are numerous archival records, such as service records and oral histories, that contain important and as yet untouched information on smaller battles and the individual human story. There are many stories still waiting to be gleaned from the living, from those who survived and from the families of those who did not. We should never be so complacent as to believe what is readily available is all there is to be found and that history is as it stands. History is only as complete as we make it. We passively let others tell us our history and then become frustrated when it doesn't give us answers or seems to be missing something. At our worst, we throw our history away like a broken toy. At our best, we squander our history by collecting it in unmarked boxes, by hiding it in unvisited museums and archives, by not speaking to our own relatives about it, let alone the world. We stifle its potential to communicate, not because that is our intention, but because we want to protect it—however, in doing so, we place it on a pedestal and forget it.

Some argue that there are problems with less official records— individuals relating what happened after the fact may forget things or may not have been privy to certain details. But do the official records contain all the information? According to Ben Morris, an oral historian, "Theories about memory open up debate among historians, many of whom are wary of it and prefer the primacy of archival research and documentary sources. As Alessandro Portelli has put it, they accept the dominant prejudice which sees factual credibility as the monopoly of written documents, refusing to even countenance that documents, like oral histories, are 'sometimes incomplete, inaccurate and deceiving.'"[1] Our wariness means we have become content to sit back and let the same stories be repeated as the only history available, denying the untold parts of history their rightful place beside those already told. The silence, the gap left by the untold parts, leaves history inevitably incomplete. Morris believes, and I agree, that

> the differences between the official history and the veterans' oral histories are not errors in memory or deceptions. Rather they are the result of the historian's starting point. By starting with the official history and triangulating back to the commander's diary and the war archives, one story emerges; whilst starting with the veterans' oral histories and comparing them with the commander's diary and the war archives reveals a different account of the same events . . . These oral histories . . . provide a "flesh and blood" recollection of life in a war zone, and recount a number of incidents which have been left out completely, incompletely recorded, or wrongly recorded in the official history.[2]

Being informed from all sides and all levels may make the telling of history more difficult but it also makes history more enriching, complete, and to the point, more human and truly ours. Taking into account all involved opens our eyes and forces us to think. And as Morris implies, one form of history over another is not the answer; we must use it all together.

Some might question why we should remember those who bombed German cities. They argue this bombing campaign was barbaric and cruel and, by extension, so were the men who flew the aircraft that dropped the bombs. But what we must keep in mind is the context of the time. Passing any sort of judgment on any person, imposing present standards on actions of the past, is unfair and involves speaking from a place of convenient hindsight. Having the full human story from the time helps us take into account the circumstances of the day. In the case of the boys of EQ-P, they died doing a job for us, the people.

They fought for our freedom. Their lives and history should count as much as those of any other person who served, and their voices should be heard. I, and all those who have contributed to bringing their history to light, just happen to be their spokespeople.

So who should remember them? We all should, not just the families and friends who loved them. Jim Mulholland, Bud's friend from Brampton who won the coin toss that saw them sign up for the air force, told me that in January 1945 he "bombed Stuttgart with one 4,000 lbs blockbuster, 6x1,000 lbs and four 500 pounders. There is no such thing as revenge but his thoughts were with me that night."[3] By war's end, Jim "had piloted 33 missions over Germany with 419 Moose Squadron and subsequently volunteered to fly the POWs back." He told me, "I have been blessed to attend Remembrance Day ceremonies every year. I was ill and in wheel chair [sic] . . . November 11, 2009, but was able to attend the services in Orillia. I laid a wreath on behalf of the Air Force. And, as I have done every Remembrance Day, I honour all those who fell. Foremost in my thoughts and memory is Bud Burt. He has not been forgotten."[4] Now "pushing 87 years," Jim still reflects on the night they flipped the coin: "At the time Bud seemed happy. God only knows would he [sic] be with us today had we used a different coin."[5]

When I stood at the cenotaph on Anzac Day 2011, I looked around the little park at the people who had come to pay their respects. Many had come, like me, as a family member of a war veteran, but most of us standing there had no firsthand knowledge of the person we had come to remember (unless, of course, that person happened to be alive and standing beside them, as my husband was with me). Even then, I question what we really know about our veterans. Some things remain locked in the private journal of one's mind for life.

Two years earlier I had known Bud only as a name, a poem, and a few pictures. The rest of the crew were strangers to me. Now they were family, they were my boys, my blood; they had become a part of me. What I found most interesting as I stood by the cenotaph at dawn, much more enlightened by my research, was that although the service was for those who had passed on, those who had served, and those still serving, not once was mention made of specific details from the lives of the men listed on the cenotaph. I listened to the words, but they did not make the dead on the stone or the living who had served real to me.

If I had stepped forward, pointed at the cenotaph, and asked, "Who are these men and what is their story?" could anyone have told me? Or would I have received a blank stare and an embarrassed shuffle of feet as people faced the reality that they did not know?

A cenotaph or memorial has its place, but if the names remain nothing more than names, their story dies with them. They are remembered as noble warriors rather than unique individuals with virtues, vices, and foibles. At best, we think of them as pure heroes, the saints and sacrificial lambs, and they become unrealistic. At worst, we forget them and stand at the cenotaph out of a sense of duty. We make them shells of their true selves. We forget they were young men, full of life, mischief, and dreams, just like us. As a result, we lack an understanding of, and empathy for, those who made the supreme sacrifice.

When I started this project I had no idea where it would take me. I wanted to know who these men were, what they had done, and what had happened to them. Only slowly did I become conscious of the fact that I was finding a way to remember and commemorate them by really getting to know the men and their lives beyond the cenotaph or memorial. In doing so, I fell in love with the real men and their individual and collective stories. In turn, I wanted to give that sense of remembrance of the whole crew to their families and to others.

You don't forget the people you love. They live on in your heart and mind, where feelings exist, not on a cold piece of stone. I want the names of the boys of EQ-P to be noted on those memorials, but I don't want them to be remembered only as people who died in a war whose names are now written on stone. I don't want them to be remembered as a general part of history told in bland terms. I want them to be remembered as distinct individuals who had lives; they were important to someone and deserve their own respected place in history.

May they be remembered forever for doing their part for our freedom.

Afterword

Separating the Geese from the Ganders

I did not arrive at my description of the events of March 15 and 16, 1944, in "Honking of Geese from Above" (Chapter 24) and "The Cold Dawn" (Chapter 25) merely by reading what others have speculated or believed. In my research I came across a good deal of primary information, even though this was not a special raid, like the ones to Leipzig or Nuremberg, which have been commemorated in books and movies. There were witness accounts, news articles, official documents, and books. Some were general references to the night, some connected to the Alsace region, and others directly linked to the boys. However, no one account or piece of documentation fully supported any other, no single source had the full story, and every source had its share of flaws. The result was the most frustrating jigsaw puzzle I have ever tried to piece together.

I questioned everything over and over as I tried to fit various puzzle pieces into the greater whole, twisting and turning them in the hope that I somehow was missing something of importance that would just fall into place if I held it the right way. If I chose to accept only one or two sources and ignored others that also had merit, I found I was leaving out crucial pieces. I rewrote the chapters numerous times, trying to decide what should and should not be said, and how I should approach it, trying to make a debate on logistics and perception into a story. That just did not work. Witness accounts, official records, questions about which aircraft were involved in the collision (if there actually was a collision), and the identities of night fighters, all posed their own problems.

With regard to witnesses, a lack of accuracy in perception or recollection, or a personal agenda, can lead a researcher astray. I believe in the sincerity of the witnesses whose accounts I've studied. They described what they honestly believed they saw on the night, sharing their version of the truth, as they recalled it, after many decades. Unfortunately, the logistics of some aspects of some accounts made me skeptical.

» Alphonse Spiller's Account

Alphonse Spiller's account raised serious doubts in my mind because of the time at which he claimed to have seen the bombers colliding and crashing, and the amount of detail he describes, even though the events occurred at a distance from him, during the dark of night.

I asked several people, including Second World War bomber aircrew and researchers, as well as enthusiasts who frequent air force forums online, for their view of Spiller's story. None accepted the story as a full possibility. Interestingly, while most dismissed the story entirely, Second World War bomber crew veterans, although skeptical, accepted the story to some degree, making allowances for such things as weather conditions and the closeness of the bombers within the bomber stream. Giving their responses serious consideration, and taking into account other information I had at hand, not just Spiller's story on its own, I was loath to remove his account. As other sources, including official documentation, proved just as flawed, I believed Spiller's story was important enough to keep and consider a little more closely.

I had two basic but opposing hypotheses and a third more likely hypothesis. The first: Spiller's story was entirely false. He dreamt it or made it up. For me, this conclusion seemed a little unfair unless I could prove his story was fabricated, which I couldn't. The second: Spiller's story was true. He did see what happened, he told the truth as he saw it, but for some reason his estimation of time was terribly wrong. Third, and most likely, he did see something that night, but what he actually saw was blurred or altered by four things: the mind's propensity to interpret/piece the events into a logical story; the information he later heard about the actual crashes, which he added to his account; other researchers' theories surrounding the events expanding his story; and the ravages of time on the mind.

At the heart of Spiller's story is his claim that he saw a night fighter attack a bomber at 0130 hours. That bomber collided with another plane, and the first bomber broke in two, while the second plane hit a third aircraft.

Spiller's story has two serious problems: the stated time of 0130, and the fact he was a considerable distance from an event happening at night. No witness accounts or documentation were found to support a time of 0130. As well, Spiller was looking into a night sky. It was not a moon period, but not full darkness either. The bombers had black bellies and were about 5,000–6,500 metres above the ground. These factors would have hindered his ability to see the events clearly and would have influenced his perception.

However, Spiller could have heard cannon or gun fire, as Louis Rudloff did in Artolsheim. He may have heard crunching or clashing sounds. Explosions or burning hulks falling from the sky would have been visible. An explosion or fire may have illuminated his view of the situation, making it possible for him to see several silhouetted aircraft. From such a distance they would have looked very close together. Considering that BQ-X, EQ-P, SR-Q, and BQ-J were all on fire before crashing, it is possible Spiller could have seen two or more flame-engulfed forms.

Taking all this into account, I felt Spiller's story deserved to be mentioned. If one chooses to disregard it, it is at least documented here as one of the stories told about this night, and so it should remain. It is the only report that suggests EQ-P was the aircraft being attacked and, after colliding with another aircraft, split in two. The fact EQ-P had split in two made it the likely choice for its positioning in my version. However, Spiller's story left me questioning which aircraft he had actually seen. Could official documents shed some light?

» Information from Official Documents

I discovered a mind-boggling array of records in the boys' service files: German documents, International Red Cross Committee (IRCC) and Casualty Enquiry records quoting German documents, and the RAF's Missing Research and Enquiry Service (MRES) forms compiled after the war. The few original German documents in some of the EQ-P crew service files consisted of one or two sheets stating the deceased's name, rank, service number, type of aircraft, date of death, and place buried.[1] The handwritten entry marking the date and time of the crash stated March 15, 1944, at 2345 hours.

Various captured German documents were translated and copied by the IRCC and Casualty Enquiry. The first was a *Totenliste* (official death list), which stated that a Lancaster had been shot down on March 15, 1944. It listed Jock, Bill, Bob, and Bud, along with J.F. Ennis (from SR-Q) and an unknown airman, as deceased.[2]

A handwritten note from the RCAF Casualty Branch recorded the information from German documents that stated a Lancaster was shot down on March 16, 1944, at 2230 near Hilsenheim. The same six men were listed and all but the unknown man were identified by their identity discs.[3] The four boys from EQ-P were buried on March 17, 1944, at Hilsenheim, while Sgt. Ennis was listed as buried on March 19 in Sundhausen, and the unknown man on March 19 at Hilsenheim.[4] Another typed copy of German documents carried the same information on the deceased as above but stated the Lancaster had crashed at 2345 at Hilsenheim on March 15, 1944.[5]

By the time the MRES began the long, gruelling, and somewhat grisly task of locating and verifying the graves of the dead or the missing and presumed dead, the war had ended. One of the conundrums it had to tackle was the confusion surrounding the boys of EQ-P and SR-Q. The two crews had been mixed together, with a number of members of both crews unaccounted for. In response, the MRES launched a casualty enquiry in an attempt to determine three specific things: the grave numbers for Jock, Bill, Bob, Bud, and Sgt. J.F. Ennis; the identity of the unknown man in Hilsenheim; and the fate of the still missing members of the crews.[6]

Another document arrived as part of the casualty enquiry, listing information from a captured German record. This record stated that a Lancaster had crashed at Hilsenheim on March 16, 1944, at 2230. Two men were killed, Sgts. J.F. Ennis and J.B. Bull,[7] and both were buried on March 19, 1944, in Sundhausen. Four bodies were unidentified.[8] An amendment to this record stated that Sgt. Bull was buried at Mussig, while Sgt. Ennis was buried at Sundhausen, both on March 19, 1944.[9]

In 1947, an initial investigative report was supplied when a member of the MRES went to Hilsenheim and visited the mayor, obtaining the following information:

A four engined bomber crashed in flames 2Kms from HILSENHEIM, on the road to WITTISHEIM,[10] at approximately 2330 hours[11] on the night of 15.3.44. The a/c [aircraft] broke in two, one portion falling near to WITTISHEIM. Seven bodies were found and buried in HILSENHEIM cemetery. The remains of the aircraft were taken away by the Germans, so no positive identification of Lancaster LL639 [an error that should have read LL637].[12]

Of the seven crewmen, three were identified.[13] "All were badly burnt."[14] The MRES was unable, through its talk with the mayor, to ascertain whether the bodies were clothed[15] and/or whether they had been buried in coffins. It was at this time that the MRES discovered that the Germans buried the bodies themselves, with no ceremony permitted, but the villagers secretly placed flowers on the graves the next night, in spite of a threat by the local German commandant.[16]

The MRES then carried out exhumations on May 16, 1947, for Hilsenheim and the day after, for Mussig. Neither cemetery exhumation confirmed the identities of the occupants. Besides charred and broken remains, only scraps of clothing were found. At Hilsenheim the cross noted four British airmen.[17] In the case of the Mussig graves the cross listed two British airmen, a Hensen,[18] and a J.B. Bull RAF, but the exact number of bodies in the grave could not be determined. Scraps of Royal Australian Air Force battle dress were found in one grave in Mussig,[19] which would be the uniform of Cecil Glenn Arthur, the only Australian in the crew. However, no verification in the form of any clearly identifiable means, such as an identity disc, was reported in the exhumation documents.[20]

In the end, the MRES and the RAF assumed the graves at Mussig held the remains of seven of the eight men of SR-Q. Ennis, upon further enquiry, turned out to be buried at Wittisheim.[21] The seven men of EQ-P were deemed to have been buried at Hilsenheim.[22]

The official record compilers, on both sides, had only collected information pertinent to their task. The result was not a clear or complete history of events but a starker outline. I felt the boys were probably buried as the MRES noted. Having been to Hilsenheim and spoken with the Steydli family, with the knowledge that the mayor was recalling events from three years prior that he may not have seen, I had a better understanding of how the information may not be as accurate as expected. It seemed possible that EQ-P and SR-Q could be linked in some sort of collision considering the proximity of both Bud's and Sgt. Ennis's bodies. It still wasn't clear proof, however, and I was left with three crash times (2230, 2330, and 2345).

» Research

Research into the Allied aircraft that went down in Alsace that night brought up more confusion. Over the decades, four Allied aircraft— EQ-P, SR-Q (the ABC-equipped Lancaster), BQ-J (which crashed in Artolsheim), and BQ-X (which crashed in Sondernach/Appenwihr and from which only Sgt. Harry C. Petty survived) have been included and placed within the story. Various permutations of which aircraft were involved, who was attacked when, and who crashed into whom have been put forward.

"La terrible nuit du 15 mars 1944," a story on the village of Wittisheim website, placed the Artolsheim crash as the first crash and commented that a little later an aircraft accidentally touched another plane and split in two during the collision, with the front half landing near Hilsenheim and the back near Wittisheim. The second aircraft fell near Mussig. No mention of a night fighter was given.[23]

In Etienne Barthelmé's book *Bombercrash in Alsace*, a different permutation is suggested. At 0130, on their way back from bombing, Lancaster SR-Q is attacked and collides with EQ-P and BQ-X.[24] Barthelmé also details BQ-J's story, attributing its demise to night fighter Heinz Rökker at 2226.[25]

In Patrick Baumann's original notes, he too initially suggests BQ-J as possibly a separate incident and EQ-P, SR-Q, and BQ-X as the three involved in the collision, but using Alphonse Spiller's account, places EQ-P as the aircraft which is attacked, possibly by Hauptmann

Reschke 1/NJG1. EQ-P then collides into SR-Q and in turn it bumps BQ-X. He also notes BQ-X has a damaged wing and that the pilot drops bombs in the region of Illhaeusern. One barn is set on fire as a result. The pilot loses control in the valley of Münster and crashes in the forest near Sondernach.[26]

In a later communication I had with Baumann, the story changes.[27] He reiterates and elaborates on BQ-X, noting from a text edition of the newsletter of the history of Illhaeusern that a bomber at low altitude, with a wing on fire, passes over Illhaeusern, headed in the direction of Münster. A few bombs from the aircraft drop on one barn. Witnesses in the valley of Münster state that a bomber circling at low altitude crashes near another farm in Sondernach. The bomber that crashed at Sondernach was BQ-X. As such, Baumann believes the accounts from Illhaeusern and the Münster valley refer to BQ-X. He also attributes, as does Theo Boiten, historian and author of the comprehensive *Nachtjagd War Diaries*, the downing of BQ-X to Major Rolf Leuchs of II/NJG6.[28] This suggests BQ-X was a separate incident.

With four aircraft listed as falling within the Alsace region and several variations on what caused their demise, the only clear thing was that none of what happened that night in the sky was actually clear. It seems likely that BQ-X was not involved, leaving EQ-P, SR-Q, and BQ-J as the probable three in Spiller's account. However, there was still the possibility that EQ-P and SR-Q had collided independently of BQ-J. This left me wondering if night fighter claims might narrow the situation further.

» Night Fighter Claims

By looking into the night fighter claims for the night, I'd hoped to be able to clear up some of the confusion, only to find more twists and turns to the night's events.

Etienne Barthelmé had attributed Heinz Rökker of 2 NJG/2 as responsible for the downing of BQ-J at 2226. Patrick Baumann suggested Hauptmann Reschke of 1 NJG/1 was responsible for EQ-P and SR-Q at 2232 and Major Rolf Leuchs of II/NJG6 for BQ-X at 2235. The original claim records were handwritten and verified through photographic evidence. Many of these documents are poorly recorded, faded, or illegible. When I looked at various claim documentation compiled by Tony Wood;[29] John Foreman, Johannes Matthews, and Simon W. Parry;[30] and Theo Boiten,[31] it was not quite so easy to come to a conclusion.

At first I too had believed Rökker to be involved. His claim—noted by Wood as well as Foreman, Matthews, and Parry—stated a four-engined bomber had been downed fifty kilometres south-west of Strasbourg at an altitude of 6,200 metres at 2226. BQ-J seemed likely. However, further research using Boiten's book and Rökker's own book[32] shows that Rökker downed a Lancaster near Aschaffenburg at 2230. Considering the four minutes between these two claims and the 250 kilometres in distance between these two positions, it would have been impossible for Rökker to have been involved in both, and with Rökker himself stating he was at Aschaffenburg, he couldn't have been involved in the downing of BQ-J at Artolsheim.

From these same sources, along with Boiten's conclusions, it became unlikely that Reschke was involved. His claim is a bomber at southwest Strasbourg, no height given, at 2232. Strasbourg is about fifty kilometres away from Sélestat.

Having considered the numerous times listed in the downing of EQ-P, I looked for anything that might work according to time and a plausible distance. First of all, the Hilsenheim mayor's estimated time of 2330 did not fit with anything in the area and, when considering the other 408 Squadron times at target (between 2314 and 2332), and the witness time of 2230 as the time the bomber stream travelled over the Alsace area, it is highly unlikely EQ-P could have been heading to or from the target. If heading over the Alsace at 2330, EQ-P would have been reached Stuttgart much later than the rest of the squadron air-craft. If heading back over the Alsace from Stuttgart, then they would have dropped their bombs over Stuttgart too early and flown directly into the incoming bomber stream.

With regard to the 2345 time, Oberleutnant Rolf Bussmann of 10/NJG5 makes two claims that might be of note. The first claim occurs at 2345 at Schlettert-Strasbourg at an altitude of 6,200 metres. The second claim takes place at 2356 near St. Die at 5,800 metres. Looking at the first claim, Boiten suggests 35 Squadron Lancaster ND708 or 466 Squadron Halifax HX341 as two possible victims. I questioned what

Schlettert stood for, as the German name for Sélestat is *Schlettstadt*. Could this have been a misspelling and as such was Bussmann suggesting a claim between Sélestat and Strasbourg? His second claim at 2356 near St. Die carries no link to a bomber. Both these times, however, would suggest EQ-P was on its way home from the target, thus without its bombs on board. Considering where it fell—within the route to the target instead of along the outbound route—and the fact the bomber stream by this point should not have been there to crash into, it all seemed a little too implausible. The second time of 2356 was even more unlikely; there would have been no logical reason for EQ-P to have turned around and flown twenty kilometres back toward the target if it had been on its way home.

The time of 2230 brought up one interesting point I could not deny. Although Unteroffizier Robert Koch is not mentioned as claiming a bomber in either Wood's or in Foreman, Matthews, and Parry's reports, he is listed in Boiten's book as the probable night fighter to have brought down BQ-J/SR-Q, making a claim for a Lancaster at southeast Sélestat at 2235. No other night fighter claims to have taken a bomber anywhere near this time or in this area. This claim not only fits the time and place, it also leaves it possible that a collision had taken place, as there was only one night fighter making a claim and three bombers that had been downed.

» My Decisions

Taking all of this information into consideration, I had to make my own decisions. It seemed likely that EQ-P, SR-Q, and BQ-J had been in close proximity to each other within the bomber stream on the way to the target. The Alsace area would have been close to where the bombers would turn onto the last leg of the route before the target. There were 863 bombers heading for Germany that night, most of them bound for Stuttgart, flying in the dark, going in the same direction in a loose formation of varying altitudes, which left them vulnerable to collision. In fact, British historian Leo McKinstry has stated that "on a maximum-effort raid, involving more than 600 heavy bombers, there would be an average of about eight collisions."[33] It was little wonder that information about what occurred in the sky seemed sketchy, whether it came from a witness or an official record.

According to Boiten, severe jamming of the night fighter and German radar communications occurred that night,[34] and thus it is likely Robert Koch had followed the signals emitted by SR-Q, which would have put him and other night fighters such as Leuchs within the bomber stream.

When examining Alphonse Spiller's account, the information surrounding Bud's last moments, and Koch's claim (the only claim in the area where three bombers came down), I was faced with a mystery that could not be unravelled. Spiller maintains he saw the first bomber being attacked before it collided with another and then split in two. As EQ-P was the only bomber to split in two it appeared likely that Koch had been after EQ-P. This fit with the information about Bud having attempted to axe his way out of the turret (something that seemed only possible if EQ-P had already been attacked and a bail-out had been ordered before the plane split in two; the movement of the tail end of the aircraft, after it split, would have made it near impossible to axe at the mountings of the turret, as he would have been pinned to the turret wall). EQ-P had likely been damaged by something before the collision and/or had incurred structural integrity issues from being attacked, which led to the bomber splitting in two. I could only speculate that EQ-P had either been directly attacked and damaged and was experiencing trouble, or alternatively, and much less likely, hit by stray bullets as one of the other two aircraft were attacked.

Koch's claim of a bomber southeast of Sélestat suggested he was focused on attacking SR-Q/BQ-J or he attacked whatever aircraft he could see and get close enough to shoot at. Considering Louis Rudloff heard cannon fire before BQ-J flew low over the houses in Artolsheim and then crashed, it seems plausible Koch was after BQ-J.

As one or more of the bombers attempted escape manoeuvres, the structural damage already incurred by a night fighter and/or by the collision itself caused EQ-P to split in two. If Koch was attacking BQ-J, it makes sense if the bomber had hit EQ-P instead of the other way around but of course none of this can be proven.

In the end, I had to make educated guesses, extracting plausible information to form a general picture of the most likely chain of events from a stack of possibilities. There is truth within all the data, and those internal truths deserve their place despite any perceptions at play. It was my responsibility to set out all the pieces in the most logical arrangement and as clearly as possible, using information from all sources and taking into account their similarities to each other. There are still gaps in the resulting picture, but I think I have presented as full an account of EQ-P's fate on the night of March 15—16, 1944, as possible at this time.

At least the witnesses had been there. They stated the bomber stream was going over the Alsace and the crashes happened at this point in the night, not after the bomber stream had long gone. Regardless of whether one chooses to believe Spiller's account of what happened in the sky that night, the realities on the ground speak for themselves.

Acknowledgements

Writing a book was not something to which I had ever given much thought. If I had known how long it would take, perhaps I would have never started, but I am glad I did. Writing requires a foundation, and my writing rests upon the assistance of a vast number of people.

I wrote this book because I was compelled by the seven young men of EQ-P. To those men, I say: You will always be an inspiration for simply being who you were. You are not forgotten. You continue to shape my life. You are in my thoughts almost every day and so you will remain.

To my family: Without my husband Michael's suggestion and constant nagging, I would have never endeavoured to write a book and send it to an editor. I owe my drive and determination, however, to my parents and my brother. You taught me to give one hundred percent, and so I have tried. Dad, if you had never planted that little seed about Bud being a tail gunner in a Lancaster bomber, I may never have gathered the curiosity to know more. Cousin Marg, creating the Burt family tree gave me the starting place from which to work. To my dear departed Ken, we did it! You were a kindred spirit. Your support and faith in me kept me going. My one regret is you did not get to see the book published.

To the families of the boys of EQ-P: Not only did you share your time, information, and photographs, you made the boys come alive through sharing your love for them. That enduring love for those boys has taken root in my heart and for that I am indebted to you.

To the wonderful people of the Alsace: Of utmost importance is the selfless love and respect shown by the Steydli family. The forethought to dig up and hide pieces of the aircraft at immense danger to your lives and the continued sharing of your knowledge and your home to the crew families will forever amaze me. Patrick Baumann, your gracious sharing of your research has shed much light into the darkness of that night and has captured the viewpoint of those on the ground. And to the villagers who defied a command and risked their lives to put flowers on the boys' graves: I respect your bravery and thank you for the honour you bestowed on the crew.

Researching also made me realize the incredible kindness of countless strangers. I do not have the space to individually name you, but I wish to thank you all for your assistance and suggestions. However, I reserve a special thank you to Kelvin Youngs for putting me in contact with George MacKillop. George, who has sadly passed, you were my rock and mentor. You saw something in my research from the very beginning and your belief in me, especially because you were a Second World War member of 408 Squadron, made a world of difference.

I have heard negative stories about working with editors and publishers. In my case I have nothing but the utmost respect and appreciation for those involved in making my book possible. To the first editor I approached but cannot remember your name, thank you for suggesting I contact Audrey McClellan when you could not take on my manuscript due to work commitments. Audrey, I could not have hoped for a better editor-author relationship. Your edits, suggestions, and shaping of the book were spot on. Your help and belief that this book should be published was heartening for an unpublished writer. The book would never have made it to a publisher without you. I cannot thank you enough.

Finally, I thank everyone at Heritage House for their support and vision. I would especially like to acknowledge Lara Kordic, who saw something worth publishing, and Jesmine Cham and Lenore Hietkamp, who spent many hours on edits, pulling together the many parts, and adding the final touches that make this a very special book for me.

Notes

PART 1: MEMORY FAILS ME

Chapter 1—Operation 5: Stuttgart

1. Theo Boiten, *Nachtjagd War Diaries: An Operational History of the German Night Fighter Force in the West, vol. 1: September 1939–March 1944* (Walton on Thames, UK: Red Kite, 2008), p. 373.

2. Kenneth H. Burt, handwritten notes of phone conversation with Kenneth A. Burt, September 1 and November 6, 2005.

3. Laurence Motiuk, *Thunderbirds at War: Diary of a Bomber Squadron* (Nepean, ON: Larmot Associates, 1998), p. 210.

4. Summary of Events, March 15, 1944, RAF Form 540, p. 3, from "408 RCAF Squadron, Linton-on-Ouse," Royal Canadian Air Force Operations Record Books, vol. 22655, Department of National Defence fonds (hereafter DND), RG 24-E-7, LAC.

5. *As It Happened: The Lancaster at War*, directed by Stephen Saunders, ASA Productions for the History Channel, off-air recording (Australia: SBS One, October 29, 2010), DVD.

6. The 4,000-pound "cookie" bomb was designed to create a blast effect, damaging buildings enough to allow the incendiary bombs access to exposed combustible materials, such as wood, and readily set it alight.

7. EMH/B Telegram en Clair 129/17, March 17, 1944 (reproduction copy number Q5-11144), from file "Lumgair, Norman Andrew J86440," "Second World War Service Files: Canadian Armed Forces War Dead" series, vol. 28021, DND, RG 24, LAC.

8. Summary of Events, March 1944, RAF Form 540, p. 3, LAC.

9. Martin Middlebrook and Chris Everitt, *The Bomber Command War Diaries: An Operational Reference Book 1939–1945* (Leicester, UK: Midland Publishing, 1996), p. 481.

10. Summary of Events, March 15, 1944, RAF Form 540, p. 3, LAC.

11. Motiuk, *Thunderbirds at War*, p. 210.

12. Detail of Work Carried Out, Stuttgart, March 15 and 16, 1944, Appendix A, RAF Form 541, p. 4, from "408 RCAF Squadron, Linton-on-Ouse," Royal Canadian Air Force Operations Record Books, vol. 22655, DND, RG 24-E-7, LAC.

13. Motiuk, *Thunderbirds at War*, p. 210.

14. Summary of Events, March 15, 1944, RAF Form 540, p. 3, LAC.

15. Bomber Command consisted of seven groups of approximately a dozen squadrons each, two squadrons often sharing an airfield. Canada's 6 Group was the only Canadian run group and was situated in the north of England.

16. Motiuk, *Thunderbirds at War*, p. 210.

17. Middlebrook and Everitt, *Bomber Command War Diaries*, p. 481.

18. Motiuk, *Thunderbirds at War*, p. 210.

19. Middlebrook and Everitt, *Bomber Command War Diaries*, p. 481.

20. Kenneth H. Burt, handwritten notes of phone conversation with Kenneth A. Burt, September 1 and November 6, 2005.

21. Boiten, *Nachtjagd War Diaries*, p. 373.

22. Pathfinders, specialized crews designated to mark the bombers' route and target, dropped a variety of "TI" (target indicator) markers/flares during a bombing operation. Target markers, depending on weather conditions, consisted of ground flares and/or sky parachute flares. Sky markers were typically green with green, red,

or sometimes yellow stars. They were easily sent off target by winds. Pathfinders were positioned throughout the bomber stream to drop new flares, as they would eventually burn out. This also helped to keep the bombers on time and on target.

23. Middlebrook and Everitt, *Bomber Command War Diaries*, p. 481.

24. Detail of Work Carried Out, March 15 and 16, 1944, RAF Form 541, p. 2, LAC.

25. Summary of Events, March 1944, RAF Form 540, p.3, LAC.

26. Information on March 15 and 16, 1944, from "Daily Operations," *No. 6 Bomber Group* website, 6bombergroup.ca/March44/March15-1644.html.

27. Middlebrook and Everitt, *Bomber Command War Diaries*, p. 481.

28. Summary of Events, March 15, 1944, RAF Form 540, p. 3, LAC.

29. Detail of Work Carried Out, March 15 and 16, 1944, RAF Form 541, pp. 2-3, LAC.

30. Motiuk, *Thunderbirds at War*, p. 210.

31. Middlebrook and Everitt, *Bomber Command War Diaries*, p. 481.

32. Summary of Events, March 15, 1944, RAF Form 540, p. 3, LAC.

33. Ibid.

34. Kenneth H. Burt, handwritten notes of phone conversation with Kenneth A. Burt, September 1 and November 6, 2005.

Chapter 2—Telegrams and Letters, Shattered Hopes and Dreams

1. Ken Burt, email to author, February 23, 2010. Ethel Burt was the author's grandmother.

2. Squadron Leader Miles for (D.S. Jacobs) Wing Commander, 408 RCAF Squadron, letter to R.W. Lumgair, March 18, 1944, from file "Lumgair, Norman Andrew J86440," "Second World War Service Files: Canadian Armed Forces War Dead" series, vol. 28021, DND, RG 24, LAC.

3. W.R. Gunn, Squadron Leader, RCAF Casualties Office, letter to R.W. Lumgair, March 25, 1944.

4. Squadron Leader Miles for (D.S. Jacobs) Wing Commander, 408 RCAF Squadron, letter to R.W. Lumgair, March 18, 1944.

5. Ken Burt, email to author, February 23, 2010.

6. Bud went by a more formal name at work and thus was called Bob, short for Robert.

7. E.L. Volkes, letter to Mr. and Mrs. Robert Burt, March 25, 1944, in possession of Ken Burt.

8. Pat Parker, letter to Mr. and Mrs. Burt, April 1, 1944.

9. Marjorie Doran, letter to Mr. Burt and family, April 3, 1944.

10. RCAF Casualties Office, letter to R.W. Lumgair, July 22, 1944, file "Lumgair, Norman Andrew J86440," vol. 28021, LAC.

11. RCAF Casualties Office, letter to Mr. H.H. Taylor, September 5, 1944, file "Taylor, William J89913," vol. 28786, LAC.

12. Madeline Hudson, letter to Clarence Hudson, November 14, 1944.

13. RCAF Casualties Office, letter to Robert Lumgair, December 6, 1944, file "Lumgair, Norman Andrew J86440," vol. 28021, LAC.

14. RCAF Casualties Office, letter to R.W. Lumgair, December 11, 1944, file "Lumgair, Norman Andrew J86440," vol. 28021, LAC.

15. R.W. Lumgair, letter to RCAF Casualties Office, January 3, 1945, file "Lumgair, Norman Andrew J86440," vol. 28021, LAC.

16. Both Bud's and Bob's formal first name was Robert. The boys from the crew likely slept side by side at Beningbrough Hall, and it is thus possible the authorities

clearing their belongings from the room had mistakenly placed some of Bud's items in with Bob's. It's not known what happened to the address book and other items.

17. Madeline Hudson, letter to Mr. and Mrs. Burt, March 5, 1945.

18. David L. Bashow, *None but the Brave: The Essential Contributions of RAF Bomber Command to Allied Victory During the Second World War* (Kingston: Canadian Defence Academy Press, 2009), p. 27.

19. Patrick Walker, email to author, May 18, 2011.

20. Patrick Walker, email to author, May 14, 2011; death certificate of William John Doran.

21. Gail Parker, email to author, June 8, 2011.

22. Pat Parker, letter to Estate Branch, August 12, 1945, file "Parker, George J85528," vol. 28375, LAC.

23. Director of Estates, letter to Pat Parker, August 21, 1945, file "Parker, George J85528," vol. 28375, LAC.

24. Estates Branch, letter to Robert Burt, November 20, 1945, reproduction copy number Q4-35021 file "Burt, Robert George Alfred R206418," "Second World War Service Files: Canadian Armed Forces War Dead" series, vol. 24972, RG 24, DND, LAC.

25. Estates Branch, letter to Myrtle Burt, January 22, 1946, file "Burt, Robert George Alfred R206418," vol. 24972, LAC.

26. Pat Parker, letter to Mrs. Taylor, June 6, 1946.

27. RCAF Casualty Office, letter to W. Lumgair, March 4, 1948, file "Lumgair, Norman Andrew J86440," vol. 28021, LAC.

28. RCAF Casualty Office, letter to W. Lumgair, August 30, 1949, file "Lumgair, Norman Andrew J86440," vol. 28021, LAC.

Chapter 3—The Beginning of a Love Affair

1. In fact, Bud was still only nineteen years old when he died. The CWGC marks age according to the closer birth date, not the actual age at the time of death.

2. The story was later removed from the website when the site was revamped.

Chapter 5—Making Connections

1. David W. Machin (nephew to Douglas Cruikshank), email to author, March 9, 2010.

PART 2: OF WHOM DO YOU SPEAK?

Chapter 6—The Background of War

1. Britain, Canada, Australia, and New Zealand each made financial contributions to establish the British Commonwealth Air Training Plan (BCATP). Canada made a significant donation, paying over half the total cost of $2.2 billion. "The British Commonwealth Air Training Plan," *Veterans Affairs Canada* website, veterans.gc.ca/eng/remembrance/history/historical-sheets/britcom.

2. "British Commonwealth Air Training Plan," *Bomber Command Museum of Canada* website, bombercommandmuseum.ca/bcatp.html.

3. "Canada in the Second World War," *Juno Beach Centre* website, junobeach. org/e/4/can-tac-air-bca-e.htm.

4. "British Commonwealth Air Training Plan," *Bomber Command Museum of Canada* website, bombercommandmuseum.ca/bcatp.html.

5. Aircraft silhouette manuals noted different features of engines, tails, wings, etc., of both Allied and enemy aircraft. Gunners would be tested in flash drills, where images or silhouettes flashed up on a screen for very short periods.

6. Students learned how to wear and maintain their gas protection gear, such as their gas mask, as well as how to detect, protect, and administer treatment in the case of a gas attack.

7. "British Commonwealth Air Training Plan," *Bomber Command Museum of Canada* website, bombercommandmuseum.ca/bcatp.html.

8. Ibid.

Chapter 7—The Boys of EQ-P

1. Evelyne Johnson, comments written down and emailed by Ken Burt to author, June 7, 2011.

2. Ibid.

3. Ibid.

4. Ibid.

5. Ken Burt, email to author, March 1, 2010.

6. RCAF Attestation Paper Form R. 100, November 20, 1942, file "Burt, Robert George Alfred R206418," vol. 24972, LAC.

7. Ken Burt, email to author, March 1, 2010.

8. Robert Oliver Burt, Attestation: Non-Permanent Active Militia of Canada, June 22, 1939, Lorne Scots Regimental Museum.

9. Robert George Alfred Burt, Attestation: Non-Permanent Active Militia of Canada, June 11, 1941, Lorne Scots Regimental Museum.

10. Ken Burt, email to author, March 1, 2010.

11. "French safe" was the term commonly used at that time for a condom.

12. Ken Burt, email to author, February 23, 2010.

13. Jim Mulholland, CD private interview by Ken Burt, June 16, 2011.

14. RCAF Attestation Paper Form R. 100, November 20, 1942, file "Burt, Robert George Alfred R206418," vol. 24972, LAC.

15. Jim Mulholland, CD private interview, June 16, 2011.

16. Robert George Alfred Burt, Statement of Services, November 22, 1942, Lorne Scots Regimental Museum.

17. Dorothy Swan, letter of reference, October 19, 1942, file "Burt, Robert George Alfred R206418," vol. 24972, LAC.

18. H.F. Loughin, letter of reference, October 19, 1942, file "Burt, Robert George Alfred R206418," vol. 24972, LAC.

19. RCAF Personal Record, October 30, 1942, file "Burt, Robert George Alfred R206418," vol. 24972, LAC.

20. J. Douglas Harvey, *Boys, Bombs and Brussels Sprouts: A Knees-up, Wheels-up Chronicle of WWII* (Halifax: Goodread Biographies, 1982), p. 24.

21. Ibid., pp. 23–25.

22. Recruits' Training Record, No. 1 Manning Depot Toronto, Ontario, December 31, 1942, file "Burt, Robert George Alfred R206418," vol. 24972, LAC.

23. RCAF Certificate of Education, February 26, 1943, file "Burt, Robert George Alfred R206418," vol. 24972, LAC.

24. Robert Burt, letter to Evelyne Johnson (née Burt), April 22, 1943.

25. Robert Fleming, CFB Trenton, email to author, March 3, 2010.

26. Gunners needed to be able to fix any issues with their guns within the confines of their turret during an operation. They would be unable to move much in the turret or see in the dark, and would be wearing gloves to keep them from getting frostbite.

27. RCAF Training Report for Air Gunner (Stage I), No. 2 AGGTS, Trenton, Ontario, June 11, 1943, file "Burt, Robert George Alfred R206418," vol. 24972, LAC.

28. Air-to-ground firing involved shooting various targets, positioned on the ground, from a moving aircraft. These targets might be dummy airfields, cutouts of ships, or buildings.

29. Air-to-air firing was usually done by gunners flying in their aircraft and shooting at a target attached to another moving aircraft. Shooting on the ground and in the air had different effects, so when they were in the air, gunners had to learn to compensate for bullet deviation from drift, gravity, their own aircraft's movement as they shot, and air resistance. In the air, the angle of the turret guns and the force of the slipstream caused bullets to move in different ways.

30. RCAF Training Report for Air Gunner (Stage II), No. 2 AGGTS, Trenton, Ontario, July 23, 1943, file "Burt, Robert George Alfred R206418," vol. 24972, LAC.

31. Robert Burt, letter to Evelyne Johnson (née Burt), no date.

32. Ken Burt, March 1, 2010.

33. Pat Johnson, email to author via daughter, April 8, 2012.

34. Ibid., November 14, 2009.

35. Ibid., April 8, 2012.

36. Ibid., November 14, 2009.

37. Ibid., November 14, 2009.

38. Ibid., April 8, 2012.

39. Ibid., November 14, 2009.

40. Ibid.

41. Ibid., April 8, 2012.

42. Ibid., November 14, 2009.

43. "Wanted . . . A Picture of Initial Training Wing Bridlington," online forum of the Stirling Aircraft Society Affiliated to the Bomber Command Association, July 19, 2011, sas.raf38group.org/forum/viewtopic.php?f=6&t=542 (accessed May 24, 2012).

44. Curve of fire/deflection refers to the adjustment a gunner has to make when positioning and shooting his guns to account for the movement of the night fighter and the distance it will shift between the time the gunner shoots and the time the bullets (also with their own movement influenced by the gun's position and winds) arrive at the target aircraft.

45. Harmonization refers to on-the-ground adjustments made so that the gunsight and guns work in harmony. The gunner lines up the gunsight so it aims where the gun fires. In the air, when shooting at a target, the bullets would then be concentrated in the area the gunner sighted for the specified distance. From "Warrant Officer Ernie Reynolds," *The Second World War Experience Centre* website, war-experience.org/lives/ernie-reynolds-w-o-raf (accessed May 24, 2012).

46. Ibid.

47. Robert Hudson, letter to Cag Hudson, no date.

48. Doug Chisholm, *Their Names Live On: Remembering Saskatchewan's Fallen in World War II* (Regina: Canadian Plains Research Centre, University of Regina, 2001), pp. 193–94.

49. Attestation Paper RCAF Form R. 100, file "Taylor, William J89913," vol. 28786, LAC.

50. Laura Smith, email attachment of Dorothy Mitchell's (née Taylor) recollections to author, March 24, 2010.

51. Chisholm, *Their Names Live On*, p. 194.

52. Laura Smith, email to author, March 24, 2010.

53. Attestation Paper RCAF Form R. 100, file "Taylor, William J89913," vol. 28786, LAC.

54. Laura Smith, email to author, March 24, 2010.

55. Laura Smith, email attachment of Edna Wagner's (née Taylor) recollections to author, December 5, 2009.

56. Frank Ast, letter of reference, November 17, 1941, file "Taylor, William J89913," vol. 28786, LAC.

57. General Remarks by the Medical Officer on his Impression of the Candidate, January 23, 1942, file "Taylor, William J89913," vol. 28786, LAC.

58. RCAF Interview Report Appendix D M.20/10, February 4, 1942, file "Taylor, William J89913," vol. 28786, LAC.

59. Occupational History Form, March 18, 1942, file "Taylor, William J89913," vol. 28786, LAC.

60. Medical Records, June 15, 1942, file "Taylor, William J89913," vol. 28786, LAC.

61. No. ITS School Letter, August 3, 1942, file "Taylor, William J89913," vol. 28786, LAC.

62. RCAF Report on Pupil Pilot—Flying and Ground Training T.58A, no date, file "Taylor, William J89913," vol. 28786, LAC.

63. Chisholm, *Their Names Live On*, p. 194.

64. Dual flights were done with a qualified co-pilot, while solo flights were done by trainees on their own after instruction and dual flights had been completed.

65. RCAF Report on Pupil Pilot—Flying and Ground Training T.58A, no date, file "Taylor, William J89913," vol. 28786, LAC.

66. Ibid.

67. Ceased Training Certificate, December 9, 1942, file "Taylor, William J89913," vol. 28786, LAC.

68. Steve Fortescue, email to author, July 5, 2011.

69. *As it Happened: The Lancaster at War*, directed by Stephen Saunders.

70. General Conduct Sheet, December 18, 1942, file "Taylor, William J89913," vol. 28786, LAC.

71. Laura Smith, email attachment of Florence Farr's (née Taylor) recollections to author (as supplied to the Carievale and District History Book, 1988), December 5, 2009.

72. R.C. Form 1, December 22, 1942, file "Taylor, William J89913," vol. 28786, LAC.

73. Air Bombers (T.81 Revised) No. 5 B&G School, March 2, 1943, file "Taylor, William J89913," vol. 28786, LAC.

74. Part II (For Air Bombers) No 1 C.N.S. Rivers, Manitoba, May 28, 1943, file "Taylor, William J89913," vol. 28786, LAC.

75. Form T.81—Part IV, para. 12 for Air Bomber Final Assessment, May 28, 1943, file "Taylor, William J89913," vol. 28786, LAC.

76. Chisholm, *Their Names Live On*, p. 194.

77. Charlie Lumgair, email to author, May 17, 2010.

78. Ibid.

79. RCAF Attestation Paper, February 12, 1941, file "Lumgair, Norman Andrew J86440," vol. 28021, LAC.

80. Charlie Lumgair, email to author, May 17, 2010.

81. Ibid.

82. RCAF Attestation Paper, February 12, 1941, file "Lumgair, Norman Andrew J86440," vol. 28021, LAC.

83. Robert Lumgair (DFC) served in 408 Squadron at Leeming and for a short while at Linton-on-Ouse before Norm arrived on the squadron.

84. RCAF Interview Report, February 9, 1942, file "Lumgair, Norman Andrew J86440," vol. 28021, LAC.

85. Occupational History Form, March 20, 1942, file "Lumgair, Norman Andrew J86440," vol. 28021, LAC.

86. RCAF Medical Board, January 27, 1942, file "Lumgair, Norman Andrew J86440," vol. 28021, LAC.

87. Fish skin is typically known today as eczema.

88. Certificate of Medical Examination, January 1, 1942, vol. 28021, file "Lumgair, Norman Andrew J86440," LAC.

89. Case History Sheet, June 6, 1942, file "Lumgair, Norman Andrew J86440," vol. 28021, LAC.

90. General Remarks by the Medical Officer on his Impression of the Candidate, June 16, 1942, file "Lumgair, Norman Andrew J86440," vol. 28021, LAC.

91. RCAF Report on Pupil Pilot—Flying and Ground Training T.58A, no date, file "Lumgair, Norman Andrew J86440," vol. 28021, LAC.

92. Ibid.

93. Ibid.

94. Ibid.

95. By now Robert was at 408 Squadron in Leeming, becoming initiated in squadron life.

96. "Bralorne Personalities," The Communicator (Bralorne Community Club) 1, no. 22, November 18, 1938, Bralorne Pioneer Museum, Bralorne, BC.

97. Patrick Walker, email to author, May 18, 2011.

98. "Bralorne Personalities," The Communicator.

99. Kitsilano Junior–Senior High School Annual, 1931 (information obtained with kind permission of the school, April 26, 2010).

100. "British Columbia is a gold mine province . . . fortunes will be made from its mines," A.E. Jukes & Co., Vancouver, BC, 1933, AM1519-:PAM1933-77, Pamphlet Collection, City of Vancouver Archives.

101. "Bralorne Personalities," The Communicator.

102. Ibid.

103. Patrick Walker, email to author, May 18, 2011.

104. General Manager, Bralorne Mines Ltd., letter of reference, April 23, 1941, file "Doran, William Lawrence J86233," vol. 25226, LAC.

105. K.G. Kern, North American Life Assurance Co., letter of reference, April 21, 1941, file "Doran, William Lawrence J86233," vol. 25226, LAC.

106. RCAF Special Reserve Interview Report, April 22, 1941, file "Doran, William Lawrence J86233," vol. 25226, LAC.

107. History of Present Condition, April 23, 1941, file "Doran, William Lawrence J86233," vol. 25226, LAC.

108. Occupational History Form, June 5, 1941, file "Doran, William Lawrence J86233," vol. 25226, LAC.

109. History of Present Condition, August 15, 1941, file "Doran, William Lawrence J86233," vol. 25226, LAC.

110. RCAF Report on Pupil Wireless Operator (Air Gunner) Air and Ground Training, Part 1 Initial Training, August 27, 1941, file "Doran, William Lawrence J86233," vol. 25226, LAC.

111. Department of Pensions and National Health Canada, January 13, 1942, file "Doran, William Lawrence J86233," vol. 25226, LAC.

112. RCAF Report on Pupil Wireless Operator (Air Gunner) or Air Gunner Air and Ground Training, Part 1, April 24, 1942, file "Doran, William Lawrence J86233," vol. 25226, LAC.

113. Part II Armament Training Gunnery, May 25, 1942, file "Doran, William Lawrence J86233," vol. 25226, LAC.

114. Board of Officers, May 25, 1942, file "Doran, William Lawrence J86233," vol. 25226, LAC.

115. William Lawrence Doran, log book.

116. Ibid.

117. Confidential Personal Assessment, December 1, 1942, vol. 25226, file "Doran, William Lawrence J86233," LAC.

118. Will, February 5, 1943, file "Doran, William Lawrence J86233," vol. 25226, LAC.

119. P/O Sveinson, promotion letter to CSO of No. 2 AOS Edmonton, April 30, 1943, file "Doran, William Lawrence J86233," vol. 25226, LAC.

120. Confidential Personal Assessment, May 10, 1943, file "Doran, William Lawrence J86233," LAC.

121. Gail Parker, email to author, June 9, 2011.

122. Gail Parker, letter to author, January 11, 2010.

123. RCAF Interview Report Special Reserve Appendix "D" M.20/10, April 15, 1942, file "Parker, George J85528," vol. 28375, LAC.

124. RCAF Order on Optician, July 25, 1942, file "Parker, George J85528," vol. 28375, LAC.

125. General Remarks by the Medical Officer on his Impression of the Candidate, September 19, 1942, file "Parker, George J85528," vol. 28375, LAC.

126. RCAF Report on Pupil Air Navigators Air and Ground Training, November 12, 1942, file "Parker, George J85528," vol. 28375, LAC.

127. Part II (For Air Navigators), March 19, 1943, file "Parker, George J85528," vol. 28375, LAC.

128. Ibid.

129. "The RAF Halton Aircraft Apprentice Scheme," oldhaltonians.co.uk/pages/news/Halton%20Story.pdf (accessed May 17, 2018).

130. Ibid.

131. J. Rickard, "No. 240 Squadron (RAF): Second World War," *Military History Encyclopedia on the Web*, July 11, 2011, historyofwar.org/air/units/RAF/240_wwII.html (accessed July 25, 2011).

132. Alan Mawby, email to author, June 6, 2012.

133. Gordon Cruickshank, email from family conveying Gordon's comment to author, April 5, 2010.

134. A drop in rank may occur for a number of reasons. It is possible he was punished for some sort of personal or on-the-job misconduct. Or perhaps he simply did not have the qualifications for a particular job and thus dropped in rank while obtaining the required training.

135. CSV Action Desk/BBC Radio Lincolnshire, "No 4 School of Technical Training (1942)—Part 1," *WW2 People's War* website (Article ID: A7798369), December 15, 2005, bbc.co.uk/ww2peopleswar/stories/69/a7798369.shtml (accessed July 25, 2011). The page is no longer available on the website.

Chapter 8—The World by Mid-1943
1. Middlebrook and Everitt, *Bomber Command War Diaries*, p. 763.
2. Armstrong, John G. "RCAF Identity in Bomber Command: Squadron Names and Sponsors," *Canadian Military History*, no. 2 (1999): Article 5, p. 47.

PART 3: HAVE WE MET BEFORE?

Chapter 9—Moving On, Moving Forward, but Never Quite Forgotten
1. Gail Parker, email to author, June 8, 2011.
2. *408 Squadron History* (Belleville, ON: The Hangar Bookshelf, 1984), p. 37.
3. Middlebrook and Everitt, *Bomber Command War Diaries*, p. 763.
4. Ibid., p. 711.
5. Bashow, *None but the Brave*, p. 26.
6. Edward Fleming, interview with author, March 20, 2010.
7. There are two working Lancasters in the UK: one at RAF Coningsby in Lincolnshire that flies in the Battle of Britain Memorial Flight; and another, *Just Jane*, at East Kirby, Lincolnshire, that takes passengers as it taxies along a wartime runway. A third working Lancaster, in Hamilton, Ontario, offers flights to civilians.

Chapter 10—To England
1. "Riots and Looting Not to Be Trifled With," *Toronto Telegram*, May 16, 1945, in *Collections—Democracy at War: Canadian Newspapers and the Second World War*, Canada War Museum, collections.civilisations.ca/warclip/objects/common/webmedia.php?irn=5074035 (accessed June 23, 2011).
2. Robert Burt, postcard to Evelyne Burt, August 7, 1943.
3. Laurie Woods, *Flying into the Mouth of Hell* (Australian Military History Publications, 2003), p. 37.
4. Edward Fleming, interview with author, March 20, 2010.
5. "Princes Pier Railway Station, Greenock," in the exhibit *Port Number One, Waterways and Recovery Bays*, on the *Remembering Scotland at War* website, http://rememberingscotlandatwar.org.uk/online-museum.
6. Woods, *Flying into the Mouth of Hell*, p. 39.
7. Ibid.
8. Harvey, *Boys, Bombs and Brussels Sprouts*, p. 31.
9. Ibid., pp. 35–36.
10. Hospital or Sick List Record Card, August 5, 1943, file "Lumgair, Norman Andrew J86440," vol. 28021, LAC.
11. RAF Training Report Pilot No. 1511 Beam Approach Training Flight, July 15, 1943, file "Lumgair, Norman Andrew J86440," vol. 28021, LAC.
12. RAF Training Report, No 15 (P) Advanced Flying Unit, RAF Form 5014, August 21, 1943, file "Lumgair, Norman Andrew J86440," vol. 28021, LAC.
13. George Parker, log book.
14. R.A.F. Training Report Air Bomber F.A.F. Form 5030, August 11, 1943, file "Taylor, William J89913," vol. 28786, LAC.
15. Duxford Radio Society (Radio Section at the Imperial War Museums Duxford), "Equipment History Summary File, Transmitter T1154/Receiver R1155 (British RAF 1941)," 2004, *Duxford Radio Society* website, duxfordradiosociety.org/equiphist/r1155/t1154-r1155-V4-jan2015.pdf.
16. RAF No. 4 AOS/(O)AFU Advanced W/T (Pre-OTU) Course Training Report, August 22, 1943, file "Doran, William Lawrence J86233," vol. 25226, LAC.
17. Robert Burt, postcard to Mrs. Burt, September 3, 1943.

Chapter 11—Becoming a Crew

1. Heavy bombers, such as the seven-man Halifax and Lancaster aircraft, were larger, more powerful aircraft that carried a greater bomb load and were able to fly longer distances than medium bombers, such as the Wellington. The boys incrementally learned their trades and moved from small to larger aircraft as their knowledge and ability progressed.

2. RAF Training Report Air Bomber No. 22 O.T.U. RAF Form 5034, November 7, 1943, file "Taylor, William J89913," vol. 28786, LAC.

3. Confidential Personal Assessment, November 7, 1943, file "Taylor, William J89913," vol. 28786, LAC.

4. Confidential Personal Assessment, Graydon Station, November 4, 1943, file "Doran, William Lawrence J86233," vol. 25226, LAC.

5. RAF Training Report 22 Operational Training Unit Sub form 5042, November 7, 1943, file "Doran, William Lawrence J86233," vol. 25226, LAC.

6. Larry Doran, letter to mother and sister Eileen, September 23, 1943. According to the Doran family, the letter did not arrive until after Larry's death in March 1944.

7. Final Training Report, November 7, 1943, file "Parker, George J85528," vol. 28375, LAC.

8. Personal Assessment, November 7, 1943, file "Parker, George J85528," vol. 28375, LAC.

9. RAF Training Report Pilot No. 22 OTU Form 5015, November 7, 1943, file "Lumgair, Norman Andrew J86440," vol. 28021, LAC.

10. RAF Training Report Air Gunner Form 5037 No. 22 OTU, November 18, 1943, file "Burt, Robert George Alfred R206418," vol. 24972, LAC.

11. E.L. Volkes, letter to Robert Burt, November 2, 1943.

12. Bashow, *None but the Brave*, p. 85.

13. Edward Fleming, interview with author, March 20, 2010.

14. Robert Burt, postcard to Mrs. Burt, December 17, 1943.

15. Robert Burt, poem to Audrey Harris, no date.

16. RAF Case Sheet—Station or Hospital Record Form 41, January 2, 1944, vol. 28375, file "Parker, George J85528," LAC.

17. William Taylor, letter to Mrs. Harry Taylor, January 20, 1944.

18. Ibid.

19. Harvey, *Boys, Bombs and Brussels Sprouts*, p. 33.

20. RAF Case Sheet—Station or Hospital Record Form 41 January 21, 1944, vol. 24972, file "Burt, Robert George Alfred R206418," LAC.

21. William Taylor, letter to Mrs. Harry Taylor, January 20, 1944.

22. William Taylor, letter to Herbert Taylor (brother), February 14, 1944.

23. February 2, 1944, file "Parker, George J85528," vol. 28375, LAC.

24. Bombers were usually attacked from behind or underneath, which meant the tail turrets were more vulnerable. The tail gunner position was assigned to the crew's more experienced gunner, who could handle the additional pressure.

25. February 3, 1944, file "Parker, George J85528," vol. 28375, LAC.

26. Training Report Crew 36 Course 6 No. 1679 HCF, no date, file "Lumgair, Norman Andrew J86440," vol. 28021, LAC.

27. Leo McKinstry, *Lancaster: The Second World War's Greatest Bomber* (London: John Murray, 2010), pp. 167–168, 155.

28. No. 1679 Conversion Flight Navigators Report, no date, file "Parker, George J85528," vol. 28375, LAC.

29. No. 1666 Heavy Conversion Flight Bomb Aimers Report, no date, file "Taylor, William J89913," vol. 28786, LAC.

30. Report on W/T Training (1666 CU), February 3, 1944, file "Doran, William Lawrence J86233," vol. 25226, LAC.

31. Training Report Air Gunner H.C.U. RCAF Wombleton, no date, file "Burt, Robert George Alfred R206418," vol. 24972, LAC.

Chapter 12—408 Squadron

1. Summary of Events, February 1944, RAF Form 540, p. 1, LAC.
2. Lucy Peltz, *Beningbrough Hall* (Swindon: History Press, 2006), p. 63.
3. Ibid., p. 59.
4. Mary Barnett, Beningbrough Hall guide, conversation with author, August 22, 2010.
5. Since 1958 the hall has been a National Trust property and is open to the public.
6. Peltz, *Beningbrough Hall*, p. 24.
7. Harvey, *Boys, Bombs and Brussels Sprouts*, p. 19.
8. Diane Elaine Lazenby, *Call of the Goose* (D.E. Lazenby, 1998), p. 63.
9. Robert Burt, letter to Evelyne Burt, February 11, 1944.
10. William Taylor, letter to Herbert Taylor, February 14, 1944.
11. Harvey, *Boys, Bombs and Brussels Sprouts*, p. 20.
12. Bashow, *None but the Brave*, p. 123 (originally from *The Crucible of War 1939–1945: The Official History of the Royal Canadian Air Force* Vol. III (Toronto: University of Toronto Press, 1994), p. 681).
13. Bashow, *None but the Brave*, p. 123.
14. Ibid., p. 83 (originally from Brereton Greenhous and Hugh A. Halliday, *Canada's Air Forces 1914–1999* (Montreal: Art Global, 1999), p. 100).
15. Summary of Events, February 1944, RAF Form 540, p. 1, LAC.
16. Norman Lumgair, log book.
17. Summary of Events, February 1944, RAF Form 540, p. 1, LAC.
18. Ibid, p. 2.
19. Brian Shields, *The East Moor Experience: 1942-1946 Squadron Operations* (Warrington, UK: Compaid Graphics, 1998), pp. 107–110.
20. Norman Lumgair, log book.
21. Summary of Events, February 1944, RAF Form 540, p. 2, LAC.
22. Ibid.
23. The "occults" Bud referred to was a system of beacons positioned along the British east coast. A second line of beacons was further inland. These beacons flashed Morse code signals to approaching aircraft to help them fix their location.
24. Robert Burt, letter to Mrs. Burt, February 10, 1944.
25. Norman Lumgair, log book.
26. Summary of Events, February 1944, RAF Form 540, p. 2, LAC.
27. Norman Lumgair, log book.
28. William Lawrence Doran, log book.
29. Summary of Events, February 1944, RAF Form 540, p. 2, LAC.
30. Ibid.
31. Earle Reid, log book.

Chapter 13—EQ-P: Birth of a Dragon

1. All descriptions in this paragraph fromMcKinstry, *Lancaster*, pp. 3–4, 167–68.
2. McKinstry, *Lancaster*, p. 17.

3. Air Ministry, UK, *Pilot's Notes for Lancaster II Four Hercules VI or XVI Engines*, A.P. 2062B (London: By Order of the Air Council), p. 6.

4. "Aircraft: Lancaster," on *RAF-Lincolnshire Info*, website of Royal Air Force and Airfield History in Lincolnshire, March 17, 2005, raf-lincolnshire.info/aircraft/lancaster.htm, 2009.

5. Ibid.

6.· Edward Fleming, interview with author, March 20, 2010.

7. McKinstry, *Lancaster*, p. 16.

8. J.J. Halley, *The Lancaster File* (Tonbridge, UK: Air-Britain (Historians), 1985), p. 72.

9. Aircraft Movement Card, Air Ministry, LL637.

10. Reid's crew was Pilot Officer J.T. Smith (Nav), Flight Sergeant G.G. Maguire (W/Op.), Sgt. J.A. May (Flt. Eng.), Warrant Officer Second Class V.C. MacDonald (AB), Sgt. R.L. Clarkson (MUG) and Sgt. J.J. Barr (RG).

11. Earle Reid, log book.

12. Ibid.

13. McKinstry, *Lancaster*, p. 156.

14. Ibid., p. 157.

15. "Lancaster Aircrew," *Bomber Command Museum of Canada* website, bombercommandmuseum.ca/lancaircrew.html.

16. McKinstry, *Lancaster*, p. 159.

17. Ibid., p. 190.

18. Ibid., p. 1.

19. Ibid., p. 240.

20. *Pilot's Notes for Lancaster II Four Hercules VI or XVI Engines*, p. 33.

21. Ibid.

22. Bashow, *None but the Brave*, p. 73.

23. McKinstry, *Lancaster*, p. 240.

Chapter 14—Berlin: A Dickey Flight

1. Middlebrook and Everitt, *Bomber Command War Diaries*, p. 472.

2. Venereal disease (VD) was much more common than one might suppose. Young men in their prime were arriving in Britain where the partners of many women were away at war, missing, or killed in action. Sex provided different things for different people—for some it kept loneliness at bay; for others it was a stress reliever (both sex and alcohol were often used). However, in a number of instances, love bloomed, and tens of thousands of British women ended up marrying servicemen from overseas and returning to Canada or other countries as war brides.

3. Hospital or Sick List—Record Cards, RAF Form 39 (id. no. 981-2 and 2493-4), February 15, 1944, file "Burt, Robert George Alfred R206418," vol. 24972, LAC.

4. Detail of Work Carried Out, Berlin, February 15-16, 1944, Appendix A, RAF Form 541, pp. 1-3, LAC.

5. Middlebrook and Everitt, *Bomber Command War Diaries*, p. 472.

6. "Canadians Prominent in Assault," *The Globe and Mail*, March 27, 1944, in *Collections—Democracy at War: Canadian Newspapers and the Second World War*, Canada War Museum, collections.museedelhistoire.ca/warclip/objects/common/webmedia.php?irn=5020724 (accessed June 23, 2011). The page is no longer available on the website.

7. Middlebrook and Everitt, *Bomber Command War Diaries*, p. 472.

8. Information from "Canadians Prominent in Assault," and Middlebrook and Everitt, *Bomber Command War Diaries*, p. 472.

9. Information on February 15–16, 1944, from "Daily Operations," *No. 6 Bomber Group* website, 6bombergroup.ca/Feb44/Feb15-1644.html.

10. Robin Neillands, *The Bomber War: The Allied Air Offensive against Nazi Germany* (Woodstock, NY: The Overlook Press, 2001), p. 293, quoted in Bashow, *None but the Brave*, p. 40.

11. John Terraine, *The Right of the Line: The Royal Air Force in the European War 1939–1945* (London: Hodder and Stoughton, 1985), 33, quoted in Bashow, *None but the Brave*, p. 71.

12. Detail of Work Carried Out, February 15–16, 1944, RAF Form 541, pp. 1–3, LAC, and Summary of Events, February 15, 1944, RAF Form 540, p. 3, LAC.

13. Middlebrook and Everitt, *Bomber Command War Diaries*.

14. Ibid. Nearly four months later to the day after Lumgair's dickey run, almost all of the Stewart crew died on a raid to Cambrai on June 12–13, 1944. Those who died are buried in Seranvillers-Forenville Military Cemetery.

15. "Canadians Prominent in Assault."

16. Ibid.

17. Middlebrook and Everitt, *Bomber Command War Diaries*, p. 472.

18. Summary of Events, February 1944, RAF Form 540, p. 3, LAC.

19. Robert Hudson, letter to Clarence Walter Hudson, February 16, 1944.

20. Summary of Events, February 1944, RAF Form 540, p. 3, LAC.

21. Bashow, *None but the Brave*, p. 100.

22. D. Stafford-Clark, "Morale and Flying Experience," originally published in the *Journal of Mental Science*, reprinted in Alan W. Mitchell, "Bomber Crews Were Men with a High Quality of Courage," *Gaggle and Stream—Magazine of the Bomber Command Association* of Canada, August 2002, 8; quoted in Bashow, *None but the Brave*, p. 100.

Chapter 15—Operation 1: Leipzig

1. Alan Cooper, *Target Leipzig: The RAF's Disastrous Raid of 19/20 February 1944* (Barnsley, UK: Pen and Sword Aviation, 2009), p. 99.

2. Harvey, *Boys, Bombs and Brussels Sprouts*, p. 48.

3. Cooper, *Target Leipzig*, pp. 99–100.

4. Harvey, *Boys, Bombs and Brussels Sprouts*, pp. 53 and 161.

5. Harvey, *Boys, Bombs and Brussels Sprouts*, p. 154.

6. Cooper, *Target Leipzig*, p. 101.

7. Harvey, *Boys, Bombs and Brussels Sprouts*, p. 154.

8. "Brunswick Is Smashed in New Bomber Attack," *The Globe and Mail*, February 22, 1944, in *Collections—Democracy at War: Canadian Newspapers and the Second World War*, Canada War Museum, http://collections.civilisations.ca/warclip/objects/common/webmedia.php?irn=5122373 (accessed June 23, 2011).

9. Detail of Work Carried Out February 19–20, 1944, Appendix A, RAF Form 541, p. 3, LAC.

10. Harvey, *Boys, Bombs and Brussels Sprouts*, p. 50.

11. Ibid.

12. The specific flares used to mark the target were altered each night so bombers knew this was their mark and would not be confused by night fighter flares. Green flares and red stars were parachute flares, used due to the cloud cover, and would easily drift off target.

13. Cooper, *Target Leipzig*, p. 101.

14. Ibid, p. 100.

15. Harvey, *Boys, Bombs and Brussels Sprouts*, p. 43.

16. Ibid., p. 51.

17. Ibid.

18. Ibid., p. 53. According to McKinstry, "It has been estimated that 80 per cent of airmen carried some sort of lucky charm or enacted a fixed pre-flight ritual, urination on the wheels being the most common" (*Lancaster*, p. 219).

19. Harvey, *Boys, Bombs and Brussels Sprouts*, p. 53.

20. George McKillop, email to author, September 17, 2009.

21. Ibid.

22. Ibid.

23. Cooper, *Target Leipzig*, p. 159.

24. Ibid., p. 157.

25. Middlebrook and Everitt, *Bomber Command War Diaries*, p. 473.

26. Ibid.

27. Cooper, *Target Leipzig*, pp. 134–135.

28. McKinstry, *Lancaster*, p. 167.

29. Quoted in McKinstry, *Lancaster*, pp. 167–168.

30. Cooper, *Target Leipzig*, p. 134.

31. Ibid., p. 123, 107.

32. Ibid., p. 108.

33. Ibid., pp. 117–118.

34. Harvey, *Boys, Bombs and Brussels Sprouts*, p. 154.

35. Information on February 19–20, 1944, from "Daily Operations" on Richard Koval's *No. 6 Bomber Group* website, 6bombergroup.ca/Feb44/Feb19-2044.html.

36. Middlebrook and Everitt, *Bomber Command War Diaries*, p. 473.

37. Detail of Work Carried Out, February 19–20,1944, RAF Form 541, p. 4, LAC.

38. "Brunswick Is Smashed in New Bomber Attack," *The Globe and Mail*.

39. Information on February 19–20, 1944, from "Daily Operations" on Richard Koval's *No. 6 Bomber Group* website, 6bombergroup.ca/Feb44/Feb19-2044.html.

40. Middlebrook and Everitt, *Bomber Command War Diaries*, p. 473.

41. Harvey, *Boys, Bombs and Brussels Sprouts*, p. 154.

42. Detail of Work Carried Out, February 19–20, 1944, RAF Form 541, p. 4, LAC.

43. "Fighter Barrier Worst Canadians Ever Met," *The Globe and Mail*, February 21, 1944, *Collections—Democracy at War: Canadian Newspapers and the Second World War*, Canada War Museum, http://collections.civilisations.ca/warclip/objects/common/webmedia.php?irn=5020899 (accessed June 23, 2011).

44. Cooper, *Target Leipzig*, p. 164.

45. Ibid., p. 108.

46. Ibid, pp. 140–141.

47. "Brunswick Is Smashed in New Bomber Attack," *The Globe and Mail*.

48. Cooper, *Target Leipzig*, p. 122.

49. Detail of Work Carried Out, February 19–20, 1944, RAF Form 541, p. 3–6, LAC.

50. Out of the twenty-eight crewmen lost, twenty-one died, six were taken as POWs and one evaded capture.

51. W.R. Chorley, *Aircraft and Crew Losses 1944*, vol. 5 of *Royal Air Force Bomber Command Losses of the Second World War* (Leicester, UK: Midland Counties Publications, 1997), pp. 83–92.

52. Quoted in McKinstry, *Lancaster*, p. 218.

53. Middlebrook and Everitt, *Bomber Command War Diaries*, p. 474.

54. "Brunswick Is Smashed in New Bomber Attack," *The Globe and Mail*.

Chapter 16—Three More Operations: Stuttgart, Schweinfurt, and Augsburg

1. "Brunswick Is Smashed in New Bomber Attack," *The Globe and Mail.*

2. Middlebrook and Everitt, *Bomber Command War Diaries,* p. 474.

3. Cooper, *Target Leipzig,* p. 144.

4. Middlebrook and Everitt, *Bomber Command War Diaries,* p. 474.

5. Detail of Work Carried Out, Stuttgart, February 20–21, 1944, RAF Form 541, pp. 6–8, LAC.

6. Information on February 20–21, 1944, from "Daily Operations" on Richard Koval's *No. 6 Bomber Group* website, www.6bombergroup.ca/Feb44/Feb20~2144.html.

7. Detail of Work Carried Out, Stuttgart, February 20–21, 1944, RAF Form 541, p. 7, LAC.

8. Detail of Work Carried Out, February 20–21, 1944, RAF Form 541, pp. 6–8, LAC.

9. "Brunswick is Smashed in New Bomber Attack," *The Globe and Mail.*

10. Detail of Work Carried Out, Stuttgart, February 20–21, 1944, RAF Form 541, pp. 6–8, LAC.

11. Middlebrook and Everitt, *Bomber Command War Diaries,* p. 474.

12. Summary of Events, February 21, 1944, RAF Form 540, p. 4, LAC.

13. "Brunswick Is Smashed in New Bomber Attack," *The Globe and Mail.*

14. Summary of Events, February 22, 1944, RAF Form 540, p. 5, LAC.

15. Summary of Events, February 23, 1944, RAF Form 540, p. 5, LAC.

16. Marjorie Doran letter to Director of Estates, August 18, 1944, vol. 25226, file "Doran, William Lawrence J86233," LAC.

17. Ken Burt, email to author, July 22, 2011.

18. Summary of Events, February 24, 1944, RAF Form 540, p. 5, LAC.

19. Middlebrook and Everitt, *Bomber Command War Diaries,* p. 475.

20. Ibid.

21. Detail of Work Carried Out, February 24–25, 1944, RAF Form 541, p. 9, LAC.

22. Information on February 24–25, 1944, from "Daily Operations" on Richard Koval's *No. 6 Bomber Group* website, www.6bombergroup.ca/Feb44/Feb24~2544.html.

23. "Canadian Bomber Group in Biggest Effort of the War," *Hamilton Spectator,* February 25, 1944, in *Collections—Democracy at War: Canadian Newspapers and the Second World War,* Canada War Museum, http://collections.civilisations. ca/warclip/objects/common/webmedia.php?irn=5020898 (accessed June 23, 2011).

24. "Canadian Bomber Group in Biggest Effort of the War."

25. Detail of Work Carried Out, February 24–25, 1944, RAF Form 541, pp. 8–10, LAC.

26. Information on February 24–25, 1944, from "Daily Operations" on Richard Koval's *No. 6 Bomber Group* website, 6bombergroup.ca/Feb44/Feb24~2544.html.

27. 408 Squadron, Lancaster II DS731, EQ-O: Sgt. Hodgins is buried at Hannover War Cemetery. The rest were taken as POW. 408 Squadron, Lancaster II DS844, EQ-X: Three are commemorated on the Runnymede Memorial. The rest are buried in Dürnbach War Cemetery.

28. Summary of Events, February 24, 1944, RAF Form 540, p. 5, LAC.

29. Middlebrook and Everitt, *Bomber Command War Diaries,* pp. 475–476.

30. Detail of Work Carried Out, February 25–26, 1944, RAF Form 541, pp. 10–12, LAC, and Summary of Events, February 25, 1944, RAF Form 540, p. 5, LAC.

31. Middlebrook and Everitt, *Bomber Command War Diaries,* p. 476.

32. Information on February 25–26, 1944, from "Daily Operations" on Richard Koval's *No. 6 Bomber Group* website, 6bombergroup.ca/Feb44/Feb25~2644.html.

33. Summary of Events, February 25, 1944, RAF Form 540, p. 5, LAC.

34. The red flares were ground flares, not sky-marker flares, in keeping with the clear sky conditions on this evening. Ground flares would not be blown off target by wind, so the bombs could be aimed accurately.

35. Detail of Work Carried Out, February 25–26, 1944, RAF Form 541, p. 11, LAC.

36. Information on February 25–26, 1944, from "Daily Operations" on Richard Koval's *No. 6 Bomber Group* website, 6grouprcaf.com/Feb44/Feb25~2644.html 6bombergroup.ca/Feb44/Feb25~2644.html.

37. Middlebrook and Everitt, *Bomber Command War Diaries*, p. 476.

38. Detail of Work Carried Out, February 25–26, 1944, RAF Form 541, pp. 10–12, LAC.

39. Middlebrook and Everett, *Bomber Command War Diaries*, p. 477.

40. 408 Squadron, Lancaster II DS791, EQ-F: This was an experienced crew nearing the end of their operations. Those who died are buried in Dürnbach War Cemetery. 408 Squadron, Lancaster II DS845, EQ-T: The crew abandoned the plane due to engine failure; five were taken as POWs and two evaded capture.

41. Summary of Events, February 25, 1944, RAF Form 540, p. 5, LAC.

42. Bashow, *None but the Brave*, p. 71.

43. Harvey, *Boys, Bombs and Brussels Sprouts*, p. 155.

Chapter 17—March Holidays and Late-Winter Stand-Downs

1. William Taylor, letter to Mrs. Stewart Smith, March 14, 1944.

2. Charlie Lumgair, email to author, September 1, 2009.

3. Robert Burt, postcard to Mrs. Burt, March 4, 1944. The "old boy" Bud referred to was his father.

4. Robert Burt, postcard to Evelyne Burt, March 4, 1944.

5. Robert Burt, letter to grandmother, March 6, 1944.

6. Summary of Events, March 7, 1944, RAF Form 540, pp. 1–2, LAC.

7. "38 Bombers Lost from Over 1,000," *The Globe and Mail*, March 9, 1944, in *Collections—Democracy at War: Canadian Newspapers and the Second World War*, Canada War Museum, http://collections.civilisations.ca/warclip/objects/common/webmedia.php?irn=5122410 (accessed June 23, 2011).

8. Detail of Work Carried Out, March 7–8, 1944, RAF Form 541, p. 2, LAC.

9. Summary of Events, March 7, 1944, RAF Form 540, p. 1, LAC.

10. Detail of Work Carried Out, March 7–8, 1944, RAF Form 541, p. 2, LAC.

11. Summary of Events, March 8, 1944, RAF Form 540, p. 2, LAC.

12. Norman Lumgair, log book. The change in planes may have been due to EQ-P receiving some damage in the Le Mans raid, but there are no records of this.

13. Summary of Events, March 9, 1944, RAF Form 540, p. 2, LAC.

14. Summary of Events, March 10, 1944, RAF Form 540, p. 2, LAC.

15. Harold Davis interview, on Imperial War Museum sound archive tape 9194, quoted in McKinstry, *Lancaster*, p. 218.

16. Summary of Events, March 14, 1944, RAF Form 540, p. 3, LAC.

17. William Taylor, letter to Mrs. Stewart Smith, March 14, 1944.

18. Norman Lumgair, log book.

19. Summary of Events, March 14, 1944, RAF Form 540, p. 3, LAC.

PART 4: GET YOUR GEESE IN FORMATION

Chapter 18—Walking in Their Footsteps

1. Isabel Reid's "To An Airman," emailed by Laura Smith to the author, October 18, 2009.

2. Yorkshire Air Museum, *Yorkshire Air Museum and Allied Air Forces Memorial Visitor Guide Book*, p. 8.

Chapter 19—Beningbrough Hall

1. James Kilner, "There Was Always Room at the Inn," December 7, 2004, on the *Gazette & Herald* website, gazetteherald.co.uk/archive/2003/12/22/ Ryedale+Archive/6663221.There_was_always_room_at_the_inn/. The page is no longer available on the website.

Chapter 20—Present Meets Past

1. Royal Air Force, "RAF Base Opens its Doors," May 19, 2008, *RAF Linton-on-Ouse* website, raf.mod.uk/raflintononouse/newsweather/index.cfm?storyid= 00A1ACEC-1143-EC82-2E5E1593DB0E42D7 (accessed June 10, 2012).

2. Alan Mawby, curator tour with author, August 23, 2010.

3. Matt Clark, "Memorial to the Lost Airmen of Linton-on-Ouse," *The Press* (York), September 7, 2011, yorkpress.co.uk/features/features/9236963.print (accessed June 11, 2012).

Chapter 21—Just Jane

1. "The Air Gunners," *Bomber Command Museum of Canada* website, bomb-ercommandmuseum.ca/airgunners1.html.

2. Robert Chester-Master, emails to author, March 29 and 31, 2012.

3. Terry Mason, letter to author, December 18, 2010.

PART 5: I REMEMBER YOU

Chapter 24—Honking of Geese from Above

1. Mr. and Mrs. Steydli, interview with author, translated by Jean-Paul Steydli, August 6, 2011.

2. Patrick Baumann, personal notes given to author, August 28, 2010; originally used for newspaper article, "Le terrible nuit du 15 mars 1944," on the fifty-year anniversary.

3. Chorley, *Royal Air Force Bomber Command Losses of the Second World War*, p. 112.

4. McKinstry, *Lancaster*, p. 364.

5. Ibid., p. 364.

6. Boiten, *Nachtjagd War Diaries*, p. 376.

7. Patrick Baumann, email to author, February 9, 2013.

8. Patrick Baumann, email to author, February 10, 2013.

9. Chorley, *Royal Air Force Bomber Command Losses of the Second World War*, p. 115.

10. Neil Deakin, Sgt. Harry C. Petty's nephew, email to Ken Burt, December 12, 2005.

11. Patrick Baumann, email to author, February 10, 2013.

12. Patrick Baumann, personal notes given to author, August 28, 2010.

13. Mr. and Mrs. Steydli, interview with author, August 6, 2011.

14. EQ-P was the only bomber to split in two, and as such I have placed them as the first bomber, according to Alphonse Spiller's account.

15. Patrick Baumann, personal notes given to author, August 28, 2010. There are some discrepancies in Alphonse Spiller's account of events, most notably that he thought he saw this at 0130, three hours after EQ-P probably crashed. I discuss the different accounts and my questions about them in the afterword.

16. Report No. 1 Missing Research and Enquiry Unit to Air Ministry, April 30, 1947, file "Lumgair, Norman Andrew J86440," vol. 28021, LAC.

17. "Andrew Charles Mynarski: World War II Hero," *Canadian Air Aces and Heroes* website, constable.ca/caah/mynarski.htm (accessed August 17, 2011).

18. Steve Fortescue, email to author, July 5, 2011.

19. Theo Boiten and Martin Bowman, *Jane's Battles with the Luftwaffe: The Bomber Campaign Against Germany 1942-1945* (London: Harper Collins, 2001), pp. 82-83.

20. Mr. and Mrs. Steydli, interview with author, August 6, 2011.

21. Patrick Baumann, personal notes given to author, August 28, 2010.

22. Chorley, *Royal Air Force Bomber Command Losses of the Second World War*, p. 115.

23. Patrick Baumann, personal notes given to author, August 28, 2010.

24. Ibid.

25. All but one crewman, a Canadian, were from the UK. All are buried at Artolsheim Communal Cemetery.

26. Report France Detachment Missing Research and Enquiry Service RAF to Air Ministry, June 5, 1948, file "Lumgair, Norman Andrew J86440," vol. 28021, LAC.

27. "La terrible nuit du 15 mars 1944," *Wittisheim* municipal website, wittisheim.fr/listeLieux00010ae5.html, November 2009. (The story was removed when the website was revamped.)

28. Patrick Baumann, personal notes given to author, August 28, 2010.

29. Report France Detachment Missing Research and Enquiry Service RAF to Air Ministry, June 5, 1948, and Exhumation Report (RAF), May 17, 1947, file "Lumgair, Norman Andrew J86440," vol. 28021, LAC.

30. Commonwealth War Graves Commission, Choloy War Cemetery, www.cwgc.org/find-a-cemetery/cemetery/2031700/CHOLOY%20WAR%20CEMETERY (accessed Dec 12 2016).

Chapter 25—The Cold Dawn

1. Mr. and Mrs. Steydli, interview with author, August 6, 2011.

2. Jean-Paul Steydli, email to author, December 23, 2012.

3. Mr. and Mrs. Steydli, interview with author, August 6, 2011.

4. Ibid.

5. Boiten and Bowman, *Jane's Battles with the Luftwaffe*, p. 29.

6. Report No. 1 Missing Research and Enquiry Unit British Forces in France, RAF to Air Ministry, August 13, 1947, file "Lumgair, Norman Andrew J86440," vol. 28021, LAC.

7. Patrick Baumann, personal notes given to author, August 28, 2010.

8. Mr. and Mrs. Steydli, interview with author, August 6, 2011.

9. Ken Burt, email to author (detailing discussion with witness Mrs. Kreger in 1981), October 12, 2010.

10. RCAF handwritten information in service file, January 8, 1946, file "Burt, Robert George Alfred R206418," vol. 24972, LAC.

11. 408 Squadron, Lancaster II LL637, EQ-P: Plt. Off. (Pilot) Norman Andrew Lumgair J/86440 (RCAF), Sgt. (Flt. Engr.) Douglas Cruickshank 620947 (RAF), Plt. Off. (Nav.) George Parker J/85528 (RCAF), Plt. Off. (Air Bomber) William Taylor J/89913 (RCAF), Plt. Off. (W. Op. Air Gnr.) William Lawrence Doran J/86233 (RCAF), Sgt. (Air Gnr.) Robert Henry Hudson 3050164 (RAFVR), Sgt. (Air Gnr.) Robert George Alfred Burt R/206418 (RCAF).

12. RCAF Casualty Office, letter to Mr. W. Lumgair, March 4, 1948, file "Lumgair, Norman Andrew J86440," vol. 28021, LAC.

13. Mr. and Mrs. Steydli, interview with author, August 6, 2011.

14. Ibid.

15. Jean-Paul Steydli, email to author, August 12, 2011.

16. Mr. and Mrs. Steydli, interview with author, August 6, 2011.

Chapter 26—A Long Walk to Be With Them

1. In 1981, Ken Burt and one of his sisters, along with their spouses, went to Hilsenheim, where Ken's sister exchanged mailing addresses with a couple in the village who spoke English. Years later, John Hudson, Bob's brother, met the Steydli family. In 1994, when John had only been able to track down the Taylor family for the fiftieth anniversary of the crew's death, the Hudsons, Taylors, and Steydlis attended the gathering to remember the crew. Two years later, Jean-Paul and his family visited the Taylor family in Canada. When they returned to Hilsenheim, the Steydlis mentioned this visit to their neighbours, who turned out to be the people Ken's sister had exchanged addresses with. Jean-Paul forwarded Ken's sister's address to the Taylors, and they wrote the sister. She let Ken know, and he contacted the Taylors, who in turn gave him Jean-Paul Steydli's address.

2. Ken Burt, letter to Jean-Paul Steydli, December 23, 2005.

Chapter 28—A Celebration

1. Ken Burt, letter to Jean-Paul Steydli, December 23, 2005.

2. Mr. and Mrs. Steydli, interview with author, August 6, 2011.

3. Ibid.

PART 6: HOW COULD I FORGET?

Chapter 31—In Memory

1. Aircrew Canadian Commemorative Geographical Feature Naming Program, google.com/maps/d/viewer?mid=1xtZDhG50xAV_AAcTTtAktVGkJ9I.

Chapter 32—Remembering the Dead

1. Ben Morris, "Permission to Speak, Sir: Official History, Whose Reality?" *Oral History Association of Australia Journal* no. 32 (2010): 3.

2. Ibid., 6.

3. Jim Mulholland, email to author, October 11, 2010.

4. Ibid., October 18, 2010.

5. Ibid., October 11, 2010.

Afterword—Separating the Geese from the Ganders

1. No title given (appears to be a death card), Ref. KE7942, no date, file "Burt, Robert George Alfred R206418," vol. 24972, LAC.

2. Translated extract from official death list (Totenliste No. 239), February 10, 1945, file "Lumgair, Norman Andrew J86440," vol. 28021, LAC.

3. Jock was buried in the collective grave with Larry, Norm, and George, so I can only surmise that the identity disc was found separate from his body and that his remains could not be distinguished from the other unidentifiable members of the crew.

4. RCAF Casualty Branch extract from KE7942, no date, file "Lumgair, Norman Andrew J86440," vol. 28021, LAC.

5. Copy of extract from KE7942, dated October 16, 1945, file "Lumgair, Norman Andrew J86440," vol. 28021, LAC.

6. Casualty Enquiry G325, December 14, 1945, vol. 28021, file "Lumgair, Norman Andrew J86440," LAC. The MRES was concerned only with obtaining the information pertinent to its enquiry. It was not responsible for finding out how the men died.

7. I have been unable to ascertain whether Sgt. J.B. Bull was the unidentified airman or a separate casualty. I have also been unable to verify if he died in the crash of SR-Q or was found elsewhere, like Sgt. J.F. Ennis.

8. Casualty Enquiry G325 (Cont), January 8, 1946, file "Lumgair, Norman Andrew J86440," vol. 28021, LAC.

9. Casualty Enquiry G325 (Contd), January 23, 1946, file "Lumgair, Norman Andrew J86440," vol. 28021, LAC.

10. The front part of EQ-P was in fact close to Hilsenheim, approximately three hundred metres from the nearest house and in a field quite far back from the road leading to Wittisheim. Wittisheim is about two to three kilometres from Hilsenheim. Bud was found in his turret somewhere on the edge of Wittisheim, although I could not determine the exact location.

11. The time of 2330 is a full hour later than the 2230 time given in French witness accounts. When considered along with the initial German record, the reported time the bomber stream was over the Alsace, and also when calculated with the average time to target for the other 408 Squadron aircraft, their drop time and return times, it seems highly unlikely the mayor's time could be a possibility.

12. No. 1 Missing Research and Enquiry Unit to Air Ministry, received August 13, 1947, file "Lumgair, Norman Andrew J86440," vol. 28021, LAC.

13. In fact, four bodies were identified by identity discs, but as stated earlier, Jock's identity disc was likely found separate from his body, which would explain why he was buried in the communal grave instead of in a separate grave.

14. The badly burnt bodies were likely those of George, Norm, Larry, and Jock, as Mrs. Steydli said the bodies she saw outside the aircraft were not burned.

15. In 1981, when Ken Burt visited Hilsenheim, he heard from Mrs. Kreder, who lived next to the Hilsenheim Cemetery, that she could see the naked bodies of the crew at the entrance to the cemetery.

16. No. 1 Missing Research and Enquiry Unit to Air Ministry, received August 13, 1947, file "Lumgair, Norman Andrew J86440," vol. 28021, LAC.

17. Exhumation report RAF Hilsenheim, May 16, 1947, file "Lumgair, Norman Andrew J86440," vol. 28021, LAC.

18. I was unable to verify who Hensen was or how he came to be listed on the cross. He was not part of this crew and does not show up in any casualties for the night.

19. Exhumation report RAF Mussig, May 17, 1947, file "Lumgair, Norman Andrew J86440," vol. 28021, LAC.

20. Today DNA is commonly used to identify bodies; however, during the Second World War, such technology didn't exist to verify the masses of unidentifiable dead. The MRES does not state it found the body of Cecil Glenn Arthur, but it knew which men would have been in which aircraft. Sgt. Bull was buried at Mussig, and there was evidence from the exhumation a RAAF member was present due to the RAAF battle dress found in the graves at Mussig; the knowledge that Arthur was the only RAAF crewman on SR-Q likely supported the belief that all crewmen for each aircraft were accounted for and buried with their own crew, not mixed with EQ-P.

21. The villages of Sundhausen and Wittisheim are close to one another. The MRES assumed that the German information stating he was buried at Sundhausen was a simple mix-up between the two villages.

22. Report from France Detachment Missing Research and Enquiry RAF to Air Ministry, June 5, 1948, file "Lumgair, Norman Andrew J86440," vol. 28021, LAC. .

23. "La terrible nuit du 15 mars 1944," *Wittisheim* website, November 2009, wittisheim.fr/listeLieux00010ae5.html. (The story was removed when the website was revamped.)

24. Etienne Barthelmé, *Bombercrash in Alsace: La Guerre aérienne 39–45 et les chutes de bombardiers alliés en Alsace. Histoire des avions et des équipages* (N.p.: Books on Demand Editions, 2009; available at books.google.ca/books?id=HntM81dvFDYC), p. 74.

25. Ibid., p. 155.

26. Patrick Baumann, personal notes given to author, August 28, 2010.

27. As more information is found and made available, the understanding surrounding the events of history changes and hopefully a more accurate assessment of what happened can be determined.

28. Patrick Baumann, email to author, February 9, 2013.

29. O.K.L. Fighter Claims: Chef für Ausz. Und Dizsiplin Luftwaffen-Personalamt L.P. (A) V Films & Supplementary Claims from Lists, Reich, West and Südfront, Jan to Apr 1944, vol. 1, Combat Claims and Casualties, don-caldwell.we.bs/jg26/claims/tonywood.htm.

30. John Foreman, Johannes Matthews, and Simon W. Parry, *Luftwaffe Night Fighter Combat Claims, 1939–1945* (Surrey, UK: Red Kite, 2004), pp. 154–155.

31. Boiten, *Nachtjagd War Diaries*, p. 373.

32. Heinz Rökker, *Chronik I. Gruppe Nachtjagdgeschwader 2 I./NJG 2. Juli 1940 bis Kriegsende 1945 Fernnachtjagd 1940–1942* (Zweinbrücken: VDM Heinz Nickel, 1997), p. 98.

33. McKinstry, *Lancaster*, p.146.

34. Boiten, *Nachtjagd War Diaries*, p. 373.

Bibliography

Published Sources

408 Squadron History. Belleville, ON: The Hangar Bookshelf, 1984.

Air Ministry, UK. *Pilot's Notes for Lancaster II Four Hercules VI or XVI Engines*. London, UK: By Order of the Air Council, June 1943.

Armstrong, John G. "RCAF Identity in Bomber Command: Squadron Names and Sponsors." *Canadian Military History* 8, no. 2 (1999): 43–52.

Barthelmé, Etienne. *Bombercrash in Alsace: La Guerre aérienne 39–45 et les chutes de bombardiers alliés en Alsace. Histoire des avions et des équipages*. N.p.: Books on Demand Editions, 2009. books.google.ca/books?id=HntM81dvFDYC.

Bashow, David L. *None but the Brave: The Essential Contributions of RAF Bomber Command to Allied Victory During the Second World War*. Kingston: Canadian Defence Academy Press, 2009.

Boiten, Theo. *Nachtjagd War Diaries: An Operational History of the German Night Fighter Force in the West. Vol. 1, September 1939–March 1944*. Walton on Thames, UK: Red Kite, 2008.

Boiten, Theo, and Martin Bowman. *Jane's Battles with the Luftwaffe: The Bomber Campaign Against Germany 1942–1945*. London: Harper Collins, 2001.

Bralorne Community Club. "Bralorne Personalities," *The Communicator* (Bralorne Pioneer Museum, Bralorne, BC) 1, no. 22 (Nov. 18, 1938).

British Columbia Is a Gold Mine Province. . .Fortunes Will Be Made From Its Mines. Vancouver: A.E. Jukes & Co., 1933.

Chisholm, Doug. *Their Names Live On: Remembering Saskatchewan's Fallen in World War II*. Regina: Canadian Plains Research Centre, University of Regina, 2001.

Chorley, W.R. *Royal Air Force Bomber Command Losses of the Second World War 1944. Vol. 5*. Leicester, UK: Midland Counties Publications, 1997.

Clark, Matt. "Memorial to the Lost Airmen of Linton-on-Ouse." *The Press* (York), Sept. 7, 2011, http://yorkpress.co.uk/features/features/9236963.print.

Cooper, A. *Target Leipzig: The RAF's Disastrous Raid of 19/20 February 1944*. Barnsley, UK: Pen and Sword Aviation, 2009.

Foreman, John, Johannes Matthews, and Simon W. Parry. *Luftwaffe Night Fighter Combat Claims, 1939–1945*. Surrey, UK: Red Kite, 2004.

Garbett, Mike, and Brian Goulding. *Avro Lancaster in Unit Service*. Aircam Aviation Series, No. 12. Oxford, UK: Osprey Publications Limited, 1970.

Garbett, Mike, and Brian Goulding. *Lancaster at War 2*. New York: Charles Scribner's Sons., 1980.

Halley, J.J. *The Lancaster File*. Tonbridge, UK: Air-Britain (Historians), 1985.

Harvey, J. Douglas. *Boys, Bombs and Brussels Sprouts: A Knees-up, Wheels-up Chronicle of WWII*. Halifax: Goodread Biographies, 1982.

Lazenby, Diane E. *Call of the Goose*. Middlesbrough, UK: D.E. Lazenby, 1998.

McKinstry, Leo. *Lancaster: The Second World War's Greatest Bomber*. London: John Murray, 2010.

Middlebrook, Martin, and Chris Everitt. *The Bomber Command War Diaries: An Operational Reference Book 1939–1945*. Leicester, UK: Midland Publishing, 1996.

Morris, Ben. "Permission to Speak, Sir: Official History, Whose Reality?" *Oral History Association of Australia Journal* no. 32 (2010): 3–7.

Motiuk, Laurence. *Thunderbirds at War: Diary of a Bomber Squadron*. Nepean, ON: Larmot Associates, 1998.

Rökker, Heinz. *Chronik I.Gruppe Nachtjagdgeschwader 2 I./NJG 2. Juli 1940 bis Kriegsende 1945 Fernnachtjagd 1940-1942*. Zweinbrücken: VDM Heinz Nickel, 1997.

Shields, Brian. *The East Moor Experience: 1942-1946 Squadron Operations*. Warrington, UK: Compaid Graphics, 1998.

The National Trust. *Beningbrough Hall*. Swindon: Acorn Press, 2006.

Woods, Laurie. *Flying into the Mouth of Hell*. Loftus, AU: Australian Military History Publications, 2003.

Yorkshire Air Museum. *Yorkshire Air Museum and Allied Air Forces Memorial Visitor Guide Book*. UK: Yorkshire Air Museum, n.d.

Websites and Other Media

"38 Bombers Lost From Over 1,000." *The Globe and Mail*, Mar. 9, 1944. Online at *Collections—Democracy at War: Canadian Newspapers and the Second World War*, Canada War Museum. collections.civilisations.ca/warclip/objects/common/webmedia.php?irn=5122410 (accessed June 23, 2011).

"Andrew Charles Mynarski: World War II Hero." *Canadian Air Aces and Heroes*. constable.ca/caah/mynarski.htm (accessed Aug. 17, 2011).

"Brunswick Is Smashed in New Bomber Attack." *The Globe and Mail*, Feb. 22, 1944. Online at *Collections—Democracy at War: Canadian Newspapers and the Second World War*, Canada War Museum. collections.civilisations.ca/warclip/objects/common/webmedia.php?irn=5122373 (accessed June 23, 2011).

"Canadian Bomber Group in Biggest Effort of the War." *Hamilton Spectator*, Feb. 25, 1944. Online at *Collections—Democracy at War: Canadian Newspapers and the Second World War*, Canada War Museum. collections.civilisations.ca/warclip/objects/common/webmedia.php?irn=5020898 (accessed June 23, 2011).

"Canadians Prominent in Assault." *The Globe and Mail*, Mar. 27, 1944. Online at *Collections—Democracy at War: Canadian Newspapers and the Second World War*, Canada War Museum. collections.museedelhistoire.ca/warclip/objects/common/webmedia.php?irn=5020724 (accessed June 23, 2011).

Commonwealth War Graves Commission. www.cwgc.org (accessed Dec 12 2016)

"Fighter Barrier Worst Canadians Ever Met." *The Globe and Mail*, Feb. 21, 1944. Online at *Collections—Democracy at War: Canadian Newspapers and the Second World War*, Canada War Museum. collections.civilisations.ca/warclip/objects/common/webmedia.php?irn=5020899 (accessed June 23, 2011).

"La terrible nuit du 15 mars 1944." *Wittisheim* website. wittisheim.fr/liste-Lieux00010ae5.html (accessed July 30, 2009).

"O.K.L. Fighter Claims: Chef für Ausz. Und Dizsiplin Luftwaffen-Personalamt L.P." (A) V Films & Supplementary Claims from Lists, Reich, West and Südfront, Jan. to Apr. 1944, vol. 1. *Combat Claims and Casualties*, Tony Wood's website. don-caldwell.we.bs/jg26/claims/tonywood.htm (accessed Mar 5, 2011).

"Princes Pier Railway Station, Greenock." *Port Number One, Waterways and Recovery Bays*, on *Remembering Scotland at War*, exhibit website. http://rememberingscotlandatwar.org.uk/online-museum (accessed Aug 10, 2010).

"Riots and Looting Not to Be Trifled With." *Toronto Telegram*, May 16, 1945. Online at *Collections—Democracy at War: Canadian Newspapers and the Second World War*, Canada War Museum. collections.civilisations.ca/warclip/objects/common/webmedia.php?irn=5074035 (accessed June 23, 2011).

Aircrew Canadian Commemorative Geographical Feature Naming Program. google.com/maps/d/viewer?mid=1xtZDhG50xAV_AAcTTtAktVGkJ9I.

BBC Radio Lincolnshire. "No 4 School of Technical Training (1942)—Part 1," A7798369. CSV Action Desk, *WW2 People's War*. Dec. 15, 2005, bbc.co.uk/ ww2peopleswar/stories/69/a7798369.shtml (accessed July 25, 2011).

Commonwealth War Graves Commission. https://www.cwgc.org.

Duxford Radio Society. "Equipment History Summary File, Transmitter T1154/ Receiver R1155 (British RAF 1941)." Duxford, UK: Imperial War Museums Duxford, 2004. *Duxford Radio Society* website. duxfordradiosociety.org/equi-phist/r1155/t1154-r1155-V4-jan2015.pdf.

Juno Beach Centre. "Canada in the Second World War." *Juno Beach Centre*. juno-beach.org/e/4/can-tac-air-bca-e.htm (accessed June 20, 2011).

Kilner, James. "There Was Always Room at the Inn." *Gazette & Herald*, Dec. 7, 2004. gazetteherald.co.uk/archive/2003/12/22/Ryedale+Archive/6663221.There_ was_always_room_at_the_inn (accessed Sept 10, 2009).

Koval, Richard. "Daily Operations." *No. 6 Bomber Group*. http://6bombergroup.ca/ Operations.html (accessed June 20, 2016).

Nanton Lancaster Society. "British Commonwealth Air Training Plan." *Bomber Command Museum of Canada*. bombercommandmuseum.ca/bcatp.html (accessed October 12, 2013).

——. "Lancaster Aircrew." *Bomber Command Museum of Canada*. bombercom-mandmuseum.ca/lancaircrew.html (accessed October 12, 2013).

——. "The Air Gunners." *Bomber Command Museum of Canada*. bombercom-mandmuseum.ca/airgunners1.html (accessed October 12, 2013).

Old Haltonian Association. "The RAF Halton Aircraft Apprentice Scheme." old-haltonians.co.uk/pages/news/Halton%20Story.pdf (accessed May 17, 2018).

Rickard, J. "No. 240 Squadron (RAF): Second World War." *Military History Encyclopedia on the Web*, July 11, 2011. historyofwar.org/air/units/RAF/ 240_wwII.html (accessed July 25, 2011).

Royal Air Force and Airfield History in Lincolnshire. "Aircraft: Lancaster." *RAF–Lincolnshire Info*, Mar. 17, 2005. raf-lincolnshire.info/aircraft/lancaster.htm, (accessed Aug, 18 2009).

Royal Airforce. "RAF Base Opens its Doors." *RAF Linton-on-Ouse*, raf.mod.uk/ raflintononouse/newsweather/index.cfm?storyid=00A1ACEC-1143-EC82-2E5E1593DB0E42D7 (accessed June 10, 2012).

Saunders, Stephen, dir. *As it Happened: The Lancaster at War*. Chartley: ASA Productions for the History Channel, 2010. DVD.

Unpublished Sources

Aircraft Movement Card. [Great Britain] Air Ministry, LL637.

"Detail of Work Carried Out," various records from Feb. 1944, RAF Form 541, from 408 RCAF Squadron, Linton-on-Ouse. Royal Canadian Air Force Operations Record Books, vol. 22655, DND fonds, Library and Archives Canada.

"Kitsilano Junior–Senior High School Annual," 1931.

"Operations Record Book," Jan. 1942 to May 1945. No. 408 Squadron. RCAF [Royal Canadian Air Force] file, Library and Archives Canada.

"Operations Record Book," vol. 1, Sept. 1943 to Dec. 1944, to vol. 2, Dec. 1944 to May 1945. No. 432 Squadron. RCAF [Royal Canadian Air Force] file, Library and Archives Canada.

Reid, Isabel. "To An Airman," ca. 1944. Emailed from Laura Smith to author, Oct. 18, 2009.

"Summary of Events," various records from Feb. 1944, RAF [Royal Air Force] Form 540, Squadron Operational Records, Library and Archives Canada.

"Summary of Events," various records from Mar. 1944, RAF [Royal Air Force] Form 540, from 408 RCAF Squadron, Linton-on-Ouse. Royal Canadian Air Force Operations Record Books, vol. 22655, Department of National Defence (DND) fonds, Library and Archives Canada.

Flying Log Books, RCAF

Burt, Robert George Alfred. Burt family collection.
Doran, William Lawrence. Doran family collection.
Hudson, Robert. Hudson family collection.
Lumgair, Norman. Lumgair family collection.
Lumgair, Robert. Lumgair family collection.
Parker, George. Parker family collection.
Reid, Earle. Reid family collection.
Taylor, William. Taylor family collection.

Service Records

Record for Douglas Cruickshank, 620947. RAF Record of Service (1920–present), Deceased Ex-Service Personnel, Ministry of Defence Veterans' Agency.

Record for George Parker, J85528. Vol. 28375, Second World War Service Files, Canadian Armed Forces War Dead, Library and Archives Canada.

Record for Norman Andrew Lumgair, J86440. Vol. 28021, Second World War Service Files, Canadian Armed Forces War Dead, Library and Archives Canada.

Record for Robert George Alfred Burt, R206418. Vol. 24972, Second World War Service Files, Canadian Armed Forces War Dead, Library and Archives Canada.

Record for Robert Henry Hudson, 3050164. RAF Record of Service (1920–present), Deceased Ex-Service Personnel, Ministry of Defence Veterans' Agency.

Record for William Lawrence Doran, J86233. Vol. 25226, Second World War Service Files, Canadian Armed Forces War Dead, Library and Archives Canada.

Record for William Taylor, J89913. Vol. 28786, Second World War Service Files, Canadian Armed Forces War Dead, Library and Archives Canada.

Correspondence and Interviews

Barnett, Mary (Beningbrough Hall guide). Conversation with author, Aug. 22, 2010.

Baumann, Patrick. Personal notes given to author, Aug. 28, 2010; email to author, Feb. 9, 2013.

Burt, Ken. Letter to Jean-Paul Steydli, Dec. 23, 2005; emails to author, Feb. 23, 2010; Mar. 1, 2010; Oct. 12, 2010; and July 22, 2011.

Burt, Kenneth H. Notes from conversation with Kenneth A. Burt, Sept. 1 and Nov. 6, 2005.

Burt, Robert. Letters to Evelyne Johnson (née Burt), Apr. 22, 1943, and undated; poem to Audrey Harris, undated; postcard to Evelyne Burt, Aug. 7, 1943, Mar. 4, 1944, and letter Feb. 11, 1944; postcards to Mrs. Burt, Sept. 3, 1943, Dec. 17, 1943, Mar. 4, 1944, and letter Feb. 10, 1944; letter to grandmother, Mar. 6, 1944.

Chester-Master, Robert. Emails to author, Mar. 29, 2012; Mar. 31, 2012.

Cruickshank, Gordon, via David W. Machin email to author, Apr. 5, 2010.

Deakin, Neil (Sgt. Harry C. Petty's nephew). Email to Ken Burt, Dec. 12, 2005.

Doran, Larry. Letter to mother and sister Eileen, Sept. 23, 1943.

Doran, Marjorie. Letter to Mr. Burt and family, Apr. 3, 1944.

Farr (née Taylor), Florence. Recollections (as supplied to the Carievale and District History Book, 1988), via email from Laura Smith to author, Dec. 5, 2009.

Fleming, Edward. Interview with author, Mar. 20, 2010.

Fleming, Robert, CFB Trenton. Email to author, Mar. 3, 2010.

Fortescue, Steve. Email to author, July 5, 2011.

Hudson, Madeline. Letter to Clarence Walter Hudson, Nov. 14, 1944, and to Mr. and Mrs. Burt, Mar. 5, 1945.

Hudson, Robert. Letter to Clarence Walter (Cag) Hudson (brother), undated, and to Clarence Walter Hudson, Feb. 16, 1944.

Johnson, Evelyne, via email from Ken Burt to author, June 7, 2011.

Johnson, Pat, via letters from daughter to author, Nov. 14, 2009; Apr. 8, 2012.

Lumgair, Charlie. Email to author, May 17, 2010; Sept. 1, 2009.

Machin, David W. Email to author, Mar. 9, 2010.

Mason, Terry. Letter to author, Dec. 18, 2010.

Mawby, Alan. Tour with author, Aug. 23, 2010; email to author, June 6, 2012.

McKillop, George. Email to author, Sept. 17, 2009.

Mitchell (née Taylor), Dorothy. Recollections via email from Laura Smith to author, Mar. 24, 2010.

Mulholland, Jim. Email to author, Oct. 11, 2010; Oct. 18, 2010; interview with Ken Burt, June 16, 2011.

Parker, Gail. Letter to author, Jan. 11, 2010; email to author, June 8 and June 9, 2011.

Parker, Pat. Letter to Mr. and Mrs. Burt, Apr. 1, 1944; letter to Mrs. Taylor, June 6, 1946.

Steydli, Jean-Paul. Email to author, Aug. 12, 2011; Dec. 23, 2012.

Steydli, Mr. and Mrs. Interview with author, translated by Jean-Paul Steydli, Aug. 6, 2011.

Taylor, William. Letter to Mrs. Harry Taylor, Jan. 20, 1944; to Herbert Taylor, Feb. 14, 1944; to Mrs. Stewart Smith, Mar. 14, 1944.

Volkes, E.L. Letter to Burt, Robert. Nov. 2, 1943; to Mr. and Mrs. Robert Burt, Mar. 25, 1944.

Wagner (née Taylor), Edna. Recollections via email from Laura Smith to author, Dec. 5, 2009.

Walker, Patrick. Email to author, May 14, 2011; May 18, 2011.

Index

Tate Needham, T8 Photography

About the Author

Born in Brampton, Ontario, Lisa Jean Russ taught primary and secondary school in Canada and Britain before moving to Australia. Inspired by her family's military history, she has spent the past seven years volunteering with the Australian Army Military Intelligence Museum, Queensland, and Army Museum Duntroon, Canberra. Russ holds BAs from Carleton University (Art History and English, hons, and Psychology, hons) and a BEd from Nipissing University. She is currently in her final year of a Bachelor of Heritage, Museums, and Conservation at the University of Canberra, with the intent of earning a PhD.